CULTURAL FACTORS

IN

INTER-AMERICAN

PREPARED FOR PUBLICATION UNDER THE
SPONSORSHIP OF THE CATHOLIC
INTER-AMERICAN COOPERATION PROGRAM
(CICOP) LATIN AMERICAN BUREAU, U.S.C.C.

CONTRIBUTORS

Rubem Alves
Ricardo Arias-Calderon
Marina Bandeira de Corvalho
Arístides Calvani
Horacio H. Godoy
João Gonçalves de Souza
Denis A. Goulet
Joseph Gremillion
Robert J. Henle, S.J.
Frank Marino Hernandez
Irving L. Horowitz

Lyle N. McAlister
Eugene J. McCarthy
Marcos G. McGrath, C.S.C.
Jorge Mejia
Gustavo Perez-Ramirez
John N. Plank
Renato Poblete, S.J.
Gustavo Romero-Kolbeck
Samuel Shapiro
M. Richard Shaull
George N. Shuster

Paulo de Tarso

CULTURAL FACTORS

IN

INTER-AMERICAN

RELATIONS

SAMUEL SHAPIRO
Editor

UNIVERSITY OF NOTRE DAME PRESS
NOTRE DAME LONDON

Library of Congress Catalog Card Number: 68-30669
Manufactured in the United States of America

Contributors

Rubem Alves teaches at Princeton Theological Seminary, Princeton, New Jersey.

Ricardo Arias-Calderon is professor of ancient and medieval philosophy at the University of Panama.

Marina Bandeira de Corvalho is secretary general of the Brazilian Basic Education Movement (MEB).

Arístides Calvani is president of I.F.E.D.E.C. in Caracas, Venezuela, and teaches in the Humanities and Education Faculty of the Universidad Católica.

Horacio H. Godoy is the director of the Latin American School of Political Science and Public Administration (FLASCO) in Santiago, Chile.

João Gonçalves de Souza is director of the Department of Technical Cooperation of the Pan American Union.

Denis A. Goulet is a visiting associate professor in the Department of Government, University of Indiana, Bloomington, Indiana.

Msgr. Joseph Gremillion is the permanent secretary of the Pontifical Commission for Justice and Peace.

Robert J. Henle, S.J., is the academic vice-president of St. Louis University.

Frank Marino Hernandez is vice-president of the Dominican University Center, Inc., in Santo Domingo.

Irving L. Horowitz is a professor of sociology at the Social Science Institute of Washington University, St. Louis.

Lyle N. McAlister is a professor of history and director of the Center for Latin American Studies at the University of Florida, Gainesville, Florida.

Eugene J. McCarthy is the senior United States Senator from the State of Minnesota.

Marcos G. McGrath, C.S.C., is the bishop of Santiago de Veraguas, Panama, and a vice-president of the Episcopal Council of Latin America (CELAM).

Father Jorge Mejia is the editor of *Criterio*, a quarterly devoted to religious and cultural issues, and published in Buenos Aires.

Father Gustavo Perez-Ramirez is the director general of the Colombian Institute for Social Development (ICODES) in Bogotá, Colombia.

John N. Plank is an associate of The Brookings Institution, Washington, D.C.

Renato Poblete, S.J., is the director of the Bellarmine Center of Social Investigation, Santiago, Chile.

Gustavo Romero-Kolbeck is the director of the Center for Economic Studies, Mexico City.

Samuel Shapiro is an associate professor of history at the University of Notre Dame.

M. Richard Shaull is professor of ecumenics at Princeton Theological Seminary, Princeton, New Jersey.

George N. Shuster is assistant to the president of the University of Notre Dame.

Paulo de Tarso is a Brazilian educator who is currently residing in Santiago, Chile.

Preface

North American interest in Latin America tends to fluctuate violently, and to focus on extreme events: an earthquake, the stoning of an American Vice President, a *golpe* (coup d'etat), an assassination, a flare-up of guerilla warfare. For a time during the early 1960's, Fidel Castro's dictatorship in Cuba, with its drumfire of newsworthy executions, expropriations, speeches, the Bay of Pigs, the missile crisis, seemed to have a permanent place on the front pages. President Eisenhower made a special tour of Latin America to counteract the bad effects of the attacks on the Vice President in Lima and Caracas, and President Kennedy gave the area a separate paragraph in his brief inaugural address and launched the Alliance for Progress to attack the economic and social maladies of the region. Latin America was a "hot" subject, and Latin American specialists had reason to be grateful for the government grants, graduate students, journalistic commissions, conferences, and other indications of popularity that came their way after decades of obscurity.

In 1968, only four or five years afterwards, a great deal of the interest and enthusiasm over Latin America has leaked away. Other, more acute problems have elbowed the southern continent aside. With a hot war against Communism in Vietnam costing 30 billion dollars a year and thousands of American lives, we cannot afford to worry as much as we once did about Communism in Cuba, Chile, or Venezuela. With our inner cities exploding into riots every summer, we are no longer as concerned as we once were about the *favelas* of São Paulo, the *callampas* of Santiago, the *villas miserias* of Buenos Aires. And with our own poor on the march and visibly present in Washington, D. C., it is natural to give a lower priority to the problems of the invisible and politically impotent poor of Latin America. With crises of the gravest kind erupting in Saigon, Jerusalem, Paris, Detroit, New York City, Los Angeles, and Chicago, we simply do not have much time, energy, attention, money, manpower, or expertise left over for our *Alianza* partners.

In addition to being obscured by other events, Latin America has also in recent years become less newsworthy in an absolute sense. Fidel Castro is still making four- and five-hour addresses to the Cuban people, still carrying on the most thoroughgoing and only Communist revolution in the Western Hemisphere; but with no further expropriations to make (everything having long ago been seized), no U. S.-sponsored invasions to fight off, and no Russian rockets to rattle, nobody seems to be paying attention. (The difficulty and expense of getting to and from Cuba, and the obstacles with which Washington and Havana confront journalists and scholars are also discouraging reports about what is happening on the island.)

Cuba, therefore, is quieter, and the once-lively dread of a Castro-inspired insurrection that would "make of the Andes another Sierra Maestra" has almost completely subsided. In Brazil, in Venezuela, in Peru, and in Bolivia the alertness of the hardline military, the inertness of the populace, and the advice and assistance of the Americans have crushed armed uprisings. Camilo Torres, the Colombian priest-turned-*guerrillero*, is dead; so is the more formidable and experienced specialist in armed uprisings, the Argentine Ernesto "Che" Guevara. Brazil, where we once worried about the leftist antics of President João Goulart, is now "safe" in military hands; so is the Dominican Republic, where we rushed in twenty thousand American troops in 1965 to avert a possible Communist seizure of power. In 1967, for the first time in over a decade, there were no successful army mutinies or illegal seizures of power. The United States, with so much trouble elsewhere to preoccupy its leaders, is satisfied with the present state of affairs, and the seven out of ten Latin Americans living under military rule have not yet found a way to express their dissatisfaction.

Beneath the surface calm, strong currents are nevertheless running. The Alliance for Progress has consistently failed to meet its modest goal of a 2.5 percent-per-year per-capita increase in income (which would raise an average Haitian's eighty dollars a year by only eight dollars after four years, provided Dr. Duvalier's murderous *ton-ton macoutes* (out-of-uniform police) did not steal it all or kill him). The housing deficit continues to grow, as the region maintains the most rapid population growth of any comparable area. Latin American economies for the most part continue to depend on one or two raw material exports, and have not yet won any concessions from the developed nations on commodity prices; the fall in coffee prices alone has cost Latin America many times the amount of foreign aid she receives. Tens of thousands of children die every year for want of proper food and medical care, and many of those who survive are like the sharecroppers in Brazil's Northeast whom Josué de Castro has described, "sad half humans crushed like cane between rollers that leave only juiceless husks behind." Nobody pays attention; when misery and starvation are normal, they are not newsworthy.

Many of the papers presented at the fifth annual meeting of the Catholic Inter-American Cooperation Program, written by educators, clergymen, religious leaders, bankers, and social scientists familiar with the area and its problems, reflect this sense of

disillusion and despair. Miss Marina Bandeira's sad confession
that the promising Basic Education Movement (MEB) in Brazil
has been throttled by the Army, John Plank's obituary of the
Alianza, and Rubem Alves' desperate call for violence to bring
an end to an intolerable social situation reflect different aspects
of the same tragic circumstances. Most of our contributors echo
Dr. George Shuster's warning that "there are real reasons for
thinking that our relationships may deteriorate rather than improve." CICOP, a small voice among the giant forces of the mass
media, has served as a forum for an impartial, unsparing look at
the two Americas and at the relations between them. If, as so
many of its speakers and other Latin Americanists believe, a
blowup is coming, few storms in recent history will have been
so widely forecast.

Samuel Shapiro

Paris
June, 1968

Contents

V THE TWO AMERICAS

UNITED STATES CULTURE AND ITS
CAPACITY FOR COLLABORATION 253
George N. Shuster

THE TWO AMERICAS: COEXISTENCE,
COMPETITION, OR COOPERATION? 266
John N. Plank

THE POLITICAL IDEOLOGY OF POLITICAL
ECONOMY 285
Irving L. Horowitz

MARKET PROBLEMS IN INTER-AMERICAN
RELATIONS 313
Gustavo Romero-Kolbeck

UNIVERSITY COLLABORATION AND
CULTURAL DEVELOPMENT 328
Robert J. Henle, S.J.

OUR LATIN AMERICAN POLICY 343
Eugene J. McCarthy

APPENDIX 351

INDEX 363

PART ONE

GENERAL CONSIDERATIONS

A THEOLOGICAL
PERSPECTIVE ON HUMAN
LIBERATION

M. RICHARD SHAULL

A number of modern historians have reminded us that the history of the West has been the history of revolutions. And these revolutions have occurred, not merely as the result of an objective crisis in society, but because a crisis was precipitated by the emergence and action of a new, dynamic proletariat. In each case this proletariat had been captured by a new vision of a new social order. Its members found themselves excluded from the benefits of the existing order or repelled by its injustices. Eventually they reached a point where their consuming passion was to bring the old order down and build a new one, and they were willing to sacrifice their lives so that this could happen.

These movements became disruptive forces in their societies. In some instances they overthrew the old order and eventually organized society on a new foundation, with new structures of economic, social, and political life. Often they failed to achieve their goals. Yet when we look back on modern history we can see that many of the most significant breakthroughs toward a more human society have occurred as a result of these revolutions.

It is hard to avoid the conclusion that the emergence of such revolutionary forces is once again the order of the day. In the United States this new proletariat has made its appearance among the black militants and the radicals of a new student generation. But it is in the Third World, and especially in Latin America, that this phenomenon is most widespread. A vanguard of men and women, old and young, of different social classes, has come to the conclusion that their situation is intolerable and must be overcome. They are convinced that the lethargy and misery of the masses, the evident social injustice, and the sclerosis of obsolete structures are due to the domination created and sustained by the wedding of colonial power with the internal structures of economic and political control by an oligarchy. They feel that a new generation must affirm its selfhood, find the road to rapid and autonomous economic development, and shape its own destiny as a nation only as this old order is overcome and a new one is built.

In the past the Christian Church has not creatively responded to the challenge of revolution. In some instances it has been one of the main bulwarks of the old order. In others it has stood on the sidelines and watched the struggle. Usually, some decades after the success of a revolution, the Church has reluctantly entered into dialogue or established a modus vivendi with it. Must this necessarily be the case? Does the very nature of the Christian faith force us to take our stand in support of the old order? Or does it perhaps offer resources for understanding a revolutionary situation and participating in a struggle for social reconstruction? I have been forced to face this question in a very existential way in Latin America, where a new generation of Christians is now in the vanguard of the revolutionary struggle, and I would like to present, very briefly, some of the theological conclusions motivated by my relation with them.

It is now a generally accepted axiom that our Judeo-Christian heritage overcame the dominance of the cyclical view of history. In its place it introduced the idea that man's historical existence was gradually moving toward a goal, and that this goal was nothing less than the creation of a new humanity, a new possibility for human fulfillment within a new social order. The original Christian symbols which provided the resources for such understanding have produced a wide variety of eschatological views, often in contradiction with each other. Nevertheless, they suggest that God is at work in human history and breaks it open to a new tomorrow, and that we are best able to understand what is going on around us and respond to it when we have our eyes open to perceive new possibilities and strive to create them.

But all this is very vague. It suggests that we can look to the future with hope, but it gives us no clues as to the nature of the historical process, the shape of the new order, or how it can be brought into existence. Can we, without attempting to create some overarching philosophy of history, say anything more specific, in theological terms, about this question? I believe that we can. In recent years, for example, a number of theologians have suggested that in the perspective of Christian faith *the history of man is the history of human liberation.* A German sociologist, Dietrich von Oppen, claims that the person and teachings of Christ have had a revolutionary impact on the world. He finds the clue to this revolution in Jesus' words: "The sabbath was made for man, not man for the sabbath." This means for Von Oppen that all institutions lose their sacral, and thus authoritarian, character. They exist to serve man, and they thus must be seen as merely functional. To the degree that this attitude toward institutions has penetrated our culture, new structures have emerged which are open, flexible, limited in their influence, and subject to constant critical examination. The gradual creation of institutions of this type signifies human liberation.

A Dutch theologian, Arend van Leeuwen, concludes that primitive societies were entirely dominated by an "ontocratic" pattern of life. By this he means that all aspects of divine and historical reality, the eternal and the temporal, were inextricably mixed together in such a way that nature and society were sacralized. They belonged to the divine order; therefore they had authority over men and could not be tampered with. For Van Leeuwen the Christian understanding of reality separated the divine from the created order and thus led to the de-sacralizing of the world. Consequently, the growing impact of Christianity on the world has meant the gradual collapse of ontocratic structures and thus has brought increasing freedom to create the future. Within this framework God's redemptive action in the world is understood as an ongoing process of human liberation. As his impact is felt, those races, classes, and communities of men that have been de-humanized move to new discoveries of human self-consciousness, new realms of experience, and thus to a new self-identity. They discover that their future is open and that, as individuals or communities, they move toward a new stage of fulfillment as they take destiny into their own hands and order their existence around the goals which they create. In a very interesting chapter in *Christianity in World History* Van Leeuwen traces the revolutionary impact of this "virus" in our Western world across the centuries.

If this is what is going on in a world in which God is at work, I find it hard to avoid the conclusion that we today have arrived at a climactic moment in that process. For it is this new discovery of selfhood and this new will to shape the future which is at the heart of the Negro revolution and the new stirrings among youth and students in this country as well as of the new developments in the Third World. And if this is the meaning of God's action, to transform and enrich human life and fill it with meaning, then we should feel ourselves closely identified with this struggle, and the achievement of this goal should be our central concern as Christians. In this case, our thought about Vietnam or Latin America will be determined, not primarily by the hope to see

Western institutions established there, or to have change without violence, or even by the desire to "stop Communism," but rather by our concern for the struggle of emerging people as they seek the freedom to develop a new way of life.

The biblical record introduces a second element into our understanding of the historical process. History moves forward, but it does not move upward in spirals, because time and again God's action for the liberation of man runs into difficulties. In the Old Testament the Messianic movement toward the new order is thwarted; it can go ahead only as God tears down in order to build up. Nowhere is this more strikingly stated than in the *Magnificat*, where the Virgin Mary speaks of the coming of Messiah as bringing a radical disruption of the established order. The powerful will be brought down and the humble exalted. The New Testament continues this same line, as the eschatological expectations for the future are intermingled with the apocalyptic. And as the imagery of the anti-Christ suggests, the growing influence of Christ in history leads to the union and dynamic activity of his adversaries, who have been called to life by his action. The liberating action of Christ sows the seeds of liberation in the lives of men, destroys the authority of those structures which block such liberation, and thus provokes a violent and often desperate reaction on the part of the old order.

In this view history moves forward by leaps, as the power of the old order is broken down so that the new can emerge. It is this which leads Rosenstock-Huessey to affirm that the history of the West can only be understood as the history of revolutions. The major steps forward in the creation of new human institutions have occurred through such confrontation and struggle. And to the degree that Christian symbols are operative in our understanding of what is going on around us, we should be prepared to recognize the importance of this element and respond creatively to the challenge it presents.

By this I mean that as Christians we are free from the self-imposed limitations of American liberalism at this point. Nothing is more common than the affirmation that we are in favor of all efforts for the liberation of the depressed classes—as long as they do not overturn the present system or run the risks of violence. Consequently we are the first to withdraw from the struggle when it no longer fits this framework. In the perspective to which I have referred, however, the problem is seen quite differently. When the old order is no longer able to serve men adequately and cannot change fast enough to keep up with events, it will have to be brought down or broken open by violence of one sort or another, and the dynamics of God's action in the world moves in that direction. In that situation the violence of the struggle will be determined primarily by those in power, for it is up to them to decide whether the old can make way for the new without total confrontation and disruption. This does not justify use of violence at any time by the agents of social change, but it does put the primary responsibility for dealing with this question where it belongs.

When I look at the world today with the biblical images in mind, I feel that they help me make sense out of what I see. A commitment to the construction of a new social order on the part of the Negro or the student in this country, or the new generation in the developing world, is being met by tremendous efforts on the part of those in power to preserve the status quo. These new forces have rejected all relationships of paternalism on the part of the powerful. Yet almost everything we do continues to express this attitude in a variety of subtle ways, as, for example, when we assume that we know the solution to the problems of development of the poor nations, or we feel that committees composed mostly of members of the Establishment can decide how to overcome the crisis in our urban ghettos. The emergence of a new self-identity of many national and ethnic groups, as well as that of a new generation, is met with extraordinarily well-organized and effective pressures for conformity, which make real independ-

ence and opposition almost impossible. And the longing of the
powerless for power to determine their destiny—here and abroad
—is met by an expanding system of domination no longer held
in check by effective countervailing power. Those in power are
so bound by their post and their irrelevant ideologies that they
are no longer able to respond creatively to the demands of a new
day. Thus those who find themselves enveloped in the shroud of
the old order have to choose between the surrender of everything
that has become important to them and an arduous revolutionary
struggle. Christian realism should lead us, I believe, to accept
this as the context within which we define our responsibility to
work for social reconstruction today.

Obviously no one can prove that there is a God at work in
history in this way. To make the wager of faith means to bet
that the dynamics of history revealed at one specific moment of
time and in one particular place do indeed offer us a possibility
of understanding the dynamics of the wider historical process,
and that the symbols and stories of the biblical tradition have
the power to make this reality transparent to us. In Christian
perspective that which is most real cannot be grasped by mere
empirical observation; it is above all the reality of the new world
that is coming to be, as the future breaks into our present and
makes it pregnant with new possibilities. In the language of the
Christian tradition, the action of the Triune God in history is
the reality in which human life is set, and it is this which pushes
man toward new possibilities of fulfillment in the midst of conflict,
crisis, and social reconstruction. To live by faith is to trust that
things work out that way and thus to participate in the struggle
in hope.

At this point a further observation is necessary. Christian faith
affirms that Christian symbols provide us with clues to the reality
of historical development and of personal existence. Jesus Christ—
crucified and risen—is both the Messiah who initiates a new era
in human history and the Second Adam, the new man. The same

dynamics which we perceive in the historical process are then operative in personal existence. As individuals, we move toward maturity and fulfillment in life as we allow the old to collapse and the new to arise. The fact that this happens in society makes new forms of personal existence possible in the world, while the new man who is formed through daily death and resurrection can be the free agent of social reconstruction.

For this reason I believe that the central Christian symbols for us today are those of *death* and *resurrection*. No modern thinker has stated this more powerfully than Eugen Rosenstock-Huessey in *The Christian Future*. He puts it this way:

Christianity is the embodiment of one single truth through the ages: that death precedes birth, that birth is the fruit of death, and that the soul is precisely this power of transforming an end into a beginning by obeying a new name. (p. 10)

In these few words we are challenged to a radical reorientation of our lives. For those who have been surprised by the irruption of the new in the midst of the old, and expect to be surprised again and again on the road to the future, death can be brought into the center of life and overcome. They are free to lose their lives in the hope of finding them, to break out of the dead end of stagnation and repetition by burying the old when its time has come and by working to give form to the new. Within this framework it is possible to contemplate and accept the loss of that which we most cherish, even though we do not yet know what will take its place. The willing acceptance of the agony of creation takes the place of security within the context of old stabilities, and those who have no future or give up the future already guaranteed for them turn out to be the ones who are free to create a new tomorrow.

If this perspective is to be transformed into a style of life, we must discover what it means to run the risk of death every day: to allow the presuppositions on which we function to be brought out into the open and called into question, to contemplate the shattering of the neat systems of thought and life in which we feel sheltered and secure, and to have the courage to start putting the pieces together once again, expecting a new design to emerge. When this happens, the Christian community becomes a parable of the coming kingdom rather than a relic of a dead order. It is the place where we serve others by forcing them to call their thought and existence into question, where we are sustained in the time of waiting, and find the courage to risk thinking new thoughts and living experimentally.

It is hardly necessary to stress the importance of this perspective in relation to the situation we now face at home or in our policy toward the Third World. For the failure of American liberalism is nowhere more evident than in its inability to bury its dead. We insist on dealing with the problems of Vietnam and Latin America in terms of an international situation of two decades ago, and thus ignore the dynamics of history and the emergence of new realities. Consequently, we use our power to destroy the most creative forces of new nations and run the risks of World War III because we are victims of our own slogans. We have allowed ourselves to be caught in a box in which we can no longer discern the real alternatives or explore new and creative possibilities latent in the situation.

If in the Christian community we are able to make these resources of our heritage operative once again, something exciting could happen. It would be possible, in the midst of a dying order, to form men and women who would be free to perceive the inadequacy of old slogans, be open to new realities, develop new perspectives, and propose new alternatives. An honest look at the insititutional Church or at the witness of history is not likely to give us much hope for this to happen in the Church as a whole. But it may well be that here and there small communities can arise that will meet this challenge in creative ways.

If this interpretation of the meaning of our Christian heritage is legitimate, it could well revolutionize our perspective on Latin

America and lead us to a commitment to a new struggle there as well as in this country. If we are free to understand what is involved in the struggle for liberation in Latin America today, then our own responsibility will be sharply redefined. To my mind the most significant work on this has been done by Professor Candido Mendes of Brazil, whose participation in the Catholic Inter-American Cooperation Program and other international Catholic movements is well known. Professor Mendes contends that underdevelopment is not simply a lack of certain resources and techniques; it is a *total social fact* which is the product of the structures of society and patterns of relationship with the outside world that developed during the colonial era. Each country was used as a source of raw materials and as a market for the products of the metropolis, and its social structures were shaped by this fact. The economic order was based on the large landowners in the country and the merchants in the city. The political system was the instrument by which this very small ruling class distributed patronage and developed a clientele. The masses were submerged in a state of lethargy; there was no independent middle class; and the intellectual and cultural life of the elite was oriented toward the metropolis.

In this context, according to Candido Mendes, national emancipation and economic development depend upon overcoming this total situation of the past. This involves the integration of the nation around nationalist goals and comprehensive economic planning moving in the direction of socialism, together with the control and disciplined use of the economic resources available. It calls for intensive efforts to awaken the masses for full participation in creating a new society and for the encouragement of a new generation of leadership oriented toward national emancipation and development. It means nothing less than the end of the old order and the creation of new social, economic, and political structures which can serve the goals of national development. And inevitably it means a radically changed relationship with the United States, because national development, by its very nature, requires that the new nations find their own solutions to their problems, build the structures most adequate for their situation, and be as independent as possible of outside economic domination.

A new generation in Latin America understands this and is committed to working for it in these terms. Especially among Catholic youth extraordinary things have been happening in recent years as they have thrown themselves into the struggle for development. But in many instances their experience has been terribly frustrating. They have discovered that the small ruling elites are not only unable to take the initiative in social reconstruction and economic development but are even willing to pay any price to remain in power and preserve their privileges. And what is even more disastrous, these Catholic young people have become convinced that the use of United States power—economic, political, and military—is the major force sustaining the old order and blocking the creation of a new one. The result is very clear. For an increasing number of these people there is only one hope: the organization of armed movements of national liberation, with all the sacrifice and bloodshed that these involve. In recent months I have been amazed to discover how many groups of Catholics and Protestants have moved to this conclusion after all their efforts to work for change by political means had been systematically destroyed.

These recent events confront all of us in the Church with a new call for decision. In the past the Church has often been the bulwark of the status quo or stood on the sidelines while the fight for a new society was going on. Fortunately our awareness today of our Christian responsibility for economic development and national emancipation has pushed us beyond that point. Yet I suspect that for most of us reliance on guerilla warfare is not an attractive prospect. We are rightly horrified by the price this would demand, in bloodshed, in the sacrifice of a new generation, and in the long delay of urgent steps toward development.

But do we have any alternative to offer? The only possibility I see is if Christians and the Church could become a catalytic force in the development of a new type of opposition to the present trend and power structures. This would mean accepting all the risks involved in creating pressure groups that would try to break the situation open: confronting the present forms of domination; insisting on freedom to build the political power of peasants, workers, and students; and supporting students, labor leaders, intellectuals, and priests who are now working to build a new order. This would not be an easy or a pleasant task; it might not have much chance to succeed. But it could open the possibility for a rebirth of hope in the political struggle for social reconstruction, and I can think of nothing that would be more important in Latin America at this time.

Those of us who remain in the United States have an even more difficult task. If we are concerned about the future of Latin America, the important thing is not for us to go there but to remain here and accept the responsibility for a long-term struggle to change a society which, by its own inner logic, has become the enemy of movements of human liberation in the Third World and here at home. And to change our policy toward that part of the world is not something that can be done by lobbying in Washington or pressing for more economic aid. It requires nothing less than a radical critique of our society, the development of a new basis of political power for radical change, and the gradual formation of a new public opinion on foreign policy. Only as these things happen can we hope, as a nation, to sympathize with and support the new forces in Latin America, encourage and permit them to develop the economic and political structures most adequate to their situation, and control the way in which United States private capital operates abroad.

Very few instruments now exist for doing this, so that today our most urgent task may be to work with other radicals in our society toward the creation of small communities willing to attack one or another of these problems on a long-term basis. In the past we have encouraged priests, nuns, and laymen to serve the peoples of the Third World by giving their lives to missionary communities in these lands. Whatever the importance of this task may still be, we now face a new challenge: to encourage this type of commitment to communities in this country that are trying to serve the rest of the world by means of intense intellectual and political efforts to transform our society and its relationship to other nations. I know of one group of twelve young people related to the North American Congress on Latin America (NACLA) who have formed such a team to work on the analysis and exposure of how United States power now operates in Latin America. To do this, they are living on a subsistence basis in New York, most of them taking part-time jobs in order to support themselves as they work at this task. I see this as only one small example of the type of communities now needed to work on a variety of issues in the university, in relation to church groups, in suburbia, and on many other fronts. Nothing less than this, I believe, will be adequate for the challenge now confronting us when we take seriously our responsibility as Christians in the contemporary struggle for human liberation.

REVOLUTION AND
RADICAL REFORM:
AN ETHICAL DILEMMA

DENIS GOULET

Violence is at the same time unavoidable and unjustifiable.

Albert Camus

A guerilla uprising cannot be brought about until all possible avenues of legal procedure have been exhausted.

All wars are cruel, the revolutionary war perhaps most of all because every citizen, whatever his wish, is or will be directly and actively involved in it by the insurgent who needs him and cannot afford to let him remain neutral.

David Galula

No revolution is even possible where the authority of the body politic is truly intact, and this means, under modern conditions, where the armed forces can be trusted to obey the civil authorities.

Hannah Arendt

The guerilla movement is not an end in itself, nor is it a glorious adventure. It is merely a means to an end: the conquest of political power.

Regis Debray

If we preach nonviolence, we reinforce established violence, that is to say, a system of production (I should say; as social system) which

16

make misery and war inevitable. However, if we enter the arena of violence, there is a good chance that we will be trapped there forever.

Merleau-Ponty

A slave who is conscious of being a slave is already half free.

V. I. Lenin

Any speaker must assume a common vocabular universe with his audience. How can this be assumed, however, when the words under discussion are "revolution" and "ethics"? No two people define revolution or radical reform identically. Academics describe revolution; they analyze it and establish "typologies." Practitioners of the art seek not to explain but to persuade; the purpose of their discourse is to recruit. And they speak the language of promises. As Francisco Juliao, head of Northeast Brazil's now defunct peasant leagues, wrote: "The first condition, and the only one, necessary to win the peasants' confidence in the revolution is to tell them, 'You will have land.'"

And what of the word "ethics"? There can be no ethics without freedom. Yet when have moral philosophers sought to justify revolution on any grounds other than its *necessity*? Is not necessity the enemy of freedom? Is Ellul right when he states that in political life a solution can only be just when it is not necessary? Indeed, if it becomes necessary, other options have ceased to exist; and can one then freely (and ethically) choose revolution? If a revolution becomes necessary, how can it provide itself with safeguards against betraying its noble objectives? Will not the requirements of efficient strategy muddy the purity of its goals? On the other hand, is not strategic efficiency a moral requirement of good revolutionary action?

Christian ethics of violence constantly stumbles over its residual links to the "just-war theory" or, when the pendulum swings to "situation ethics," over a subjective model of the right conscience. Regamey insists, on the other hand, that the problem of violence places a Christian in an "ethics of distress situation." This apostle of nonviolence, faced with the contradictions inherent in violence itself, is obliged to say that

The worst distress possible for a Christian is to be forced to recur to violence. I think I see an extreme case of this in Camilo Torres of Colombia. I would go so far as to say that in such a case the man can be not only a hero but even a saint.

The real dilemma for Christians is that they must either advocate nonviolence, thereby becoming accomplices of exploiters, or justify violence and thus sanctify history's aberrations in the name of a gospel which preaches love and respect for life.

Marxist moralists face different but equally perplexing problems: How to keep history open-ended, How to keep their means from becoming ends? Their basic constraint, however, comes from the dogma which refuses (with minor exceptions among contemporary Czech Communists) to dissociate social alienation from religious alienation. Consequently, Marxists need to rewrite history to prove to "religion-beguiled" masses that Christ, or Buddha, or Brahman-Atman is their kind of social revolutionary.

My conclusion is that no ethical doctrine of revolution exists. There are only free and responsible ethical options for or against revolution. But after the option, what then? In the words of I. F. Stone,

For the Revolution, as for the Church, the world is full of snares and pitfalls: the unavoidable minimum of intercourse with things-as-they-are, the need for trade to earn one's bread . . . and the logic of statecraft which demands weapons, technology, compromise and duplicity. With the assumption of temporal power, the Revolution, like the Church, enters into a state of sin.[1]

Or, as Thomas Merton put it, "We are delivered to the god of power that we adore—our punishment is to have what we want."

In conventional usage, revolution means the illegal conquest of central political power for the purpose of tearing down the old social order and building up a new one. Social scientists, however, generally define it as any far-reaching change which transforms men's outlook, behavior, self-image, or life style. Thus they speak of technological, communications, and sexual revolutions, while often they pay scant attention to the time dimension. One wonders if disagreement over what is revolutionary or evolutionary, reformist or radical, would endure if all observers synchronized their discussion to fit the same time span.

Eric Wolf sees revolution as a "process by which varying components of the middleman layer and of the peasantry are mobilized and brought into contact with each other."[2] Fanon regards it as a method by which the oppressed man cuts the umbilical cord that links him to exploiters and, more importantly, heals his psyche by an act that purges him of his inferiority.[3] For Camus, revolution is the establishment of universal human justice after revolt has overthrown injustice. And Debray restates the classical Marxist doctrine that the purpose of revolution is the conquest of political power.

Revolution is, in effect, a special kind of total warfare, involving the violence of arms, rationing, the impressment of men and property, manipulative propaganda. Its aim is to seize power and alter the process of decision-making. Though it enjoys dramatic moments, revolution also knows the tedium of simply holding on when victory appears impossible and of painfully rebuilding institutions after the triumph. Mao in China, the fellagha in Algeria, and Fidel in the Sierra Maestra have all illustrated the institution-building function of guerilla activity. Leaders are summoned to administer small communities in harmony with revolutionary ideals. In so doing they serve a political apprenticeship for the day when they will govern the larger society.

In his dialogue *The Statesman* Plato imagines that

The government of human beings was originally government by gods. In their control of the world things improve as if they were wound up on a spindle to achieve a high tension and power control. Then at a certain point the gods decide that they will let this unwind, and this is the period when

human beings take over. After this happens, human beings become worse
and worse at the art of government, until finally government degenerates
into a kind of chaos, anarchy, tryanny, and so forth. When it gets bad
enough, the gods decide they will take over again, and so they begin—
perhaps through a man—to wind up the process again, and it begins to
improve.[4]

This essay takes revolution to mean the illegal seizure of the
central organs of political power, with the declared aim of insti-
tuting new arrangements for running society, especially in its
economic and political spheres.

We now move to our second term: "ethics." Ethics presupposes
freedom, and where freedom is, there is responsibility. A man
acts ethically when he could have acted otherwise or refrained
from acting. Responsibility is both accountability and the ability
to respond to challenges issued by events, things, other men.
Whenever freedom or responsibility is absent, there is no ethical
problem. There may be the human problem that man ceases to
be human. But there is not the ethical problem that he ceases
to be good.

The original title of this article was "Ethical Quagmire: Concomitant of Radical Change." Quicksand morality is not concomitant with every radical change, however. Religious conversion,
for instance, is radical change; it goes to the roots of one's beliefs
and meanings. Yet it leaves a man secure in his ethical stance,
not wallowing in doubt or indecision. Peopling a new frontier also
entails radical change in the pioneer's life. But there is no ethical
quagmire involved because a break has been made with the
past on the basis of hope, and dedication to the future poses no
insoluble "case of conscience" to those engaged in the adventure.

That special kind of radical change we call revolution does,
on the other hand, confront the conscience with a dilemma. One's
choice of alternatives is such that one cannot avoid committing
evil in one way or another. In the face of moral perplexity moralists of the past told men to choose the lesser evil and set their
consciences to rest. This advice helps little in the case of revolu-

tion, for one cannot weigh on the same scale two different *kinds* of evil, the first present and unbearable, the second future and unpredictable. If history teaches us anything about revolutions, it is that the revolutionary himself does not know where his acts will lead. This is why many people conclude that there never has been a good revolution. Their point is, as Scott Buchanan explains, "that what the revolutions started out to achieve never came off. The people who started them suffered a good deal, destroyed a good deal, and never realized their original vision." This verdict is hardly acceptable because it assumes that revolution is not about anything very important. All revolutions, in fact, do go through a stage during which they must reconsider, and perhaps even lose, their original aims and set new aims in the light of lessons learned during the revolution. A revolution, a real revolution, is a very profound thing. It means that the people who revolt, as well as the people against whom they are revolting, become reeducated.[5]

We are placed in an ethical dilemma. Revolution can be good as well as bad. Its ethical justification, I believe, always rests on necessity. Moralists often consider revolution to be dangerous, possibly even positively bad. Yet, the argument goes, men are at times so cruelly victimized that they must revolt, even if only to defend their humanity. The evolution of Camilo Torres illustrates the point. In 1963, speaking as a priest, he disapproved of violence as contrary to Christian morals. As a sociologist, however, he sought to refrain from value judgments, lest he confuse positive science with normative science. Three years later Camilo wrote that

The people do not believe in elections. The people know that legal paths have been exhausted. The people know that only armed battle remains open to them. The people are in a state of despair and are resolved to risk their lives so that the next generation of Colombians will not be slaves. . . . Every sincere revolutionary has to acknowledge that armed combat is the only alternative that is left.[6]

In a recent publication of the National Council of Churches we are asked,

Is it lawful for the Christian actively to patricipate in revolutionary movements that may resort to violence, in cases where the goal of social transformation does not appear viable by any other means, but which is indispensable from the point of view of social justice and human well-being?[7]

Once again a plea is made to allow violence because there is no other way.

My argument is that if we have no alternatives, we have no dilemma. Moralists have always taught that no one is obliged to do the impossible. If social justice is impossible except through violence, we are not morally bound to use futile, nonviolent means. Furthermore, ethics forbids the use of "intrinsically bad" means. Yet it has always condoned police coercion, defensive war, military assistance given to embattled allies. Violence, in a word, has never been treated as an intrinsically bad means. Many contemporary moralists, it is true, condemn atomic, bacteriological, and chemical warfare as inherently evil. But these are hardly the weapons used by insurgents! We therefore ask moralists, "Why have you not always preached that revolutionary violence is unequivocally good? In the light of your own principles it has to be good because it is not intrinsically bad and it is sometimes the only option *possible*." A dilemma exists because we speak of ethics, which presupposes freedom, while pleading necessity, the antithesis of freedom.

Ellul contends that no political solution can be just if it is necessary, if it is not free. In delicate political matters justice depends primarily on the moment at which decisions are taken rather than on any lofty conception of justice on the part of their author, his good intentions, or the particular political line he follows.

A decision must be reached [he says] before irreparable acts have been committed, before public opinion has been aroused. . . . In effect, when a situation is nascent, it is not *necessary* to intervene; consequently, the act runs the risk of seeming gratuitous. . . . A just solution can in fact be found only in the freedom of the decision-maker who has a gamut of solutions and possible combinations before him. Once circumstances evolve and solutions get progressively eliminated, the freedom of the actor diminishes at each step and finally there remains but a single solution which imposes itself of necessity. It thus becomes necessary; and we may say that in all such cases this solution simply reflects the greatest measure of power, but *never* of justice. In politics a solution imposed of necessity is never a just solution.[8]

We can now explain why there is a dilemma. Ethics assumes revolution to be good because it is inevitable. Once revolution becomes inevitable, however, it is too late to build into its conduct the safeguards against absolutizing its means, against betraying the justice and brotherhood of its cause in the name of strategic efficiency. Revolutionaries argue that any realistic ethic posits strategic efficiency as a moral requirement of good revolutionary action. Even the Gospel warns us against building a tower unless we can finish it or launching a war unless we can see it through. In a word, ethics can easily justify launching a revolution but is at a loss to impose limits on its conduct.

If we reject this analysis of political justice, determinism then nourishes both our good conscience and our dilemma. Our good conscience, because we justify revolution as necessary. Our dilemma, because we cannot control revolution. By its very nature revolution forces us to tread paths whose destination is unknown. Its goals change as it proceeds, and its participants are educated to a truth yet to be revealed. Perhaps we can "free the present from the past," but who will free the future from the present? Is not Djilas right when he says that

Throughout history there have been no ideal ends which were attained with non-ideal, inhumane means, just as there has been no free society which was built by slaves. Nothing so well reveals the reality and greatness of ends as the methods used to attain them.
If the end must be used to condone the means, then there is something in the end itself, in its reality, which is not worthy.[9]

Purists want both revolution and love simultaneously, but these two things are incompatible. Revolution consists in loving a man

who does not yet exist. "But the man who loves a living being,"
says Camus, "if he loves him truly, can only be willing to die for
that living being, not for a man who does not live yet."[10] To the
Marxist, who argues that his ethic spurns love in favor of justice,
Camus replies that when morality is formal it devours, for no one
can be virtuous by dictate.

Revolution moves men by denouncing the injustices they suffer.
Yet it perpetrates new injustices on that flesh in the name of an
idealized man who lies at the term of history. This is why, if it
wishes to be human, revolution must come to terms with relativity.[11] The virtue of adversaries resides in their choice of means,
for in the last analysis the goals of all the combatants are good.
At its ultimate level the debate is over two acts of faith. Any
revolution must wed power to love. The crucial question is, Will
love bow in submission to power because it is too weak to triumph in the real world? Or will power accept love's gentle yoke
in recognition of its own impotence to serve human purposes?
Fanon believes "that only violence pays. . . . The exploited man
sees that his liberation implies the use of all means, and that
of force first and foremost."[12] But Thomas Merton places his
act of faith in love:

> the non-violent resister is persuaded of the superior efficacy of love, open-
> ness, peaceful negotiation and above all of truth. For power can guarantee
> the interests of *some men* but it can never foster the good of *man*. Power
> always protects the good of some at the expense of all others. Only love
> can attain and preserve the good of all. Any claim to build the security
> of *all* on force is a manifest imposture.[13]

Transcending rational discourse on the ethics of violence there
lies the option for one of these faiths. In both cases the believer
falls into an "ethics of distress" situation. Whatever he chooses,
he cannot predict or control the outcome of his options. Violence
on behalf of justice can become repression under the banner of
"eliminating counterrevolutionaries." Nonviolence for love's sake
just as readily paves the way for the greater violence of despera-

tion. Once cannot avoid taking chances; and if he is lucid, his conscience is in distress. Lucidity is essential; so is advertence to the ambiguity of the word "necessity." Marx calls class struggle a necessity. Even when "enlightened" exploiters carry out reforms, they may unwittingly deepen class antagonisms and prepare the day of ultimate violence. History moves ineluctably toward conflict, and we must attempt to alter history's dialectics ahead of history's apocalyptic deadline.

For Ellul, necessity signifies the failure to meet freedom's deadline and the resulting loss of options. Not that it is wrong to begin a revolution, but once revolutionaries have burned their bridges, they have no leverage to counter the tendency of revolution to subordinate purity of goals to efficiency of means. The revolutionary has to parody Christ: "he who is not with me is against me." Both insurgents and counterinsurgents need every citizen and "cannot afford to let him remain neutral."[14] Under both kinds of necessity ethical choices lose their meaning; they become either impossible or superfluous.

There is no Christian ethic of revolution. There are attempts by Christians to interpret complex issues in ethical terms. Many such efforts have foundered on the shoals of the just-war theory. This theory posits a number of criteria for a just war:

a. War must be declared by legitimate authority.

b. The cause must be just. This has usually been interpreted to mean self-defense or helping a beleaguered ally under attack.

c. Leaders waging war must preserve a right intention. Their goal must remain peace, not war; reconciliation, not vengeance; equity, not conquest.

d. Only lawful means are permitted. That is, means must be morally indifferent or inherently good. This criterion urges moderation in destruction and advocates "proportionality" between damage inflicted and benefits obtained. The principle of licit means obviously assumes the operational difference be-

tween combatants and noncombatants, and knowledge of what
constitutes a good or bad instrument of violence.[15]

Some years ago these principles were revised to fit revolutionary situations. They now read as follows:

a. It must be certain that legitimate authority has lost its mission, that is, become tyrannical or incapable of administering
the common good.
b. All peaceful means must be exhausted before revolutionary
violence is lawful.
c. Revolution's anticipated "good" effects must outweigh the
harm it causes.
d. Revolutionary leaders must entertain reasonable hope of
success.
e. No intrinsically evil means can be employed.
f. It is forbidden to exacerbate the prerevolutionary situation
in order to precipitate the outbreak of violence.[16]

My intent is not to refute this doctrine point by point as it applies to revolution, for these criteria, even refurbished, obviously
ignore political realities. Let us take the first principle, for example. Who will judge whether or not legitimate authority has lost
its mission? A majority of voters? But what if voters represent but
a minority of citizens? A revolutionary minority party? By whose
mandate do they speak for the body politic? The masses? A particular class? Through what mechanism can this judgment be
tested, according to what rules?

As for exhausting all peaceful means, what should a budding
revolutionary group do if it expects to be wiped out unless it con-
ceals its opposition to the ruling elite until ready to engage in
combat? And who can predict a revolution's possible "good" and
"bad" effects? How does one gauge a "reasonable" prospect of
success? Holden Roberto's GRAE (*Governo Revolucionario de
Angola no Exilio*)[17] has now been fighting seven years and still

seems far from victory. Nevertheless, if we are able to believe Mao and Ho Chi Minh, the revolutionary who perseveres to the end is certain to win. Indeed, it took the Algerians more than seven years to win their battle. There is no need to belabor the point. The just-war theory fails to come to grips with the psychological and political realities of revolutionary situations. It is worthless.

What of some form of Christian situation ethics? There is something to recommend this approach, it is true; it is often quite hardheaded. But it provides no norms other than purely subjective ones for evaluating objective situations. There is good reason to fear that a man's ideology, class interests, occupational bias, heredity, environmental conditioning, to say nothing of his personality characteristics, go far toward inclining him toward violence or nonviolence. Can any right conscience truly exist if the ultimate appeal is to subjective persuasion? At best the direction such a position can take is that of moral ambiguity. Niebuhr was right in arguing, thirty-five years ago, that

the struggle for a social justice in the present economic order involves the assertion of rights, the rights of the disinherited, and the use of coercion. Both are incompatible with the pure love ethic found in the Gospels. How, then, do we justify the strategy of the "class struggle"? We simply cannot do so in purely Christian terms. There is in the absolute sense no such thing as "Christian socialism."[18]

The Gospels contain no ethic of socialism, of the status quo, or of revolution. All ethical positions, in personal life as in political affairs, compromise Jesus' "pure love principle." Where Niebuhr's analysis falters, I believe, is in assuming that pure love is meant to be an ethical norm. Christianity urges the dynamics of love, but love's demands cannot adequately be expressed in juridical terms. Jesus advocated love of one's enemies, eschatological hope in God's defense of the victimized, the sacrifice of one's rights for the sake of brotherhood, not as moral laws but as a spiritual ideal which will constantly thrust us beyond ethics and beyond the realistic dictates of political or personal wisdom. The worst distress for a Christian is, indeed, to be forced to recur to violence. Distress means not being free to work on behalf of love without, even if tentatively and temporarily, professing one's impotence to love, to forgive, or to transmute his earthly despair into eschatological hope. It is no weakness of Christianity or bankruptcy of the Gospel that breeds distress; it is man's condition in history. Were man more than human he could create goodness, justice, and freedom for all men without having to destroy them in those he calls enemies. If man did not live in history, he could "free the present from the past." Yet, no revolutionary can totally achieve this. Destruction never leaves the destroyer unscarred and free to build with a blithe heart and a clear conscience. Revolutionaries, like ecclesiastics and politicians, cannot avoid compromises.

Revolutionary situations confront one with a dilemma whose only issues are heroism or compromise. One can of course escape distress by fleeing reality or by abdicating ethics, but these are pseudo-solutions. Even the man who cannot rise to heroism must avoid escapism. If he wishes to be moral, he can never resign himself to the determinisms of violence or the passivities of nonviolence. Neither violence nor nonviolence can be absolute; total nonviolence is connivance with the violence of exploiters, whereas total violence is rationalization of evil.

We must consider next the Marxist approach to revolution. In 1850 Engels wrote that

The worst thing that can befall a leader of an extreme party is to be compelled to take over a government in an epoch when the movement is not yet ripe for the domination of the class which he represents, and for the realization of the measures which that domination implies. What he can do depends not upon his will but upon the degree of contradiction between the various classes, and upon the level of development of the material means of existence, of the conditions of production and commerce upon which class contradictions always repose. What he ought to do, what his party demands of him, again depends not upon him or the stage of development of the class struggle and its conditions. . . . Thus he necessarily finds himself in an insoluble dilemma. What he can do contradicts all his previous actions, principles, and the immediate interests of his party, and what he ought to do cannot be done. In a word, he is compelled to represent not his party or his class, but the class for whose domination the movement is then ripe. In the interests of the movement he is compelled to advance the interests of an alien class, and to feed his own class with phrases and promises, and with the asservation that the interests of that alien class are its own interests. Whoever is put into this awkward position is irrevocably lost.[19]

As sadly as any purist Christian, Engels laments the betrayal, not of Gospel love, but of proper class interests. Like contemporary Christians, he sees his elite in the grip of an insoluble ethical dilemma. Engels, like Ellul, defines political ethics as a function of time, the moment in the history of class struggle, and not of right objectives or lofty and sincere personal goals. Interestingly, he concedes that revolutionary leaders must lie to and manipulate men. "Whoever is put into this awkward position," he concludes, "is irrevocably lost!"

Marx regarded violence as an ontological necessity whose use poses no problem of principle.[20] But times have changed. There may well be, in the words of I. F. Stone,

something anachronistic in Castro's Cuba and in Che's mission to build a new and bigger Sierra Maestra in the Andes. The hard realities of the hemisphere are very different from the revolutionary clichés of Castroism. How do you create new managerial and scientific cadres to replace the old oligarchies and American aid? How do you inspire and organize for hard work for many hungry years an illiterate mass quite different in its conditioning and past from, let us say, the immemorially productive people of China? For after the music of the Revolution dies down, everybody still has to go to work.[21]

Let us grant with Debray that the goal of guerilla warfare is the conquest of political power; what does one do with political power after the revolution is successful? Is he, as Engels feared, simply trapped by the objective conditions of history's capricious moment?

The history of Marxist revolutions in the Soviet Union, China, and to a lesser extent in Cuba, cannot leave us very optimistic about the possibilities of revolutionary governments maintaining an open-ended attitude toward the future. The mobilization of the oppressed by the use of an ideology whose central themes are class struggle and the suppression of exploitation almost necessarily elicits, engenders, or reinforces simplistic allegiances to a dogmatic utopianism ill prepared to be self-corrective once power has been gained. Mannheim challenges Communism for requiring its adherents to draw a blank check on their future:

> The dangerous fallacy in the communist argument is that its champions promise to pay for every inch of lost freedom in the intermediary period of dictatorship with an undated check on a better future. . . . Once a dictatorial system, whatever its social content, seizes the educational apparatus, it does everything to obliterate the memory and need of free thought and free living; it does its utmost to transform free institutions into tools of a minority.[22]

Djilas' query about means and ends has never been satisfactorily answered by Marxists. No doubt leading Communist theorists —Garaudy, Althusser, Adam Schaff, and a few others—embrace dialogue. A joint Communist–Christian group is even now debating the possibility, in Marxist terms, of dissociating religious alienation from social alienation. By and large, however, Marxist ethics is in a state of disarray and raises more questions than it can answer. China's cultural revolution, for example, seriously undermines the assumption of all revolutionaries since 1789, namely, that a radical act of violence will burst open the door to a better society. As *The Economist* commented a year ago (January 14, 1967, p. 99),

> It is this belief that Chairman Mao has now finally and perhaps decisively put in doubt. . . . What is needed, and what he has set himself to achieve, is perpetual revolution—to be precise, a regular succession of upheavals, following each other at intervals of a generation or less. He believes that nothing short of this will keep the original revolutionary impetus alive.

Yet Mao is charged with heresy by the Holy Office of Marxist orthodoxy, and he is challenged by many of his old Yenan revolutionary comrades. Even if Mao is proved right, why should down-trodden men sacrifice their all for a revolution that then needs to be discarded every fifteen years?

The present travail of Marxist revolutionary ethics reveals that old doctrinal certitudes are being eroded by the realities of political life. Even wily old Togliatti complained before his death that Communists were incapable of recognizing the new forms of alienation they had generated in their own societies. In a word, Marxist revolutionary ethics also founders in a quagmire.

We now come to an ambiguous term: "conclusions." Nothing I have said is definitive or final; on the contrary, it is all very inconclusive. To conclude, however, also means to finish, not just to close debate. And what has our excursion along the thorny paths of revolutionary ethics shown us?

First, that we are still in a quagmire, but we know how we got there and why we are stuck. If to be conscious of one's state of slavery is already to be half free, then we are better off than when we started. The problem is necessity: to the extent that determinism limits ethical choice, so freedom and the scope of ethical goodness are reduced. This is so whether we take necessity to mean simply the lapse of options with the passage of time or the impersonal determinism of history's laws.

Second, I have argued that there is no ethics of revolution. There are only ethical (that is, free and responsible) options for or against revolution. Since the old just-war theory and situation ethics are both powerless to untangle our perplexities, the only options left, short of heroic witness to love and human goodness, involve compromise. Each man must therefore choose the causes for which he will compromise: revolution, law and order, tradition, gradual change, reform, socialism, and so on. He can never fully convert another man to his point of view, because if he is perfectly lucid, he cannot fully convert himself. Certain positive values are served by each of the options, but no single individual or group can fully bear witness to all of these values.

This is why Regamey, who preaches nonviolence, can recognize heroism and, yet, even sanctity in a Camilo Torres!

My third conclusion can be phrased as a question, After the revolution, what? If successful revolutions are invariably tempted to become idolatrous, they must tolerate dissent. In the words of Camus,

a revolutionary is also a revolted man or he ceases to be a revolutionary. But if he is revolted, he will end up opposing the revolution. . . . Every revolutionary ends up being either an oppressor or a heretic. In the purely historic universe which they have chosen, both revolt and revolution lead to the same dilemma: either the police or folly.[23]

After the revolution there abide the twin problems of perpetual renovation and of technology's hold over romanticism. What happens when revolutionary fervor confronts the impersonal logic of advanced technology? How does one avoid those new modes of alienation, unknown to Marx, which afflict all developed countries today irrespective of their ideologies?

A fourth conclusion is that we must insist on basic definitions: each theorist of radical change must be made to define his concepts with precision. The efforts of Furtado, Hirschman, and others to establish typologies of revolutionary situations is a positive step, but typologies are descriptive, never normative. Fals-Borda has moved further and incorporated overt value positions in subversion and revolution into the very fabric of his social science analysis. His boldness may well constitute a major breakthrough in overcoming the communications barrier between different kinds of experts on revolution.

My fifth conclusion is that no one can feel very secure about passing on moral enlightenment to others regarding the ethical dimensions of revolution. I echo Domenach's advice:

Carry on your revolution if you wish; in the extreme case, wage your war if you wish. But stop preaching someone else's war. When the moment comes to take up guns, then let the intellectual resort to arms, but not to words which place bullets inside guns at a distance! . . . What weight can we give to the bad conscience which preaches war without waging it—or the good conscience which preaches peace and justice without forging the the means to establish them?[24]

My final word is the very first word contained in the epigraph to this article: "Violence is at the same time unavoidable and unjustifiable."[25]

NOTES

1. I. F. Stone, "The Legacy of Che Guevara," *Ramparts* (December, 1967), 21.

2. Eric R. Wolf, "Reflections on Peasant Revolution," Carnegie Seminar, Indiana University, April 3, 1967 (mimeographed), p. 10.

3. Frantz Fanon, *The Wretched of the Earth* (New York: Grove Press, 1966) *passim*.

4. Scott Buchanan, *On Revolution, a Conversation* (Santa Barbara, California: Center for the Study of Democratic Institutions, 1962), pp. 1–2.

5. *Ibid.*, p. 6.

6. *Camilo Torres*, in the collection *Sondeos*, No. 5 (Cuernavaca, Mexico: CIDOC, 1966), p. 116, second citation, p. 374.

7. "A Theological Reflection by Latin American Christians on Violence and Non-Violence," *Latin American News Letter*, National Council of Churches, 66 (December, 1967), 9.

8. Jacques Ellul, *L'Illusion Politique* (Robert LaFfont, 1965), p. 190.

9. Milovan Djilas, *The New Class: An Analysis of the Communist System* (New York: Frederick A. Praeger, 1957), p. 162.

10. Albert Camus, *The Rebel* (New York: Vintage Books, 1956), p. 96.

11. *Ibid.*, p. 290.

12. Fanon, *op. cit.*, p. 48.

13. Thomas Merton, "Blessed Are the Meek: The Christian Roots of Non-Violence," Fellowship of Reconciliation Reprint (July, 1967), p. 7.

14. David Galula, *Counter-Insurgency Warfare, Theory and Practice* (New York: Frederick A. Praeger, 1964), p. 76.

15. P. R. Regamey, *La Conscience Chretienne et la Guerre* (Cahiers Saint-Jacques, n.d.), pp. 31–40.

16. Gerardo Claps G., "El Cristiano frente a la revolución violenta," *Mensaje*, 115 (1963), 142.

17. John A. Marcum, "Three Revolutions," *Africa Report* (November, 1967), 8–23.

18. Reinhold Niebuhr, "The Ethic of Jesus and the Social Problem," in Harry K. Girvetz, ed., *Contemporary Moral Issues* (Belmont, California: Wadsworth, 1963), p. 315.

19. Friedrich Engels, *The Peasant War in Germany*, in Lewis S. Feuer, ed., *Marx & Engels, Basic Writings on Politics & Philosophy* (New York: Anchor Books, 1959), p. 435.

20. Gustave Thibon, "Ya-t-il une doctrine chrétienne sur la violence?" in *La Violence, Recherches et De'bats* (1967), p. 122.

21. I. F. Stone, *op. cit.*, p. 21.

22. Karl Mannheim, *Freedom, Power, and Democratic Planning* (New York: Oxford University Press, 1950), p. 28.

23. Camus, *L'Homme Revolte* (Gallimard, 1951), p. 305.

24. Jean-Marie Domenach, "Un Monde de violence," in *La Violence*, p. 37.

25. Albert Camus, "Reponses a E. d'Astier," in *Actuelles I, Pleiade*, II, 355, cited in Thomas Merton, "Terror and the Absurd: Violence and Non-Violence in Albert Camus," August, 1966 (mimeographed), p. 23.

VIOLENCE AND
COUNTERVIOLENCE

RUBEM ALVES

We are becoming more and more aware of the basically violent
character of the world in which we live. The main reason for this
new awareness is primarily, not the increase in the use of violence
on the part of the powerful (although this is an undeniable fact
today), but rather the new fact that those who were and are
under violence, those who are paralyzed, deprived of their capacity of speech and action by it, began to be aware of their
situation of bondage, began to have hope for new days, and
decided to act accordingly in order to liberate themselves. Their
protest and action toward liberation uncovers the violence under
which they exist and triggers new forms of terror as strategy
for their containment, terror intended to dissuade them from
their project.

In the "golden days" when the slaves were still unable to
speak the language of protest and hope, when they could not
act but in obedience to their masters, violence presented itself
under benevolent disguises. Colonialism was considered the civil-

izing and Christianizing thrust of the Western nations which
would liberate the natives from their barbaric preindustrial culture and values. It was never acknowledged as a form of exploitation. The wealthy nations of the world even today cannot recognize the causal relationship between their wealth and the poverty
of the Third World. Their wealth is attributed to their Puritan
heritage, their Calvinist morality, their ingenuity, but never to
the exploitation of the Third World. When the "underdeveloped"
world is referred to, the connotation is that it is a world which
lags behind, not a world which is under the power of the wealthy
nations, as even the word so compellingly suggests. Segregation
was not seen as a form of injustice and violence, but rather as a
necessary protective measure on the part of the whites to avoid
the contamination of their women, their stores, barbershops, and
restaurants, by a barbaric and inferior race unfit for freedom.
The *military interventions* in Hungary, Santo Domingo, and Vietnam were, and are, regarded, not as the exercise of power on
the part of the masters, as violence, but rather as the protection
of freedom for the sake of peoples who were not intelligent and
organized enough to take care of themselves.

Those were the "golden days," when the power of the masters
was so overwhelming that it made men unable to speak and
unable to move. No action for change. No protests. Silence.
Paralysis. Stability. Violence was thoroughly successful. It was
able to destroy the slave's will so that he could not oppose or
resist his masters. Nobody was able to shout VIOLENCE. This
word is always shouted by the oppressed in their rejection of
oppression, in their hope for liberation. But they were not yet
fully human. They did not yet know how to speak, let alone shout.
The masters, in their turn, would only say: peace, stability, civilization, Christian values, law, order, legality. Violence thus
remained hidden. Legality and order were the names for oppression. So, the ideology and even the religion of the oppressors
de-historized the Indian and the Negro in order to justify violence.

What a remarkable similarity to the crucifixion of Jesus Christ, who was killed in the name of law and order, by the supreme embodiment of law and order, the Roman Empire, and in the name of God by the supreme embodiment of piety and spirituality, the Judaic religious structure of that time. We see then how intimate the relationships between order, legality, piety, and violence are.

With the emergence of the colonial people from passivity into history, their silence and paralysis are over. They reject the violent situation in which they exist. They refuse to adjust themselves to the social reality that is determined by violence. They find themselves in bondage in Egypt, and they search for the ways to their Exodus, toward a new tomorrow. They have learned two things: first, that the masters never willingly give up their power, their hold upon the slave. As Marcuse indicates, "they are able to improve the conditions of the slave, and to improve their exploitation." And, second, that the masters, once their ability to pacify the slave by the improvement of his conditions fails, once they perceive that the slaves will not succumb to the temptation of the "flesh pots of Egypt," do not hesitate to use terror and naked violence to dominate those they are unable to domesticate.

From the point of view of the oppressed it is idle to ask abstractly if violence can be used to achieve goals of justice. For them violence is not an abstract problem but the hard daily reality of their lives. They do not ask abstractly about violence but, from their experience with it, demand that violence against them be stopped at once. It is interesting that both, masters and slaves alike, now speak the same language: they talk about their concern for peace, about the need to bring violence to an end. But they mean two completely different things. What the masters say is: "Give up your ideas of freedom and I will not use violence any more. I use violence to dissuade you from your project. Become domesticated, adapt yourself to my rule and I will even make it possible for you to get fat." The slave, in turn, says: "No. My vocation is freedom. I want to be free to organize my world and my children's world as we want, according to our choices and needs, not according to yours. From my suffering, created by your violence, I will press forward against your violence which wants to stop me."

From the perspective of the slave the use of violence is completely rejected. Violence is power used to dominate. When the slave decides to become free, he is rejecting the validity of violence. His project is liberation, not domination. But he knows that the master will not give up his power willingly. The masters do not liberate the slaves. The slaves liberate themselves, and in this act they liberate the masters for a new type of relationship. If they have to reject violence, as the basic master-slave relationship, they have to exercise counterviolence, that is, power used against violence, power directed toward liberation. The question "How is counterviolence, in the context of violence, going to take shape?" cannot be decided in the abstract. The answer is a question of circumstances and strategy. It takes shape contextually, as the answer of power for liberation, in opposition to the forms of violence—power for domination—which the masters are using.

A COMMON HISTORY OF
THE AMERICAS?

SAMUEL SHAPIRO

In a famous presidential address to the American Historical
Association, Professor Herbert E. Bolton argued that Anglo-
America and Latin America had had essentially similar histories.[1]
Both societies were established during the same outward surge of
Europe in the sixteenth and seventeenth centuries; both were
formed by the mingling (in different proportions and under different circumstances) of Europeans, Indians, and Negro slaves;
"likenesses in the colonial systems were more striking than differences." The American Revolution was a continental affair, lasting
for half a century after 1776; the new nations went through similar turbulent eras of disorder, civil war, and foreign intervention;
"the essential unity of the Western Hemisphere" was revealed
again in World War I.

Bolton's idea of stressing hemispheric history, the "Epic of
Greater America," buttressed by a lifetime of brilliant teaching
and able scholarship, was an attractive one. His scholarly affirmation of the essential idea behind the Monroe Doctrine, the Good

Neighbor Policy, and the Alliance for Progress has stimulated a
great deal of research and controversy, some of it conveniently
collected by Lewis Hanke.[2] Hanke's rhetorical question is best
answered by an equivocation: Yes, in some ways they do, and
No, in some ways they do not. The purpose of this paper is to
survey some of the general similarities and differences in the
history of the two Americas as an introduction to the essays in
this volume.

Table I lists some two dozen arguments that support the
Bolton thesis, common factors in the history of the United States
and our hemispheric neighbors to the south. We are all, to begin
with, products and parts of Western Christendom, with all that
that phrase implies. Christianity (and not Buddhism or Islam),
the Western alphabet (and not the Greek, or Arabic, or Chinese
ideograms), the classical heritage from Greece and Rome,
related Indo-European languages, a common origin in Renaissance Europe, a common artistic and musical patrimony—all are
ties that bind the Americas more or less strongly. A North American would never feel as lost, as alienated, in Buenos Aires or
Santiago as he might in Bangkok or Saigon. He can make some
sense of the newspapers (even if he does not know Spanish or
Portuguese), he can attend reasonably familiar religious services,
he will recognize the painters and the themes in the art museums.
He will *not*, on the other hand, encounter anything as bewilder-
ing to Westerners as Oriental calligraphy, cow worship, Sinitic
languages, or ritual suicide.

TABLE I

COMMON FACTORS IN THE HISTORY OF THE AMERICAS

1. Origins in Europe as offshoots of Western Christendom
2. The Frontier: empty lands to be occupied
3. The American Indian: exploitation or extermination
4. Plantation systems: Virginia, Mississippi, Cuba, Brazil
5. Negro slavery

6. Geographic proximity (Cuba, Mexico, the Spanish Border-lands)
7. Colonial eras: rule from London, Lisbon, Madrid
8. Wars of independence: Washington, San Martín, Bolívar, Martí
9. Republican principles (if not practices): empires and mon-archies fail
10. Raw material export economies (lumber, cotton, silver, coffee, sugar, etc.)
11. Expansion (United States and Brazil)
12. "Newness": all are the children of Columbus
13. Federalism (United States, Mexico, Brazil)
14. The "new" immigration of the nineteenth century: Irish, Ger-mans, Italians, etc.
15. Modifications of language: "American" English, Rioplatense Spanish, Haitian Creole, etc.
16. Modifications of law
17. Mingling of cultures in Arizona, New York City, Florida, Puerto Rico, etc.
18. Labor shortage: low ratio of man to land
19. Feudal survivals: the encomienda, capitania, patroonship, seignory, proprietorship
20. The Monroe Doctrine—political expression of the Bolton thesis
21. The Good Neighbor Policy
22. The Organization of American States
23. The Alliance for Progress

A second common theme in the history of the Americas is the existence of the Frontier—prairie, plains, *llanos*, pampa—in most countries. We cannot, in this brief paper, touch upon the enor-mous historical literature dealing with this key element in the history of the United States, Brazil, Venezuela, Argentina, and other nations. But there can be no doubt that the existence of vast areas of empty land has been a major factor in shaping that history, and that it has had some similar effects upon the cowboy and the *llanero*, the pioneer and the *bandeirante*. Huckleberry Finn's flight from civilization ("I can't stand it. I been there before.") is an echo of *Martin Fierro*, José Hernández' epic of the Argentine gaucho:

> Mi gloria es vivir tan libre
> Como el pájaro del cielo,
> No hago nido en este suelo
> Ande hay tanto que sufrir;
> Y naides me ha de seguir
> Cuando yo remonto el vuelo.
>
> [My glory is to live as free
> As the birds of the air,
> I make no nest in this land
> Where there is so much sorrow;
> And no one need to follow me
> When I take to flight again.]

And on the lower cultural levels, as on the higher ones, the dream of the wilderness, the TV Western, the Mexican shoot-'em-up film, the gaucho movies of Argentina, the glorification of the Brazilian *bandeirante* are all variations on a common theme.

A similar, and related, element in hemispheric history is the presence of the Indian: Inca and Iroquois, Aztec and Arawak, Taino, Tehuelche, Toba, Sioux, Yahgan, and all the rest. Scattered as these original settlers were from northern Canada to southern Chile, and living at vastly different cultural levels, they had very different roles to play in different areas. Many—generally the most primitive tribes, those first encountered, those living on land coveted by the whites—were exterminated. Columbus' men running amok on Hispaniola, the American frontiersman with his slogan of "the only good Indian is a dead Indian," and the agents of the Brazilian Indian Service today, with their ghastly record of terror, torture, and murder, are playing the same role in the same terrible tragedy. In some parts of Latin America (Mexico and her neighbors, Ecuador, Brazil, Peru, Bolivia, Paraguay) as in some American states (the Southwest), the Indian survived as a major element of the population. These countries and these states face the same problem of incorporating the poverty-stricken, marginal Indian or *mestizo* into the larger society.

A fourth similar factor in hemispheric history is (or was) the existence of the plantation system, vast estates dedicated to the production of tropical or semitropical crops, usually worked by some form of coerced or unfree labor. The sugar plantations of French Haiti and Gilberto Freyre's Brazil have obvious points of resemblance to similar establishments in the pre-Civil War American South. Many recent and highly interesting studies of slavery (Frank Tanenbaum, *Slave and Citizen;* Stanley M. Elkins, *Slavery;* Herbert S. Klein, *Slavery in the Americas*) compare the institution as it existed on both sides of the Rio Grande, and try to account for the differences in Negro-White relationships, the ease of emancipation in Brazil, and so on. Here, in the field of race relations, is one area in which we North Americans should go to school to the more wise and humane among our hemispheric neighbors.

The sixth item on our chart refers to the fact that some Latin American nations are very close neighbors indeed. Havana, as we are reminded from time to time by journalists or politicians in election years, is only ninety miles from Miami, and a ghostly TV reception of one of Fidel Castro's interminable harangues is one of the cost-free blessings of a Florida vacation. Mexico is even closer to our Southwestern states, just a short walk across a bridge to Tijuana, Ciudad Juárez, or Nuevo Laredo. Geographic proximity of this kind has been a major influence on the history and culture of every Caribbean and Central American nation. Other Latin nations, on the other hand, are really not neighbors at all. Brazil, for example, is much closer to the western bulge of Africa than it is to any part of the United States, and the southernmost parts of Chile and Argentina are seven thousand miles from the Texas border—farther than Moscow is from New York City.

Our seventh and eighth items indicate the broad general pattern of hemispheric history during the three centuries after Columbus. Everywhere in the hemisphere a colonial system prevailed, with varying relationships between the imperial European metropolis and the local governments in Williamsburg, Boston, Philadelphia, Mexico City, Lima, and Buenos Aires. Board of Trade and Casa de Contratación, royal governor and viceroy, House of Burgesses and *cabildo,* despite many differences, confronted the same problems and often solved them in similar fashion. And the revolutionary leaders of 1775 and 1810 suffered similar economic and fiscal grievances, felt the same resentment of Creole against peninsular, and justified themselves in the language of the Enlightenment. Except for their dissimilar endings, the careers of George Washington and José de San Martín have obvious similarities: birth into a good position in colonial society, service with the imperial armies (in Spain and in western Pennsylvania), disenchantment with European rule, development into an unorthodox, but skillful, military leader (crossing the Delaware and crossing the Andes), refusal to become a monarch or a dictator when the opportunity offered. Unlike the old states of Europe and Asia, almost every nation in the Western Hemisphere has some nineteenth-century founder as its father.

Western Hemisphere nations were also alike in rejecting monarchy as a form of government at a time when that institution was almost universal in the Old World. Brazil did have a successful imperial regime down to 1889, but the other efforts to set up kings or emperors were short-lived: the abortive attempt to find an Inca ruler for the old La Plata viceroyalty; the brief reigns of King Henri I of Haiti, an enforced suicide in 1820; Agustín I of Mexico, exiled after ten months, shot in 1824; and the Emperor Maximilian, precariously maintained for three years by French bayonets and executed in 1867. We have had dictators in quantity, but kings, emperors, kaisers, czars, and crowned, hereditary monarchs in general were eliminated here long before they went out of style in Europe and Asia.

The colonial and early nineteenth century economies of the new nations also resembled each other. Lacking home markets, capital, and industrial techniques, the New World relied on raw material exports with which to purchase European manufactured goods. Mexican and Peruvian silver, Argentine hides and beef, Uruguayan wool, and Brazilian coffee did for Latin America what Virginia tobacco, New England timber, Illinois wheat, and California gold did for the United States. And, during the era of Great Britain's industrial hegemony similar shipments of cloth, cutlery, china, rails, locomotives, steam engines, and such would be made to all the cis-Atlantic states. The United States, in the decades after the Civil War, was able to break loose and develop industrial independence; most of Latin America, unfortunately, is still overdependent on one or two raw material exports and suffers severely when price declines, tariff barriers, and wars damage a nation's import capacity.

In geographic growth, the eleventh item in our table, only Brazil shares the American experience of expansion. These two countries, through successive exploration, treaties, and wars, have grown into 3-million-square-mile giants. The "normal" Latin American experience is for a nation to be smaller now than in 1810: Argentina losing Uruguay and Chile, former parts of the viceroyalty; Mexico losing half its territory to the United States in 1848; the breakup of Central America into five quarreling, little principalities the size of small American states; Paraguay decimated and dismembered by her giant neighbors in 1870; Bolivia and Ecuador, the luckless eternal losers of South American politics, chopped down to fragments. The aggressive, optimistic American spirit, bred out of effectiveness, prosperity, and success in war and diplomacy, is far removed from the brooding sense of loss and failure and missed opportunities in so much of Latin America.

One factor that is common to all the Americas is the newness of their societies, the fact that the oldest of them (if we except the pre-Columbian past) go back less than five centuries. European and Asiatic cities—London, Paris, Rome, Moscow, Tokyo, Peking—go back thousands of years, their origins lost in obscurity, and the remembrance of an ancient past still preserved in street names, buildings, broad avenues where ancient fortifications once stood. For most American cities, on the other hand, the names and dates of their foundation are known to us; many date from the eighteenth, nineteenth, or even twentieth century (Gary, Indiana, founded 1902; Brasília, proclaimed a new capital in 1960). The "new" immigration, the postcolonial nineteenth-century flood across the Atlantic, is newer still. Because the United States was closer to Europe, because passenger service was cheaper and more regular, and because economic opportunity here was much greater than elsewhere, the United States got the lion's share of the immigrant tide, some 40 million people in the century before 1914. But the same phenomenon, on a smaller scale, was taking place in Brazil, Argentina, and Chile at about the same time, with settlers from the same countries (Ireland and Germany in the earlier part of the century, Italy and Eastern Europe later). And if the numbers of immigrants to the southern part of the hemisphere were smaller, their relative impact was greater in Argentina than anywhere else: the percentage of foreign born in Buenos Aires rose from 5 percent in 1810 to 49 percent a century later. Thus the coalition of immigrants' children who elected Franklin Roosevelt in 1932 finds a counterpart in the immigrant Radical party victory that made Hipólito Irigoyen president of Argentina in 1916. Brazil's Juscelino Kubitschek, Chile's Eduardo Frei, like our Presidents Eisenhower and Kennedy, are descendents of nineteenth-century immigrants.

Throughout the Americas, as a result of the colonial past, the influence of the native population and new geographic conditions, and the mingling of peoples in the nineteenth and twentieth centuries, we find similar modifications of English and Iberian law, of the English, Spanish, Portuguese, and French languages. Henry L. Mencken has produced a superb three-volume study of what he calls "American" English; similar changes in pronunciation, neologisms, assimilations of Indian words, mixtures of German, Italian, Yiddish, Polish, and so on can be found in Haitian Creole, French Canadian, Brazilian Portuguese, Rio-platense Spanish. Sometimes it appears that the line between a dialect and a new language has been crossed: the Creole spoken in Port-au-Prince is hardly intelligible to a Parisian, and the texts of Argentine tangos with their admixture of *lunfardo* (underworld slang), Creolisms, and Italian inflections would baffle a member of Royal Academy in Madrid. The transatlantic versions of the three major languages have, at any rate, prevailed over their English and Iberian ancestors through weight of numbers, and standards are now set on this side of the ocean. English, Spanish, and Portuguese law have gone through a parallel transformation, with new institutions and practices developing to meet New World needs.

Many of the similarities listed above are fortuitous, the result of similar circumstances, with no di. .t connection between events in Anglo- and Latin America. Thus Virginians did not take lessons in slaveholding from Brazil, nor did the American frontiersmen kill Indians because of the example set in Hispaniola or Chile. In some areas, however, there has been a direct confrontation, a mixing of the two ways of life. The very names of our Southwestern states and cities—Arizona, Montana, Colorado, Los Angeles, San Francisco, San Diego—testify to their Hispanic origins, and millions of American citizens who speak Spanish and have Iberian and Mexican-Indian ancestors still live in that part of our country. Other, more sharply concentrated and more recent, Spanish arrivals are the Puerto Rican migrants to New York and other cities since 1946, and the hundreds of thousands of Cuban refugees centered in Miami, but tending to fan out over the country as the Castro regime solidifies itself in power.

From these Spanish people in our own country we have learned to eat *tacos* and chili con carne, to dance the merengue and the cha-cha, and to use words like ranch, lariat, silo, stevadore, hoose-gow, and mustang.

A final, general condition which has prevailed throughout most of the Americas during much of their history is the low ratio of people to land, and the consequent generalized shortage of labor. Haiti and El Salvador, with about 420 and 370 people per square mile, are as crowded as parts of Asia; but Brazil (26), Argentina (21), and Chile (30) clearly could, with effective economic organization, support larger populations. Some of the many consequences of this basic fact have been fortunate; others not. High wages in the United States, the meat-eating habits of Argentines and Uruguayans, geographic mobility and attempts to build utopian societies in the wilderness are some of the products of our God-given *Lebensraum*. The darker side of the picture, of course, is the lawlessness of the unsettled regions, the destructive use of the soil by Virginia cotton planters and Latin American slash-and-burn agriculture, and the African slave trade, a tragic system of labor recruitment. Since labor was scarce and land plentiful, feudal institutions like the Dutch patroonship, the Canadian seigniory, and the various North American propri-etorships did not long survive. In Latin America, where the encomiendas and capitanias of colonial days did evolve into the haciendas, fundos, and fazendas of our time, exploitation was based on race and culture, not, as in feudal Europe, on a scarcity of land.

These common factors, or at least the most creditable among them (one does not boast, nowadays, of the heritage of Negro slavery!), have for a long time formed the background of Ameri-can foreign policy. We have insisted, in the Monroe Doctrine (1823), in the Pan-American movement (1889–   ), in the Good Neighbor Policy (1933–1945), in the formation of the Organiza-tion of American States (1948), and in the Alliance for Progress

(1961–   ), that there was a special relationship between the Americas, that we were called upon to protect the Latin American states against extrahemispheric aggression, to set their internal affairs in order (by intervention, if necessary), to give them special assistance in economic development. In today's world, with the global commitments of the United States, this special American sense of power and responsibility in the Americas has no doubt seen somewhat diluted. Still, it is noteworthy that we have been willing to stand by while nations like Tibet and Czechoslovakia were overrun by the Communists, but we reacted strongly in similar situations in Guatemala (1954), Cuba (1961 and 1962), the Dominican Republic (1965), and Bolivia (1967).

Latin Americans, of course, have rejected the imperialistic aspects of the Monroe Doctrine, although they find it useful in claiming funds from the United States Treasury. And historians from both sides of the Rio Grande have, in general, rejected the Bolton thesis, although they find it useful as a stimulus to research. Canadians and Brazilians and Argentines in particular have rejected the idea of an American unity, and insisted on the uniqueness of their own culture. Professor Freyre emphasizes Brazil's ties with Africa and speaks of a special tropical Luso-Brazilian civilization; Domingo F. Sarmiento long ago passionately insisted that Argentina was not part of "South America"; and our nearest southern neighbors proudly insist that "*Como Mexico, no hay dos*" (There is only one Mexico).

Setting aside the very real and immensely important differences between one Latin country and another, between Peru and Panama, Chile and Colombia, we may indicate also one major factor which separates all of them from the United States: their Iberian origin. In Table II are listed some dozen cultural and political factors which run, not north and south in the hemisphere, but across the Atlantic to Spain and Portugal. Some of them are indisputable and obvious matters of fact, others arguable and subjective, still others operative in only a few countries; but all are points, and generally significant ones, against the unity of the Americas proposed by Bolton.

TABLE II

LATIN AMERICAN TIES WITH SPAIN AND PORTUGAL

1. Language and literature
2. Catholicism: Iberian origins, Indian and Negro admixtures
3. The *patronato:* a state-supported-and-controlled Church
4. The latifundio
5. More relaxed race relations: the mestizo; an easier end to slavery
6. A more rigid class structure
7. Caudilloism: "absolutism tempered by assassination"
8. *Machismo:* the cult of virility
9. Bullfights (in a few countries only)
10. The Hidalgo mentality: valuing of leisure, philosophy, professions where your hands do not become dirty
11. A relaxed attitude toward time: the siesta and fiesta
12. Warmer climate: houses of stone and adobe
13. The arts: music, painting, architecture, city planning
14. Centralization: dependence on the capital
15. Localism: the *patria chica*
16. Attitude toward government: "the law is obeyed, but not put into effect," tax evasion, smuggling

First, and most obvious, is the heritage of Spanish and Portuguese language and literature. While young Americans are (we hope) reading Shakespeare and Coleridge, Dickens and Durrell, their Latin contemporaries will be studying *Don Quixote, Os Lusiadas,* Lope de Vega, Quevedo, Calderon, and Machado de Assis. Even today, despite the (probably pernicious) penetration by North American mass media, translations of *Life* and *The Reader's Digest,* TV comedy and Westerns, rock-and-roll records and the like, the Iberian languages and habits of thought, learned in infancy, persist. George Bernard Shaw once wittily declared that England and the United States were separated by a common language, but the linguistic gap between the two Americas is a much wider one. In a literal sense we do not understand each other. And the passionate struggles over language in so many parts of the world (French vs English in Canada, French vs Flemish in Belgium, English vs Afrikaans in South Africa, English vs Spanish in Puerto Rico, and so on) should warn us not to underestimate language as a unifying or divisive force.

Similarly pervasive and undeniable is the massive, omnipresent influence of Iberian Catholicism. From the very beginning the English colonies in North America were mixing places of Anglicans, Puritans, Separatists, Quakers, Lutherans, with a scattering of Mennonites, Baptists, Methodists, Catholics, and Jews thrown in. Neither the king nor the founders of colonies (except for Roger Williams and William Penn) really believed in pluralism and religious liberty, but it worked out that way just the same. The Iberian colonies, on the other hand, with their tradition of a seven-centuries'-long religious crusade to free the homeland, founded by the Catholic Kings in the same year that the Jews were expelled from Spain, developed and to some degree still maintain a Catholic unity. It is, to be sure, very often a perfunctory Catholicism, a folk religion with a single sacrament (baptism), imperfectly understood, focused on saints' days, fiestas, processions, and magic. In Brazil, Haiti, and Cuba it is deeply, often inextricably, mixed with African cults, and in parts of Indian America it is confused with various pre-Columbian religions. It has been exposed to persecution far worse than any of the anti-Catholic crusades in the United States (the expulsion of the Jesuits in 1767, the anticlericalism of the Revolution and the 1920's in Mexico, and so on). But, like Popocatepetl, Chimborazo, and Aconcagua, it is *there,* and seemingly as permanent; ask a Mexican farm worker who has never been to church in his life, who has a scattering of illegitimate children, two wives, and a couple of mistresses, if he is a Catholic, and he will often reply, *¡Como no!* (Of course!), as if the answer were self-evident.

Along with this all-but-universal Catholic heritage (and Spain today still has fewer than thirty thousand Protestants out of a population of 33 million) goes the heritage of the *patronato,* the uniquely state-supported and state-controlled Church. Papal bulls of 1493, 1501, and 1508 gave the Spanish Crown remarkably complete control of ecclesiastical appointments, tithes, diocesan boundaries, buildings, and the like: not even priests or papal bulls could pass to the Indies without royal approval. From this circumstance have arisen many unfortunate consequences which the United States, with its eventual separation of Church and state, has generally managed to avoid: heresy trials, the Inquisition, clerical exploitation of the natives, Church affairs as a burning political issue.

A fourth basic Latin heritage from Spain is the latifundio, the large estate with one family as owner and a hundred, a thousand, or ten thousand laborers bound to it. The comparable Southern plantation system was abolished a century ago, but the hacienda, or fazenda, or fundo, with its inefficiency and injustice, has survived in Spain and in many parts of Latin America down to our own day. And these large estates in Granada, in Valencia, in Colombia, in the Mexico of Porfirio Díaz, in Chile's Central Valley, do not produce: *hacienda no es negocio* (the landed estate is not a [profitable] business). An American family farm, with its machinery, fertilizers, insecticides, and hybrid seeds, feeds twenty persons per farmer, overfeeds many Americans, and produces mountains of exportable surplus. The hacienda, and its counterpart, the tiny *minifundio* of one or two acres, can barely feed itself.

If Ibero-Latin American agricultural knowledge and practice is deplorably weak, race relations have been reasonably good—in comparison with what went on in North America at any rate.

The American Indian and the Negro slave (and after 1877, the Negro freedman) were at the mercy of a ruthless, hard-driving white majority, often unrestrained by any institution or inner sentiment. The result was genocide, the reduction of the slave to the level of a chattel with no human rights, the fanatical determination to preserve white supremacy at any cost. As our remaining Indians languish on reservations, and our cities decay into Negro ghettos with evermore frequent explosions, we may well admire and hope to learn something from the Spanish and Portuguese experience. Slavery was brutal enough in Brazil and in Haiti, and Indian tribes were exterminated in the Caribbean, Chile and Argentina, and Mexico. But there were, at some times and in some places, mitigating factors. The Crown tried to protect the Indians and Negroes as subjects and souls; the Church insisted that they were men, to be treated as such. Race prejudice certainly exists in Latin America, but "money whitens": a Negro, an Indian, a mulatto, a mestizo who educates or otherwise elevates himself will not encounter the caste barriers that confront even the most successful Negro in the United States.

If race relations in Spain, Portugal, and their American offshoots have been relatively relaxed, the opposite is true of class lines and the social structure. The North American rags-to-riches story—the Horatio Alger legend come true in the lives of men like Jackson, Lincoln, Carnegie, Rockefeller—symbolizes the social mobility that is a very real part of North American life. Millions, tens of millions, of Americans have moved upward along what Samuel Lubell calls "the old tenement trail," from farm work and unskilled labor to success in the professions, in business, or in politics. In Iberia and Ibero-America, except for the lightning-bolt luck of a conquistador, a bullfighter, or a lottery winner, one must expect to remain in the career and circumstances of one's ancestors. Free education, the escalator to success in North America, is not available; the land is locked up in a few hands; politics is the monopoly of a few dozen families. One does not expect to rise; as a Peruvian peasant put it to Richard W. Patch of the American University Field Service:

Our destiny depends on divine will. Because God wills it, some are rich, some know how to read and write, some are masters while we are the servers. . . . We are blind, ignorant brutes [*chunchos*] because God has permitted it to be so. He has permitted this hacienda to exist, and that we be its servants.

This rigidity of class lines, the worried anxiety of the ruling few to keep what they have rather than to expand the economy, and the immense waste of human resources among the lower classes, have kept Spain and Portugal the poorest countries in Europe, and continue to hobble the nations they founded across the Atlantic.

At the top of the sharply stratified social pyramid sits the *caudillo,* the strong man who dominates life in the Iberian nations in a way unknown in North America. Santa Anna and Porfirio Díaz in Mexico, Juan Manuel de Rosas and Juan Domingo Perón in Argentina, Dr. Francia and the López father and son in Paraguay, a whole string of more or less durable, more or less grotesque tyrants, constitute practically all the national life of countries like Haiti, Venezuela, and the Dominican Republic. In 1968, as the United States approached two hundred years of independence without ever having experienced a single coup d'etat or dictatorship, both Spain and Portugal, along with three-quarters of the Latin American people, were controlled by authoritarian regimes. The Bolton thesis is utterly invalid when applied to governments; the real parallel is between Franco and Salazar in the Old World and Silva e Costa, Onganía, Stroessner, Duvalier, Somoza, and others in the New.

Still more pervasive, though harder to describe objectively, is *machismo,* the cult of virility, masculinity, and the martial spirit that goes back to the wars of the Reconquest and before. Without the hair-raising bravery and recklessness of the conquistadores there would have been no Iberian America to begin with. And there is certainly something very attractive about daring, the courage that does not count the odds, the spirit that led an anonymous Marine sergeant to shout back at his lagging squad, "Come on, you ——! Do you want to live forever?" Other manifestations of *machismo* are less pleasant: drunkenness, quarrelsomeness, readiness to use violence, abuse of women—the Western badman personified. The *torero*, in his aloneness, his defiance of death, the arrogance of his poses in the arena, is a good exemplar of *machismo;* it should be pointed out, however, that the bullfight survives only in Lima and Mexico City among New World metropolises, and that it is heavily overshadowed everywhere by either baseball or soccer.

Akin to *machismo,* and even more pervasive, is the Hidalgo mentality, the overwhelming desire to live without working, the abhorrence of manual labor by the upper classes, the avoidance of activities and professions that get your hands dirty. Laziness, to be sure, is a human, and not an Iberian, trait; but it is certainly true that the settlers of Latin America, while willing to risk great hardship and even their lives, did not cross the ocean, as most North Americans did, to work for a living. Here are some comments by Spanish authors during the colonial era attesting to this trait among their compatriots:

(A report from Honduras, 1536, testifying that the writer had seen gentlemen) "sowing the fields with their own hands, something he had never seen before."

(Don Gonzalo, a Nicaraguan Indian chief): "What is a Christian, what are Christians? They ask for maize, for honey, for cotton, for women, for gold, for silver; Christians will not work."

(Rodrigo de Albornoz, *contador* of New Spain in Cortez' time): "Since the land is rich in food and in mines of gold and silver, and everyone becomes swollen with the desire to spend and possess, by the end of a year and a half he who is a miner, or farmer, or swineherd no longer will be so, but wishes to be given Indians, and so spend everything he has on ornaments and silks."

(Juan de Delgado, Philippine Islands, 1750): "Do Spaniards work the soil and plant crops in these islands? Certainly not! On reaching Manila, all become gentlemen."

The shortage of agronomists, engineers, skilled craftsmen, foremen, and entrepreneurs in Latin America, the failure to organize large-scale industry, the channeling of capital into luxury apartment houses and Swiss banks, the primitive state of agricultural and industrial techniques, the backwardness in science and technology, all owe something to the Iberian world view. One should not, of course, paint all Latin Americans with the same brush. The lower classes for the most part work very, very hard (if ineffectively), because they have to in order to stay alive, and there are plenty of hard-driving, hard-nosed executive types in places like Mexico City and São Paulo. Still, the attitude of many well-to-do Latins reminds one of the mandarin visiting Hong Kong, who, after watching a strenuous game of tennis between British officials, politely asked if "they could not hire two coolies to do all that running around for them."

Yet another facet of the same personality trait is a relaxed attitude toward time and money, and an amused superiority toward the North American aphorism that equates the two. I well remember how my students in Argentina found Benjamin Franklin's "Way to Wealth" amusing, and rather contemptible; there were so many more important things than saving time and making money. The North American, when he can, holds two or three jobs in order to get more money to buy more things. Murderous inflation may force a Chilean white-collar worker to do the same thing in order to have enough to eat; but there is an underlying preference for leisure, rather than money. The self-denying drive of the North American entrepreneur, the grim determination to "keep up with the Joneses" and to make sure that your children surpass Jones, Jr., the whole complex of attitudes we call the Protestant ethic—all are about as rare in Latin America as Protestantism itself is. The easy tempo of life, the elastic sense about appointments and deadlines, the restaurants that lock up between mealtimes, careless generosity with money, willingness to save money for months and spend it all in a few days of fiesta—these are attitudes and habits of great importance derived from the Iberian origins of these countries.

Along with personal warmth goes climatic and geographical warmth. The Spanish and Portuguese empires in Asia, Africa, and the Americas were founded in tropical areas only; a few explorers pushed up into eastern Siberia and what is now the central United States but, characteristically, decided to let these frigid areas alone. The British and French, crossing over at higher latitudes, founded new societies in the great forests of eastern North America; the Spanish in places of low latitude and high altitude. In place of the log cabin and wooden balloon-frame house the Spanish built with stone and adobe. The Spanish village, city, or metropolis developed along lines exactly opposite to those in the English settlements. Where Lima, Caracas, and Bogotá have fine homes in the center, clustered around the main plaza, with slums on the outskirts, the North American city has been compared to an apple with a shining skin (the suburbs of Beverly Hills, Shaker Heights, Scarsdale) and a rotten core (the inner city, Watts, South Chicago, Harlem). Even the houses are mirror images of each other with everything reversed: the Latin narrow sidewalk, blank front wall, small windows with iron bars on them, a fence with bits of broken bottles fixed in concrete, all life going on in the hidden patio out of sight; and the extroverted American house with a big front lawn, picture windows, and an open backyard where the life of the owners is exposed to the common view.

The arts have, similarly, taken divergent, and not Boltonian, paths in the Americas. For example, for reasons we may leave to the art historians, Great Britain has produced only one or two eminent painters and sculptors. There is Gainsborough, per-haps, and Turner, but nobody to rank with Velasquez, El Greco, Goya, Picasso, and a host of secondary men. The United States,

England's heir, has never produced anything in the plastic arts but *Heimatkunst,* folk artists, portrait painters, Whistlers, Sargents, and Pollocks. Latin America, while not reaching the heights of the Old World, has had its Aleijadinho, its School of Cuzco, its anonymous builders, sculptors, and painters for the great cathedrals, its Orozco, Diego Rivera, Siqueiros, and Tamayo. England's achievement has been, not in painting or music, but in literature, and here the United States has produced Hawthorne, Whitman, Thoreau, Melville, Clemens, James, Hemingway, and Faulkner, men of far more note than any American painter or musician.

Yet another way in which Latin America resembles Iberia rather than the United States is in governmental centralization, the feebleness of local government, and the hypertrophy of the capital. Mexico City, Lima, Santiago, Havana, Montevideo are giant heads mounted on a feeble body and spindly legs, far too grand for the national economy to support. Greater Buenos Aires, where seven of Argentina's twenty-one million people live, can be compared only to Paris or post-World-War-I Vienna in its monopoly of government, industry, foreign trade, and intellectual activity. Twenty nations have a larger population than Argentina, but Buenos Aires is the eighth largest city in the world, and by far the greatest in the Southern Hemisphere. A North American equivalent would be a supercity of 60 million people, handling 80 percent of the nation's export trade and half its manufacturing, with a virtual monopoly of meat-packing, publishing, movie-making, light industry, and university life as well. The American pattern of dispersed government and industry, with the capital in one city, publishing and the money market in another, and the automobile, steel, film, aircraft, meat-packing, and rubber industries still elsewhere, has been healthier and more successful. Very Hispanic and unfortunate, too, has been the atrophy of local government in Latin America, the feeling that improvements in paving, the schools, parks, and so forth must come from politicians in the capital, while local authorities fold their hands and hope.

Along with this reliance on *la capital* and *el presidente*, who, lacking resources and unable to do everything, generally fail you, goes a strong attachment to the locality, the *patria chica*. The feeling of separateness, of localism, the desire to secede is far stronger in Catalonia and the Basque country than in Wales or Scotland. The very language is different, and separatist movements are serious, often bloody affairs. The same failure to merge into a nation is evident in most parts of Latin America: the breakup of Central America and of the La Plata viceroyalty, the Mayan revolt, the long grueling war between Buenos Aires and the provinces, the gulf between Havana and Oriente, between São Paulo and the Northeast. An inability to organize, to work for the common good, to *hacer patria* (build up the nation), is one of the legacies of Iberia to the disunited states of Latin America.

The final item on our chart, a product and corollary of others discussed above, reflects Latin America's pervasive distrust of politics and politicians, weary cynicism (usually justified) about the government, and acceptance of tax evasion, smuggling, and bribery as a way of life. Dishonesty, again, is not an Iberian or Latin American monopoly, and a nation that has produced Boss Tweed and the Syndicate is no perfect exemplar of administrative efficiency and respect for the law. Still, there is a difference: in England and the United States the system *works*. People do, overwhelmingly, pay their taxes and obey the laws. The federal, state, and local governments have ample revenues; they do build highways and schools, and when a grievance becomes acute enough, something is generally done about it. In Latin America— in Mexico especially—"external administration" is necessary to get a license, a permit, an official piece of paper to which you are entitled, and which you could get in the United States in a few minutes or by mail. Low salaries and an ambience of accepted dishonesty make the *mordida* (bite, bribe) a way of life. Here is another important argument against the validity of the Bolton thesis.

TABLE III

THE ENGLISH HERITAGE OF THE UNITED STATES

1. Language and literature
2. English law: habeas corpus, jury trial, protection against unreasonable search, independent judiciary, protection against *ex post facto* laws and bills of attainder, etc.
3. Representative government and civilian rule
4. Protestantism and the Protestant ethic
5. Religious liberty
6. Antipathy to Spain: 1588 and 1898
7. Successful industrialization
8. Inventiveness and scientific achievement: Newton, Faraday, Darwin, Arkwright; Franklin, Edison, Ford, Westinghouse
9. Forest civilizations: cold climates, wooden houses, coal
10. Naval power and empire
11. Alliances, World War I, World War II, NATO

Our third and last table, listing Anglo-American ties and similarities, resembles the second and provides additional disproof of Bolton's theory. Most Americans are not of English origin, and the parents of many came to the United States during the present century. Yet—such is the power of the melting pot and the overwhelming significance of nationalism in a developed country—English is our native tongue, and English literature from Chaucer to Joyce accessible and familiar to us. English law—jury trial, the independent judiciary, the protections of the Bill of Rights—is as firmly established here as in its land of origin. Our representative form of government derives, ultimately, from Magna Carta and medieval parliaments, evolved through the centuries in Great Britain. Our founding fathers were able to govern the new nation after 1776 because they had had practice at self rule for a century. In Latin America, as Bolívar lamented, the inhabitants were

not prepared for secession from the mother country; secession was suddenly brought about. . . . The Americans have risen rapidly without previous knowledge, and, what is worse, without previous experience of the conduct of public affairs, to enact upon the world stage the important roles of legislators, magistrates, financial administrators, diplomats, generals, and every position of authority.

Inexperienced, riven by racial and class distinctions, confronted with financial and organizational problems they could not solve, the new Latin nations fell apart into quarreling, impoverished fragments. It is instructive to compare the final years of the founding fathers of the two Americas: Washington, John Adams, Madison, Jefferson, dying in peaceful old age, heaped with honors, crowned with success; and Bolívar, San Martín, Hidalgo, Sucre, dying in exile, executed, assassinated, embittered by treachery and failure. "America," Bolívar declared shortly before his death, "America is ungovernable. Those who have served the revolution have plowed the sea."

A basic reason for the success of England and her transatlantic offspring lay in the character of the English people, in their pragmatic, materialistic, common-sense, energetic pursuit of wealth, what Max Weber called—perhaps not quite accurately—the Protestant ethic. "A nation of shopkeepers," Napoleon deprecatingly called the English; and in his famous essay *Ariel* the Uruguayan writer José Enrique Rodó passionately made the same charge against the United States, a nation which "subordinates all its activity to the egotism of personal and collective well-being." Cuba's José Martí, Nicaragua's Rubén Darío, and a hundred others before and since have denounced Yankee materialism, Anglo-Saxon cold-bloodedness, and the difference in soul and spirit between the two Americas, and they are probably closer to the truth than Bolton was. The difference between the two Americas is the difference between such culture heroes as the Cid and Henry Ford, Don Quixote and Benjamin Franklin, Manolete (the great Spanish bullfighter who died in the ring a decade ago) and Vince Lombardi (the successful Organization Man coach of the Green Bay Packers football team, whose profession does not call upon him to risk his life in the arena).

The underlying differences and latent animosity between the two societies, exacerbated by religious differences, have often flared to the surface. Even a casual acquaintance with Elizabethan literature reveals the violent Hispanophobia of England's greatest cultural age: the stage Spaniard is proud, "fantasticall," bigoted, treacherous, a confirmed enemy of the English Church and people. John Quincy Adams, while he posed in public as a friend and protector of Latin American nations, was in fact as hostile to them as the first Elizabeth's ministers were to the Spain of Philip II:

> They have not [he told Henry Clay in 1821] the first elements of good or free government. Arbitrary power, military and ecclesiastical, is stamped upon their education, upon their habits, and upon all their institutions. . . . I have little expectation of any beneficial result to this country from any future connection with them, political or commercial.

When the two societies did come into direct contact—in Texas, during the Mexican War, in 1898, in New York and Miami today—the result was a most un-Boltonian antipathy. The memoirs of veterans of the Spanish American War almost invariably record their dislike of the Cuban people they had come to liberate: they were poor, dirty, diseased, illiterate—and *Negroes!* It is significant that Bartolomé de Las Casas' *Brief Relation of the Destruction of the Indies,* a mine of anti-Spanish propaganda and the source of the Black Legend of Spanish cruelty and duplicity, was translated into English in 1583, a few years before the Armada, and reprinted in the United States in 1898 shortly before another war against perfidious Spain.

The seventh item on our chart, referring to the growth of industry in England and Anglo-America, is yet another example of transatlantic, rather than hemispheric, unity. The Industrial Revolution, as we all know, got its start in England. Blessed with coal, good harbors, a fortunate geographic location, and an industrious, inventive people, England in the nineteenth century became the workshop of the world. The Americans, with the same enterprising spirit and even greater geographical advantages, overhauled the parent country around 1900 and became incomparably the greatest industrial power ever known. Spain, Portugal, and their former colonies limped along in the rear, poor relations at the feast of geometrically increasing wealth and power. Short of coal, suffering from misgovernment and instability, lacking capital, markets, and a mobile, trainable labor force, the Latin American capitalist was a timid and unenterprising fellow in comparison to his northern contemporary, the Captain of Industry. There are, as a result, North American cities that make more steel, or automobiles, or television sets than good-sized Latin American countries. Even giant Brazil produced no automobiles to speak of until the mid-1950's, and Latin America today is unable to produce a single airplane, computer, or atomic energy plant on her own.

A rough, but convenient, way to emphasize this gulf between the interests and capacities of the Anglo-Saxons and the Iberian world is to consider major inventions and the nationality of the scientist, engineer, or inspired amateur involved. English and American names come readily to mind: Newton, Darwin, Faraday, Arkwright, Davy, Cavendish, Bacon, Rutherford in England, Franklin, Edison, Ford, Bell, Fulton, Whitney, the Wright Brothers, Morse, Goodyear in America—the list could be extended to hundreds of names. Iberia and Ibero-America have produced great warriors, painters, sculptors, saints, poets, dramatists, but comparatively few pure or applied scientists. Some geographers and botanists during the colonial period (though two of the best known, the German Alexander von Humboldt and the Frenchman Charles Marie de la Condamine, were foreign); the Cuban Carlos Finlay, who identified the *Stegomyia* mosquito as the carrier of yellow fever; Dr. Oswaldo Cruz of Brazil; Argentina's Nobel Prize winner Dr. Bernardo Houssay; Santos Dumont, a Brazilian pioneer in aviation—the list is not a long one. The gap between the levels of scientific investigation and engineering practice in the two parts of the hemisphere is a large one, and, as the tools of technology continue to grow more complex and expensive, it will probably continue to widen.

In geography, too, that persistent overt and covert influence on civilization, we again find the similarities to run east-west across the Atlantic. Spain, with a century's head start, explored a few of the colder regions of North America, made some tentative settlements on the Great Plains, but in the end confined herself almost exclusively to tropical America. The English, coming from a northern, forested area, settled in regions whose climate was not unlike their own.

Both Great Britain and America, from an imperial, military point of view, were resoundingly successful societies. In the ages of sail and steamship, when control of the passageways between oceans was a key element in economic and naval power, Great Britain dominated all but one of these strategic points, and she had a treaty granting her equal rights to that one, the Panama passage. For nearly three hundred years, from the time of Dutch decline to the war of 1914-1918, Britain controlled the world's oceans. And then, in decline herself, she passed her hegemony on to her American allies, whose fleets now dominate the Atlantic, Pacific, and Indian oceans, and the Mediterranean Sea. Spain, on the other hand, was a naval power only very briefly, almost reluctantly, and as it were by accident. It is noteworthy that some of the most famous sea captains who sailed under the banners of Castile were foreigners: the Italians Columbus, Vespucci, and Cabot, the Portuguese Magellan. Within a few decades of the Discovery, Dutch and French and English pirates and merchants —the distinction was not an easy one to make in those days—were successfully challenging Spanish naval power with their fleets; in 1588 the British demonstrated their superiority at sea; by the next century Spain had to rely on foreign ships to maintain her commercial links with the Indies. The Spanish, for all their bravery, have not been a maritime people; their naval wars have been a series of disasters, from the Armada to Trafalgar to Santiago de Cuba.

I have spoken above of the Anglo-Spanish antipathy, based on imperial and commercial rivalries, and on national religion, that most virulent breeder of hatred and war. The nineteenth century, which saw direct conflict between the two civilizations in the Mexican and Spanish American wars, saw the reforming of transatlantic ties between Madrid, Lisbon, London, and their former colonies. Spain, it was recalled anew, was the mother country; Pan-Hispanism emphasized the virtues of Spain and Spanish civilization; during the war of 1898 many Latin Americans sympathized, not with their hemispheric neighbor, but with the dying imperial glory of Spain.

Between England and the United States, after the bitterness and hatreds of the Revolution and the War of 1812 had worn away, an even stronger bond was forged. An unofficial, and later a formal, alliance was made; the two nations fought as allies during both World Wars; their partnership was the cornerstone of the North Atlantic Treaty Organization. In a century that has seen so many strange shifts of friendship and enmity among the great powers the Anglo-United States tie has remained firm. This alliance, and the eighty-odd other European, African, and Asiatic nations with whom we have treaties of mutual defense, must detract a good deal from our supposed special relationship with Latin America.

We have then, in our three tables and comments upon them, provided a kind of debating-team handbook on the Bolton thesis by supplying arguments for both sides. Which arguments, viewed from the perspective of the present, have more weight? Should Latin America attempt to develop with North American help (through the Alliance for Progress), without American aid (as Argentina's Juan Perón and Guatemala's Juan José Arévalo argued), or in determined opposition to American influence (as Fidel Castro stridently recommends)? Increasingly, it seems to me, Latin American students, statesmen, labor union leaders, and other influential people are coming to reject the Bolton thesis, the *Alianza*, the Organization of American States (OAS), and the whole network of Pan Americanism. The world, they feel, is divided, not by a north-south line drawn through the Atlantic and Pacific oceans, but by a meandering east-west line that divides the rich and the poor, the developed and the under-developed, the affluent and the hungry nations; and they are south of it.

That line, dividing Russia from China along their immense Asiatic border, explains the Sino-Soviet split and the seemingly irreparable division of world Communism. And that line, running along the Rio Grande, separating the Cuban *guajiros* from the vacation hotels of Miami Beach, divides the Americans just as effectively. We may paper it over with slogans and speeches; we may provide token amount of economic aid; we may ally ourselves with the soldiers and dictators who promise to keep their nations in the "free-world" camp. But economic and political realities—our wealth, their poverty; our power, their impotence—must eventually come to the surface. Then it will be the turn of the United States to reevaluate our relationship with Latin America, and to devise a newer, more honest, more realistic, and more just basis for living together in the hemisphere.

NOTES

1. See Herbert E. Bolton, *Wider Horizons of American History* (Notre Dame: University of Notre Dame Press, 1967).

2. *Do the Americas Have a Common History?* (New York: Knopf, 1964).

PART TWO

BUSINESS, THE MILITARY, POLITICS

FLOW OF CAPITAL
IN LATIN AMERICA

JOÃO GONÇALVES DE SOUZA

The subject upon which I have been asked to comment is one of those about which little reliable information exists. It is a topic beset by stereotypes, prejudices, and distorted views. I shall divide my presentation into two parts. One will deal with the general question of the outflow of capital from Latin America. The other will be devoted to describing my experience as director of the Development Plan for the Northeast of Brazil (SUDENE). I will begin, then, by examining the scope and magnitude of capital export in Latin America as a whole, and then consider a specific case, the current attempt at regional development in the Northeast of Brazil. This is an immense underdeveloped region whose economy is dormant or almost nonexistent, and which needs to attract funds from other regions of Brazil and from abroad on a massive and increasing scale.

A question currently being asked in many quarters concerns the extent to which capital flight takes place in Latin America. This idea is closely connected with the possibility of net capital

69

outflows from the region to the rest of the world. It is true that capital outflows include some capital that leaves Latin America for a safer environment, but on the whole it is made up of outflows which are related to either autonomous movements or to compensatory finance.

By capital flight one usually means outflows of capital funds from countries where government action or the general unhealthy economic conditions involve great risks for the owners of such funds. Where such situations exist, the capitalist looks for external safekeeping of his money. When such transfers are prohibited by law, he engages in secret and illegal actions. Capital flights are therefore not reported to national authorities, and official statistics cannot be relied upon to measure the magnitude of such a movement. Statistics compiled by recipient countries cannot be relied upon either, because in some cases the authorities are engaged in a policy of secrecy just to attract these sorts of funds through overevaluation of imports or the underevaluation of exports.

It is therefore extremely difficult to give an accurate estimate of the amount of capital flight from Latin America. For one thing, it is not known to what extent exports are undervalued and imports overvalued. For another, the net "errors and omissions" item in the balance of payments, though giving hints of the probable magnitudes, is not a reliable indicator, because it is a balancing item which includes the errors involved in estimating the accounts. What part of this item can be charged to the estimating error and what part to omissions is anyone's guess. Available statistics do, however, give some idea of the flows both in capital and current accounts.

Recent studies made by the Secretariat of the Inter-American Committee of the Alliance for Progress (CIAP) point out the following trends in the region's international situation:

1. Since 1964 the region has incurred increasing deficits in its current account, that is, it has imported more goods and services

than it has sold to the rest of the world. The future prospects are for a continuation of this tendency because of the precarious outlook for the region's exports and its increasing needs for imported capital goods and raw materials, which will increase with an acceleration of the region's growth of income. For the years 1964 through 1967 the region's deficit in current account has amounted to 631, 446, 878, and 1,410 million dollars respectively.
2. During the same period the region has experienced an additional net outflow due to greater repayments by the public and monetary sector than what they have received in official disbursements, including transfers. The data are as follows:

PUBLIC BALANCE OF PAYMENTS

	(in millions of dollars)			
	1964	1965	1966	1967
1. Repayment (amortizations of the public and monetary sectors)	1272	1922	1462	1329
2. Disbursements	1138	1125	1325	1420
Net (−) means outflow, (+) inflow	−137	−797	−137	+91

3. Registered capital investment during the same period has fluctuated from a decrease of 290 million dollars to an estimated 500 million dollars surplus in 1967.
4. There has been a noted reduction in "supplier's credit," banking credit, and extension of exchange agreements since 1964, when the region received an estimated one billion dollars of new short-term credits.

With respect to the net flow of private capital it is opportune to quote a recent CIAP study which concludes that in 1966 for the first time in several years a net positive increase was obtained in private foreign investment. This relatively small increase is attributable to the reduction of foreign capital repatriation, particularly from Argentina, Brazil, and Venezuela. Preliminary data on the increased flow of private capital from the United States, and the prospects for a further decrease in repatriation, give some basis to the estimate of a net increase of 500 million dollars in 1967, which represents an increment of nearly 350 million dollars above the preceding year. It is, however, extremely difficult to estimate the development of this item, since it is so very sensitive to changes in local conditions and has a high propensity to experience pronounced fluctuations. In the context of the CIAP work it has been estimated that for 1967 the region's additional capital requirement was between 500 and 800 million dollars. This means that after account is taken of all possible sources, this amount was still needed in order to permit the region to finance its deficit in current accounts, its commitments to the international financial community (amortizations of the public and monetary sectors), and a modest increase in the region's reserve position.

Whether there is a substantial net short-term capital outflow from the region due to interest rate differentials is a matter which needs to be studied in detail. There is the presumption, however, that this sort of capital is sensitive to interest rate differentials, even when one considers the existence of negative rates of interest in some Latin American countries in which the rates of inflation have been rather high. In these cases profit rates and liberal credit policies may compensate for interest differentials and cause capital to stay at home.

As it has already been stated, it is difficult to determine the size of the capital outflow from Latin America. We can, however, form some idea of its magnitude. For this purpose let us consider how capital flight is undertaken. Someone must take out goods, gold, or money. When exported goods bring money into the country, there is no capital flight. Likewise, if gold or money is taken out and goods of foreign origin are imported, there is a commercial transaction and no capital flight. Now we can see that the upper limit of capital flight must be the total of all the goods, money, and gold taken out less what is brought into the country in exchange. It will generally, of course, be much less than this upper limit because what is taken out is often genuine investment, payment due for earlier services, donations, and a few other matters.

On the basis of such rough estimates, we can venture a guess that the capital flight from all of Latin America in 1967 probably amounted to more than one billion dollars. Of course, there are huge differences from country to country, but some outflow probably will take place from every single Latin nation. Now what does such a magnitude mean? A billion dollars is about the same as the total annual flow from the World Bank, the Monetary Fund, the Inter-American Development Bank, the United States Agency for International Development (AID), and similar Washington-based official agencies to Latin America. This, in turn, may be from 5 to 20 percent of the region's yearly capital and other expenditures to take care of its economic and social development needs. This percentage may be much less. But, if we take capital flight at one billion dollars, it means that a billion dollars worth of foreign goods and services could have been obtained for Latin America had the people engaged in capital flight chosen to obtain these goods and services for use at home, rather than to leave their capital abroad.

These are impressive and somber statistics. It is obvious that capital flight does great harm to Latin America. And it must be remembered that the lack of capital goods and technical know-how is one of the main sources of poverty and social unrest in Latin America. Having established this, we must find out what has caused capital flight in the past.

The oldest, but probably no longer very important, cause is political in nature. Some governments in the nineteenth century and earlier simply confiscated the property of the wealthy. This probably is unacceptable in most countries today, but as the fear persists, it may take centuries to eradicate. Moral suasion, education, and appeal to public virtue may help.

Second, there is a fear that the government, in carrying out its social and political programs, might try to bring about a redistribution of wealth through taxation. Closely connected to this is the fear that governments may heavily tax property or income to finance activities of the public sector which are thought to be in the common interest and socially just. Finally, there is fear that unwise government policy may cause a destruction of wealth that is kept at home. To illustrate this last point, keep in mind that all wealth must be held in the form of financial assets or real property, and that both forms can decline sharply in value owing to inflation or disorder.

The obvious cure for the disease of capital flight is intelligent and moral behavior on the part of governments and wealthy individuals. Comprehension of the social doctrine of the Church can play an important role in achieving this. Governments must learn economics and behave in a moral way so as not to confiscate property capriciously for the benefit of a few. Wealthy individuals must be convinced that private property is not only a right but also a social obligation, that it must be used in socially constructive ways, and that the authorities are entitled to transfer a certain amount from the rich to the poor and to insist that the rich be willing to bear a much heavier burden than heretofore in financing worthwhile economic and social programs. Such a change in outlook is essential in a Latin American society where, until recently, wealth was considered exclusively a privilege and not an obligation, and where what social obligations were recognized took the form of charity and alms, sometimes with the Church as intermediary, but never with the government as main agent of transfer.

The moral and ethical aspect of the whole problem can also be looked at in a different way. Capital kept at home cannot be hidden and therefore can be easily taxed. Capital transferred into a huge industrially developed country frequently can be hidden or made subject to much lower taxation by the authorities of the foreign country who try to attract this capital. It is natural and justifiable if Latin American governments try to put an end to all capital flight motivated by this fact by means of laws which heavily punish perpetrators of the crime of capital flight. But this is not enough. No government has ever been able to control such flights by force. On the contrary, punitive laws against capital flight usually have the opposite effect from that intended, because they increase apprehensions about the intention of the government and thus induce further capital flight.

This impasse can be solved only if, on the one hand, the authorities follow long-term policies which eventually convince potential perpetrators of capital flight of the social responsibility of such governments and of the benefit of such policies. On the other hand, there must be a change in attitude on the part of Latin American capitalists, so that they recognize that it is immoral to break laws aimed at furthering the welfare of the nation. They must also understand, that, law or no law, they have a moral obligation to utilize their wealth in a way which is in accordance with the best interests of the nation. This is an area in which government, Church, and lay leaders have a very important role to play. Many of them are actively working to improve the situation.

Latin America's future economic growth does not depend solely on what is done internally. The efforts of most governments in the region have been significant, but they are not sufficient to finance all development programs. The export prospects for the next few years are not too bright, and the needs will be increasing as more programs are launched to change the social and economic situation. One of the greatest problems of our time is that rich countries are not paying enough for the basic products from these poor countries. The financing gaps will have to be filled by the international financial community.

Since there is no doubt of the economic potential of the region, foreign private capital will have greater incentives for investment when new plans for economic integration begin to be implemented in the near future. During the past five years most private investment in the region has originated in the United States. During the period 1960 to 1965, according to the Organization for Economic Cooperation and Development (OECD), the total bond issues of certain Latin American countries on OECD capital markets reached US$490 million, of which 390 million dollars were bond issues of Mexico. Latin American regional institutions are trying to channel European financial resources to the region. In addition, the multilateralization of the Alliance for Progress Program should proceed at an ever-increasing pace.

I would like to emphasize the fact that my "guessing game" has been intended more for illustrative purposes than as a technical estimate of capital outflows from the region. One can say with certainty, however, that there is a significant capital outflow from Latin America. We must echo the conclusion of an article written in 1965:

There is some incontrovertible evidence in U.S. statistics of an appreciable outflow of capital from Latin America and some indirect indications in Latin American statistics of further large outflows. But to derive precise figures from such evidence as exists would be an excessively hazardous task.[1]

In the near future perhaps we will have further research into the complex problems involved in making accurate and reliable estimates on capital flight in the developing countries.

I shall turn now from these general considerations to examine the regional experience in the Brazilian Northeast and the efforts which are being carried out by private capital and savings to promote development there. For many planners and ideologists of today the development of a region such as this one would be possible only by means of extremely harsh and violent measures, under a banner waved by divinely inspired leaders. Our case, however, is an example of the overall development of a vast region whose population is larger than that of almost all Latin American nations. The program comprises policies and mechanisms aimed at simulating development, using capitalist and democratic ingredients without hampering other measures which were taken or should be taken on behalf of social justice. The transformation which is occurring in the Northeast is of the greatest importance for Brazil and for the hemisphere.

Let us begin with some basic data. The Northeast is a vast region, with 1,600,000 square kilometers. Among the countries of South America only Argentina exceeds it in size. It is by far the largest and most populated underdeveloped area in Latin America. The per-capita income there is US$130. In the entire Western Hemisphere only Haiti, Bolivia, and Paraguay fail to exceed this figure.

The region is well endowed with natural resources and with an active, intelligent population. Its economic base has been agriculture and livestock raising, traditionally affected by three negative factors: periodic drought, low prices for its export products, and a low level of technology. In addition, between 1956 and 1963 the equivalent of US$150 million originating from its exports left the Northeast for the South. Above all, the region was not creating sufficient employment for an extremely prolific population. The result was that those persons who were not able to leave the region to seek work elsewhere were naturally receptive to an ideological message. The "peasant unions" which were set up then had the purpose of arousing the awareness of the rural peasantry that the situation had to explode, and thus open up a bridgehead for international Communism.

Pressed by these factors, the government decided to take action. An overall development plan for the region was prepared and approved by the Congress in 1959. SUDENE was created. Up to now it has been operating on the basis of three-year plans which are periodically modified to take experience into account. The plans are not politically oriented. The interests of parties and individuals do not negatively affect their preparation and execution, the appointment of leaders and technicians, or the placement of the great industrial and agricultural projects, and infrastructural or communal services. SUDENE has outlived governments, external pressures, and other difficulties. It was able to mobilize close to one thousand technicians from the region itself who would otherwise have departed for the more developed South. Almost all of them had completed university training, and many had taken specialized courses and graduate courses in the South or abroad. The region was aroused to its future of growth. Regional leadership joined hands without regard to political or religious cleavages. The universities and technical institutes are changing their traditional structures, curricula, and programs to fulfill their role in the struggle. The government and the Church, although differing on other matters, joined forces in the need to confront the problems of the Northeast.

The result is that today the Northeast is the region in Brazil which is experiencing the greatest development. In the last four years this region achieved an economic rate of growth of more than 7 percent per year. A steady technological flow is being directed to the region, together with the installation of hundreds of industrial and agricultural projects which will provide 200,000 new jobs at higher salary levels.

The development of this entrepreneurial surge is primarily the result of an intelligent policy of public and private investments gathered almost entirely from Brazil itself, with external financial and technical assistance required only in supplementary form. These external resources emanate from multilateral and bilateral agreements, particularly with the governments of the United States, Germany, France, Japan, Israel, and others.

Public investments from the federal government and from the states are directed to those sectors which are inherently related to government action, such as infrastructure projects (transportation, electric power, water supply), education, health, research, and scientific exploration of the natural resources of the Northeast. Some international loans have also been directed to these vital sectors. In this way the government creates conditions which in turn attract interest, know-how, and capital from rich and developed regions to the underdeveloped Northeast. Efforts of a profit-making nature, particularly in the industrial and agricultural sectors, are reserved to private capital, which is attracted by the infrastructure projects and by various other incentives.

For private capital thus plays a decisive role in this process of development in the Northeast. Attracted by financial, tax, and other incentives, private capital began to appear in the region itself. It had previously been thought that local savings were not available because all of these had been transferred to the South or abroad. Experience proved that the situation was contrary to what stereotyped thinking led one to believe. An investigation carried out by Professor Asimov from the University of California at Los Angeles showed that it was possible to uncover and mobilize capital in economically backward areas of the Northeast itself provided that specific opportunities existed. All that was needed were projects which were technically and economically viable, capable of offering security and profit for the investment.[2]

In addition to local savings, attracted by them and strictly associated with them, we have witnessed growing flows of capital from the South which is earmarked for developing the Northeast. How was this semimiracle achieved? When the National Congress approved the Second Director Master Plan, it introduced amendments which, by their simplicity and ingenuity, provided a new dimension to the institution's work. It consists of a system of incentives which entails the following main features:

1. *A 50-percent income-tax deduction.* Any juridical person, national or foreign, can deduct income tax and any other additional tax to which he may be subject up to 50 percent of the value of the tax in order to reinvest it or apply it to industrial, agricultural, or telecommunication projects in the area of

SUDENE's jurisdiction which have been declared by this agency to be essential to the development of the region.

2. *Contribution on the part of private capital.* In order to recover the 50 percent deduction which the government granted, the legislation requires that the enterprise agree to the financing of the total projected capital investment from its own resources (never less than one-third of the total capital planned for the project) and, second, that the enterprise conform to the standards of priority established by the agency.

3. *Exemption from import duties.* The law ensures the exemption from any duties on the importation of machines and equipment not produced in Brazil and which are indispensable to the projected enterprise.

4. *Other incentives.* The states of the region also offer tax exemptions for periods ranging from five to ten years to those companies which move to places designated by the agency as priority areas for the region. There is also an import license without the usual requirement of an exchange cover. In addition, the firm is allowed to reinvest its profits without having to pay income taxes. Funds earmarked for the area can be deposited in the Bank of the Northeast in a blocked account without interest. The company has a maximum of three years in which to apply these resources. If this is not done, the right to them will be lost. The Bank of the Northeast and SUDENE work in complete agreement as parts of the same program and of the same process.

There are two main systems for private investment under the plan:

1. *Without financing.* A sum of 100,000,000 cruzeiros can be applied, with 25 million cruzeiros from the firm's own resources and 75 million cruzeiros from deposits coming from the income taxes.

2. *With financing.* In this case the firm's resources are added to the deposits from income taxes and to loans from the Bank of the Northeast. The plans compare as follows:

WITHOUT FINANCING		WITH FINANCING	
Own resources	25%	Own resources	15%
Income taxes	75	Income taxes	45
Company capital	100%	Financing from the BNB	40
		Investments	100%

A project is approved by SUDENE only after a complete study has been made as to its financial viability and technical feasibility. Its relationship to the priorities of the plan is established, and the competence of the management and shareholders must be verified. The approval or rejection of any project is not subject to the slightest political influence.

Even though it has only recently been created, this system is bringing about a revolution in the country's investment policy in the Northeast. More than twenty thousand income tax payments collected by the Bank of Northeast Brazil have netted some NCr$850 million (U.S. $300 million). To these will be added another 300 million dollars obtained from private resources and from complementary financing. This legislation has thus brought more than US$600 million of new investment to the Northeast. Two-thirds of these resources were committed to 350 industrial and agricultural projects approved as of December, 1967. The remaining one-third is being committed to 150 projects which SUDENE is currently studying and approving.

We know that there are many problems still without solution. There are serious doubts as to the capacity of this program to provide all the jobs needed in the region. And there are serious questions as to the way in which these benefits have been distributed. This program is, however, creating 200,000 new jobs at salaries higher than the traditional ones of the region. An industrial park more modern than any in the South is being constructed. The agricultural sector is beginning to gain momentum, although more slowly than industry. This region's natural resources, cheap manpower, large potential market, and favorable local conditions are at last being understood and exploited.

Professor Albert O. Hirschman of Harvard University, who visited the Northeast late in 1967 on a mission for the Brazilian government, stressed, among other things, two points which deserve emphasis. He stated that this incentives policy "is by far the most significant economic forward move to take place in Brazil's Northeast for many decades" and that "The advantages of (this) service will make this particular policy instrument attractive to 'developers' in other lands."

Before concluding I should like to explain what the Church is doing in the Northeast. The Church most assuredly has had and is continuing to have a role in handling this complex problem. In the Northeast the Church brings into play its own definite views and ideas on social action and economic development. It has been an active force in the discussions on the problems of the Northeast, including those concerned with the migration of know-how and capital. It has played a part in creating the awareness, in the region itself and throughout the country, of the urgency of finding a solution to this problem of the Northeast in a planned manner. It was even able at times to persuade the government to back projects for which it signed assistance agreements.

The Church assisted in clarifying the problems. The episcopate of the Northeast in particular, confronted with the challenge of the surrounding society, was anticipating the Church of the second Vatican Council itself. In summary, the Church encouraged the Northeast to discover and appreciate its natural and social potential. It called the attention of the developed regions of Brazil to the underdeveloped Northeast, a clear threat to national integrity itself. It attracted interest, resources, and technical leadership from outside of the region. Finally, it is providing an example to other episcopal conferences of the so-called Third World.

Members of the Church are also presently discussing new parts of SUDENE's working plan, designed to improve and adapt it to present-day reality. I do not suggest that the Church should intervene in problems which belong to the specific sphere of action of the government. Brazil has had a policy of separation of the two powers which is reflected in its republican tradition and in the national Constitution.

But the Church most assuredly has a responsibility of its own in the sense of discussing the topic, suggesting appropriate solutions to it in terms of its social doctrine, and mobilizing public opinion to solve the problem.

At this point I should like to mention a problem we have encountered. There is a need to define clearly what the role of the religious sector should be with regard to economic development. There has been some confusion on this question that has engendered a certain amount of tension with civil authorities. In addition there is resentment that certain religious authorities limit themselves to criticizing, in harsh terms, the existing poverty without, however, helping to do anything to alleviate it. It is hoped, however, that the recent recommendations given by the Council on the Development of Peoples, and also the common sense of both religious and civil leaders, will lead them to effective and useful cooperation with each other. The success of such cooperation in the Northeast has been so successful that it is now being extended to Amazonia.[3]

Instead of speaking about theories relative to the flight of capital, I have considered it more useful to focus attention on an actual example in our own hemisphere. The Northeast was a region which seemed destined by fate to become another field for the infiltration of international Communism in America, perhaps even another Vietnam. Now, in spite of so many problems still to be solved, this area is witnessing the most positive experiment in regional planning in the entire hemisphere.

NOTES

1. Poul Host-Madsen, "How Much Capital Flight from Developing Countries?" *Finance and Development,* II, 1 (March, 1965), 32–33.

2. The Project Rita. More information is obtainable from AID's Office of Development Finance and Private Enterprise, New State Building, Washington, D.C. 20534.

3. The executive branch and Congress have recently implemented legislation and plans, similar to those of the Northeast, that are adapted to the needs and the potential of Amazonia. A regional planning agency has been created, Superintendency of Regional Development (SUDAM), in addition to the approval of incentives by legislation even more liberal than that described for the Northeast.

THE IMPACT OF
MILITARISM ON LATIN
AMERICAN SOCIETY

LYLE N. MCALISTER

The imposing scope of the subject to be discussed compels me at the outset to enter a number of caveats. First, the term "militarism" itself offers some serious conceptual and semantic problems. Perhaps the best definition of the phenomena as it has been traditionally conceived in the Western world is offered by Albert Vagts. It is, he says, a system characterized by

the domination of the military man over the civilian, an undue preponderance of military demands, an emphasis on military considerations, spirit, ideals, and scales of values in the life of states. It has also meant the imposition of heavy burdens on a people for military purposes, to the neglect of welfare and culture and the waste of the nation's best manpower in unproductive army service.

Militarism, Vagts adds, has strong imperialistic overtones.

According to this definition, militarism has been nonexistent or at least a rare phenomenon in Latin America. Probably the closest analogues in the region to the militaristic archetype have been the program of the Group of United Officers (G.O.U.) in

Argentina, Paraguay under the dictatorship of Francisco Solano López, and possibly Chile in the mid-nineteenth century. Militarism as applied to Latin America has meant something else: the extrusion of the armed forces beyond their normatively defined mission of defending the state, the constitution, and law and order against aggression from the outside and subversion from within. Historically it has been essentially a political phenomenon involving "military intervention," the overt or subvert employment of violence by the armed forces for political ends. It is in this sense that I shall use the term, although I do so with some misgivings. In recent years the Latin American military have become interested in or engaged in developmental and modernizing programs. This role is normally not explicitly mentioned in constitutionally defined missions. Whether it constitutes intervention or is a form of militarism is an open question. It must, however, be taken into account in any evaluation of the impact of the armed forces on contemporary Latin American society.

Second, there is the problem of generalizing about the role of the military, or for that matter any other social phenomenon, in an area so vast and diverse as Latin America. The level, frequency, and duration of militarism varies throughout the region as does its impact, so that any generalization may be countered with the observation, "Yes, but that is not the way it works in Mexico or Bolivia or Argentina." In the space available I am forced to generalize and thereby place myself at the mercy of regional and national specialists.

Third, surprisingly little is known about the Latin American armed forces and their interaction with civilian institutions. What information we do have consists of (1) some fairly reliable data on their strength and organization, (2) some empirical observations about their more overt forms of political behavior, (3) some high-level models and typologies of the military role, (4) a set of generalized propositions about why the armed forces behave as they do, and (5) a body of value-laden judgments about the effect of militarism.

The lack of firm data is due in part to the fact that only within the past decade has the Latin American military been the subject of systematic investigation, but due more fundamentally to problems of research peculiar to the subject. The armed forces in Latin America are sensitive organizations and are inclined to surround even their routine functions with security restrictions. They are particularly touchy about their political role. Thus an investigator who is overly aggressive may at best be frustrated and at worst find himself *persona non grata*. It is these difficulties which led Professor Frank Bonilla to lament:

And I do think the fact that Latin Americans have not studied the military really stems from the fact they have made a wiser choice about research or they have discounted the importance of this, but it is largely related to the fact that both to Latin Americans and us non-Latin Americans who go to Latin America to make studies of this kind, the military are in fact powerful enough to shield themselves from any kind of serious examinations, as I have found out through bitter experience. So I will just say I think we can largely forget about getting serious answers to a great many of these questions because of the fact that the possibilities of carrying out any kind of really useful research in this [are few].

Perhaps Bonilla is too pessimistic. In any case I shall have to base my remarks on whatever information is currently available.

Fourth, quite aside from the problem of data acquisition, the study or observation of the role of the Latin American military has other peculiar attributes. Militarism is a highly value-laden concept. In both liberal democratic and Marxist terminology it is a bad word. Therefore, much of what is written about Latin America's armed forces and their relations with civilian institutions tells us more about the author's feelings than about the structure and functioning of the system.

In a similar vein, the problem of the role of the military in Latin America has become closely associated with United States foreign policy. A high proportion of the published and unpublished studies that have been made have been subsidized either directly or indirectly by our State and Defense Departments or by private foreign-policy groups. In these studies primary empha-

sis is, not on an objective analysis of systems of civil-military relations, but on the extent to which the United States is responsible
for their existence and what we should do about them.

Turning now to observable or identifiable forms of military
behavior, Samuel Finer offers the concept of "levels of intervention" as a convenient device for classifying such phenomena
in Latin America. The first level he calls "influence," that is,
the use of more or less logical persuasion by military leaders
to achieve institutional objectives, as, for example, budgetary
allocations, the adoption of this or that weapons system, or quasi-
personal ends such as promotions, key appointments, and the
like. This level of intervention, or perhaps it would be better to
say, participation, is quite legitimate and conducted within the
legal and normative forms of civil control. It is, in fact, universal
in modern states; we are all familiar with the lobbying activities
of military personnel and military interests in our own system.
In Latin America, however, in contrast to the United States, influence tends to be more direct. It is exerted by service ministers
directly on the center of power, the head of state, rather than
upon congressional committees or through a civil bureaucracy.

The next higher level of intervention Finer classifies as "pressures" or "blackmail," that is, threats made by military leaders
that if their wishes are not met, some form of sanctions may
be forthcoming. The threats may be quite specific, that is, if a
certain minister is not removed, if certain institutional interests
are not met, if the government adopts certain economic or social
policies which the military opposes, then specific action will be
taken. The threat may be implied or it may be direct, in the form
of an ultimatum.

Pressures or blackmail may assume a general and continuing
form, that is, a government may be given to understand that
there are certain limits of action beyond which it will incur a
military veto. Thus, in Peru President Belaunde is well aware
that in tax or land reform, negotiations with foreign oil companies,

and dealings with *Alianza Popular Revolucionaria Americana* (APRA) or leftist students and intellectuals there are certain limits he cannot exceed without risking military displeasure.

In employing influence or blackmail the military is "working upon and through civil authorities," generally behind the scenes. The third level of intervention is direct. The military acts forcibly to depose a ministry or a president and replaces them with another administration more amenable to their wishes. Displacement may be accompanied by provisional military rule while the armed forces negotiate the succession or provide for new elections whose outcome they are in a position to influence. A case in point is the *junta militar* which assumed power in Peru after the *golpe* of 1962. The highest level of displacement occurs when the armed forces depose a government and replace it with a military rule which is intended to be of indefinite duration. Cases in point are the present regimes in Argentina, Brazil, and Paraguay.

These phenomena are easier to observe and describe than to analyze and explain. Thus we begin to encounter methodological problems when we are confronted with the questions: Why is the Latin American military militaristic? Why does it intervene, and what circumstances cause it to adopt one form of intervention rather than another or determine it to act today rather than tomorrow?

Historically many "causes" of intervention have been identified or hypothesized. First, there are the ambitions of individual officers. Many cases where this was a factor may be drawn from Latin American experience, beginning with the imperial aspirations of Agustín de Iturbide in Mexico to the behavior of Manuel Odría and Marcos Pérez Jiménez. Second, there are institutional corporate interests. These have ranged from rather primitive desires for loot to affronts to military honor, dissatisfaction with a budgetary allocation, and perceived threats to the integrity of the institution. The latter may involve efforts on the part of civilian leaders to tamper with internal matters such as promotions and assignments. In some cases the military may feel that its security or very existence is threatened. Thus, a chronic factor in the behavior of the Peruvian military has been the apprehension that if APRA came to power, it would dismantle the army. On a more general level the Latin American armed forces have been extremely sensitive about Communist influences. While their attitude is in part ideologically inspired, it also derives from the conviction that should the Communists have their way they would destroy existing military establishments.

The military may also intervene in response to their evaluation of national need, a concept of function which has been termed the supermission. Thus if a government appears to have come to power by processes of doubtful legitimacy, or if there are rival claimants to power, the armed forces may interpret their responsibility to defend the constitution and the laws as demanding intervention. Or if they feel that a government, even one of immaculate constitutionality, is faltering in meeting its responsibilities, they may construe their mission even more broadly so as to justify its elimination. These elements appear to have been present in Argentine military thinking since the fall of Perón.

A checklist of the causes of Latin American militarism would be incomplete without including the attitudes and actions of the United States. There is general agreement that our policy has some influence, but differences of opinion exist as to whether it is beneficial or not. The more popular view may be summarized as follows: (1) United States military assistance encourages militarism in Latin America in that it not only increases the capacity of the armed forces to act against civilians but, by inflating their ego, encourages them to do so. (2) United States military missions sometimes connive with Latin American officers to depose governments when it is in the interests of our foreign policy to do so. Specifically, such charges have been made in the case of the overthrow of the Goulart government of Brazil and the Bosch administration in the Dominican Republic. (3) United

States recognition of and aid to a military government in Latin America encourages the armed forces in other republics to depose constitutional regimes.

It is contended by some that the shift in Pentagon hemispheric defense policy from concern with invasion from without to the control of internal subversion further encourages militarism. First, it involves the military in decisions which are essentially political. Second, it provides the armed forces with a justification for actions against elements which it views with disfavor; third, counter-insurgency equipment and training produce a type of operational unit which, for purposes of *golpes*, coups, and internal control, is more effective than conventional forces.

The basic counterargument offered by our own military is that these propositions have not been demonstrated systematically but are based on more or less logical assumptions, political gossip, and coincidence. In a more positive vein they argue that Latin American officers, through attendance at service schools in the United States or through social and professional contacts with North American attachés or assistance groups at home, somehow acquire a notion of the proper role of the military in a democratic society.

There is a fairly general agreement that increasingly since the 1930's the character of Latin American armies has been changing in fundamental ways. First, traditional elites can no longer count on the military to defend the status quo. Second, what Janowitz calls "designed militarism," that is, positive action undertaken simply for the acquisition of power and the perquisites it conveys, is being replaced by "reactive militarism," that is, intervention, often reluctant, undertaken in corporate self-defense, in an attempt to correct perceived faults in the polity or society, or in response to civilian requests or expectations. Third, action tends to be institutional; it represents the collective will of the military rather than the interests of individual officers or factions. As a consequence, in the case of displacement or supplantation the instrument is no longer the military caudillo but the *junta militar* ruling in the name of the armed forces. Fourth, the armed forces tend increasingly to regard intervention as a temporary action to correct a specific situation and are reluctant to assume long-term responsibilities for the conduct of government.

These trends are commonly attributed to changes taking place both within the military institution and in general society. In the former case the increasing recruitment of commissioned personnel from middle and lower-middle social sectors is assumed to have weakened the ties of officer corps with traditional elites, while professionalization decreases their political interests and develops stronger institutional identification. With respect to general social change the proposition is that as societies become more complex, as interest groups proliferate, and as countervailing sources of power emerge, the military simply finds it increasingly difficult to intervene and even more so to govern.

Paralleling or in connection with these structural changes, the nonmilitary role of Latin America's armed forces has acquired a new dimension: support of and participation in processes and programs of modernization and development. This type of activity, while not prescribed by the constitution and the laws, is not forbidden by them. It is not of course new. Since at least the late nineteenth century the military have been engaged in development work—road construction, mapping, basic literacy training, and the like—which was closely related to their military missions. What is new is the notion that the armed forces, by virtue of their possession of technical and logistical competences which are in short supply in developing societies, should employ these resources more extensively, more explicitly, and in areas which may have no direct relation to purely military requirements.

The developmental role of the military is today generally described as *acción cívica militar*. Civic action, however, has two meanings. First, there is broad-scale participation on a variety of fronts, sometimes in conjunction with a general national effort.

Thus in 1963 President Belaunde appealed to the Peruvian armed forces to "join with civilians, using their discipline and technical skills in making war on unacceptable social conditions." The military responded by adopting civic action as a formal component of their mission and announcing it as their contribution to the President's program of *Acción Popular*.

Civic action also has a more specific meaning; the cooperation of military units with rural communities in the construction and operation of basic services such as schools, utilities, sanitary systems, and the like. While such activities have developmental and modernizing functions, they also have objectives that are essentially military, that is, forestalling insurgency by winning the confidence of villagers in the national governments and conciliating and reconstructing areas affected by insurgency.

The idea of a positive and extensive developmental role for the military has a complex rationale. Within the armed forces themselves it represents an honest conviction of many officers of the post-World War II generation. The majority of these are the products of national military academies; they have undergone advanced training in command-and-general-staff schools, and very likely they are graduates of superior war colleges. Their schooling has included instruction not only in military science but also in the humanities and the natural and social sciences. At the war-college level it will have included studies of problems of national development. They are therefore well aware of the social, economic, and political ills of their countries and the various theoretical and pragmatic formulae prescribed by experts for their cure. They are also likely to be serious-minded and patriotic officers who feel that their institution is obligated to place its expertise and resources at the disposal of the nation. Thus, for example, the founder and moving spirit of the Peruvian *Centro de Altos Estudios Militares*, General José del Carmen Marin, was convinced that the effectiveness of national defense was in proportion to the value of that to be defended. Initially, therefore, seven months of the school's ten-month term were devoted to studies of national, social, and economic problems.

Aside from the enlightenment they receive in their own educational institutions, many of the new generation of officers have received advanced or specialized training in Europe or, more frequently, in the United States. Schooling abroad provides them with an opportunity to compare conditions in their own countries with those in a developed nation. The experience can be quite traumatic.

The participation of the armed forces in developmental-type programs, however, is not entirely disinterested. It affords them an opportunity to demand a larger share of the national budget and, in view of North American support for civic action, to ask for increased military assistance from the Pentagon. Moreover, proper public relations treatment of civic action programs may serve to brighten the public image of the armed forces.

Finally, it should be noted that neither military nor civilian support of civic action is unanimous. Some officers believe that it is essentially nonprofessional, that it diverts time and resources from their primary mission, which they continue to regard as the defense of the national territory, the constitution, and the laws. In the case of civilian leadership my own observation is that attitudes are largely negative. They range from a rather resigned belief that as long as the military is there, it may just as well be put to work constructively, to an apprehension that it may give the armed forces an exaggerated notion of their obligations to the nation.

Unquestionably, the nonmilitary use of the military has political implications. It involves them in the formation of public policy in areas unrelated to their primary missions; it may provide them with an excuse to demand larger budgets; and it may improve their public image, thus to increase their leverage in dealing with the government or civilian interest groups. At another level, military concern with development and modernization may provide the "supermission" with a new dimension. When civilian governments fail to respond effectively or responsibly to demands for change, impatient officers may ask the question once posed by Colonel Gamal Abdel Nasser: "If the army does not do this job, who will?" While it would be difficult to identify an actual intervention in Latin America that was based exclusively or even primarily on such a motivation, Nasserist sentiments have certainly existed in Argentine military circles and, in Peru, among officers associated with the *Centro de Altos Estudios Militares.*

An analysis of levels, motivations, and forms of military intervention in Latin America does not, of course, do justice to the complex interaction of personal, institutional, and environmental factors which invariably characterize specific situations. The military themselves are not a monolithic institution with a clearly defined ideology or program supported by internal consensus. Within the armed forces normally exist cleavages based on personal, class, or sectional loyalties; conflicting ideological positions; interservice rivalries; different interpretations of the military mission; and divisions of opinion over the relative weight to be assigned to civic action as against conventional tasks. Disagreements also may exist over the circumstances which might justify intervention or the timing, level, and form of political action. It is likely that preceding a modern *golpe* an intense internal struggle will take place before a solid institutional front or the appearance of one is achieved.

Motivations for intervention, moreover, are rarely clear-cut. In following a universal form of rationalization, individual, group, and institutional interests may be identified with national interest. Motivation, moreover, may change as action develops. As a consequence of the temptations afforded by the possession of power, a *golpe del estado* undertaken for essentially disinterested motives may evolve into an unprincipled and corrupt dictatorship. Finally, intervention is frequently not a unilateral action on the part of the military but is undertaken because of invitations or pressures from civilian factions or groups that are dissatisfied with programs or actions of incumbent governments or that aspire to power. Professor John J. Johnson terms this type of interaction "civilian militarism."

If it is difficult to explain systematically the structure and functioning of Latin American militarism, it is even more frustrating to attempt to evaluate its impact. It is empirically observable that military intervention in the Dominican Republic interrupted the first national experiment with democratic constitutional government. What is not observable is whether, if the military had abstained, democratic evolution would have proceeded without interruption.

On the more positive side, it is empirically observable that the armed forces in Latin America are creating functional literates, training technicians, and building roads. What is not observable is whether with appropriate budgetary reallocations civilian agencies might not do these things more efficiently and economically or whether such activities threaten democratic institutions. We do not know, moreover, in any particular case the proportion of the military's contribution to the total national effort.

In any case it is simplistic to base evaluations of impact on scattered observations of phenomenon that may be essentially ephemeral. What really concerns us is change over time, and the question then becomes, What is the impact of militarism on long-range developmental processes in Latin America? And herein lies the real problem. Quite aside from the methodological problem of measuring rates and directions of change and development, there are sharp differences of opinion as to what type of society should be the ultimate goal and the means by which it should be achieved. Evaluations of the role of the military, therefore, tend to be highly value-influenced. They will depend on the observer's judgment of whether what the military does or might do inhibits or expedites the achievement of goals he regards as desirable. I would like now to attempt to construct a typology of such judgments.

The first type I shall call the traditional conservative. It is based on a commitment to the status quo, a doctrinaire or pragmatic conviction that the best system is the one that has always existed, and the best government is one dominated by the traditional elite. While the traditional conservative may accept the inevitability of change, he believes that it should be gradual and organic, not imposed or planned by human agency. The function of the military is to support the traditional system, if necessary by direct intervention. There is not too much room here for military civic action; it might induce social change. This view continues to be held by many Latin American oligarchs and is shared by some public officials in the United States for whom stability in Latin America is a primary objective of policy and who regard the armed forces as the chief bulwark against Communism. It is essentially anachronistic and unrealistic. It disregards the tremendous pressures that exist for a basic restructuring of Latin American society, the increasing reluctance of the military to ally themselves with traditional elites, and their incapacity to block change even should they wish to do so.

At the other end of the spectrum is the doctrinaire revolutionary, generally but not necessarily of one of the several Marxist persuasions. He is convinced that the proper solution to Latin America's problems is the destruction of the existing order by revolutionary violence and the creation of democratic "peoples' republics." Like the traditional conservative, he regards the military as the defender of the existing order, and, as a corollary, he views the United States as the principle supporter of militarism in Latin America. Civic action is looked upon as simply an opiate employed by North American imperialists and their local lackeys to dull the masses' awareness of their true conditions and prospects. A primary objective of the revolutionary, therefore, is the subversion and destruction of the regular armed forces and their replacement by a people's army at the service of the revolution. If one grants his basic premise, his view of the military makes sense. It does not, however, take into account the prospect of the substitution of one form of militarism for another. In a revolutionary state the armed forces are the political instruments of a new establishment.

In between these extremes two other positions are identifiable. One of these might be termed the doctrinaire liberal position. Its ideal is the achievement of liberal, constitutional, and social democracy in Latin America. The doctrinaire liberal regards the Latin American military as maleficent. They absorb resources which might otherwise be devoted to constructive purposes, but even worse they are a reactionary force which through intervention thwarts the democratic aspirations of the Latin American people. The doctrinaire liberal is skeptical of the accomplishments of civil action and doubts the sincerity of its rationale. Like the doctrinaire revolutionary, he identifies the Pentagon as a villain in the case in that its programs of military assistance and counterinsurgency encourage the Latin American armed forces to misbehave. This view is held by the democratic left in Latin America, and with some justification, because they have in fact seen their programs frustrated by military intervention. It is shared by the majority of North American intellectuals, by a number of our senators and representatives, and by elements within our Department of State.

I subscribe fully to the objectives of the doctrinaire liberals but regard their views of the impact of the military as based on questionable assumptions. The ratio of military expenditures to GNP in Latin America is low, and it cannot be demonstrated that if military budgets were cut to the bone, any substantial impetus to development would accrue. Moreover, in a statistical exercise correlating military expenditures and ordinal indices of levels of democracy, Charles Wolf finds that larger military programs do not appear to be associated with more restrictive or authoritarian political institutions. On the contrary, he finds a positive relationship between level of democracy and domestic defense expenditures, and suggests that this result should not be unexpected because of the generally positive correlation between both variables and per-capita income. It might be added that Wolf also detected no significant correlation between the amount of United States military assistance and levels of democracy.

More fundamentally, I cannot accept unconditionally the assumption that if the conventional Latin American armed forces were abolished or rendered politically sterile, liberal, constitutional democracy would inevitably ensue. The regular military is but one form of organized violence, and in societies where violence is an accepted alternative to peaceful resolution of political issues, the means of violence will be created if established military institutions are not available. Thus, when the old army was abolished in Bolivia after the 1952 revolution, civilian factions proceeded to create armed militias to support their political objectives. Indeed, throughout the nineteenth century much of what is called militarism was the product of armed bands led by civilians, rather than interventions by the regular armed forces.

Finally there is the position of what might be called the pragmatic liberals. Like their doctrinaire brethren, they regard liberal constitutional democracy in Latin America as a desirable and achievable goal, and in principle oppose military intervention. They realize, however, that the forces of democracy are still weak and unorganized and that democratic governments are hard put to meet urgent popular demands for reform, development, and modernization. If they falter, the right or, more threateningly, the left is ready to pounce. In this unstable situation the military may serve useful functions. While democratic forces and institutions nurse their strength and develop their capabilities, the military, employing intervention if necessary, may act as a moderator among parties and factions and prevent the political pendulum from swinging to extremes. Or to put it more concisely, the military may be used to buy time for evolutionary forces to withstand revolutionary pressures. In the meantime, the pragmatic liberals maintain, the armed forces, employing programs of civic action, may contribute directly to the achievement of desired goals.

Inasmuch as I sometimes pass as an authority on the subject, I suppose I am under some obligation to reveal my own notions. I will do so. In colonial times the military was juridically a component element in the polity. Although the juridical relationship was abolished by the liberal constitutions of the nineteenth century, the armed forces continue to constitute de facto institutional interest groups; they are publicly recognized and accepted as such. There is no military establishment in Latin America today that would attempt to displace or supplant a democratically elected government if it anticipated determined and united civilian resistance, and if it tried to do so in the face of such resistance, it is unlikely that it would succeed. The concept of intervention, therefore, is not appropriate, for how can an entity that is an integral part of the system intervene in it? What we, also rather inappropriately, call militarism is simply the interaction of the armed forces and civilian groups and institutions in a situation which is not comparable with Anglo-Saxon experience. This relationship is likely to prevail for the foreseeable future, but I am of the opinion that as civilian interest groups proliferate and gain strength and self-confidence, the relative influence of the armed forces within the system will decline and ultimately vanish. In this connection I would like to offer the proposition that the reason the Mexican military is nonpolitical today is precisely because it was not excluded from the revolutionary family but rather was admitted to full membership. Thereafter it was absorbed and eventually neutralized.

If I must make a commitment on the impact of militarism, that is, offer a value judgment, I suppose I would classify myself as a pragmatic liberal, but with two sets of reservations. First, there are substantial numbers of progressive, reform-minded, and even revolutionary officers in Latin America's armed forces. By and large, however, they are of junior and middle grade and thus relatively uninfluential. Also younger officers inevitably become older officers whose identification and loyalties are institutional, rather than programmatic or ideological. The Latin American military, furthermore, remain essentially conservative and loyal to the system which gave them existence and continues to provide them with sustenance and status. While they may undertake developmental missions, these tend to have technical rather than broadly social objectives. It is quite unlikely that they would voluntarily accept a role which would threaten the established order; if they did, they would resist a rapid rate of change. I doubt also that they have the capabilities to perform a major developmental role without diverting the bulk of their resources from their military mission, and this they are not willing to do.

With respect to the influence of the United States, it has not been demonstrated to my satisfaction that military assistance programs encourage Latin American armed forces to misbehave, though I suspect that in certain circumstances and under certain conditions this may be the case. I have seen no direct evidence that North American military personnel have deliberately encouraged Latin American officers to overthrow democratic governments, and I doubt that they have done so. I doubt also whether United States recognition policy has any real deterrent or encouraging effect on the political behavior of the Latin American military. On the other hand, I am skeptical about the proposition that Latin American officers acquire democratic, apolitical attitudes through rubbing shoulders with their North American counterparts. I am more inclined to think that through contact with the marvels of our way of life they may develop profound dissatisfaction with their own societies and their own lots. The political implications of such attitudes are obvious.

In any case, I think that we are inclined to overestimate the influence we can or do exercise on fundamental institutions and forms of behavior in other lands. Militarism in Latin America is an indigenous phenomenon. It is a response to tensions in societies which have not yet achieved true national identities or established basic norms of political legitimacy. While it would be foolish to deny that North American policy and personnel have some impact on the thinking of the Latin American military, the influence is peripheral.

More fundamentally I think it is presumptuous for North Americans to prescribe the proper forms of social and political organizations for Latin America or the proper means of achieving them. I agree with the late Winston Churchill that democracy is absolutely the worst form of government except all the rest. But, in considering the question Whither Latin America? the experts should bear in mind that despite their present difficulties, Latin Americans are talented and creative peoples with rich cultures and histories. It is conceivable that eventually they will work out some democratic sociopolitical system that fits their particular traditions, values, and aspirations, and it may not necessarily conform to the Anglo-Saxon liberal democratic model or the Marxist people's democracy.

POLITICAL OPTIONS IN
LATIN AMERICA TODAY

RICARDO ARIAS-CALDERON

The most significant development in Latin American political thought in recent years is the emergence of a "scientific" pattern of thought, in the sense this term is employed in the social disciplines. As sign and factor of this emergence, one can point to the establishment in 1966 of the Latin American School of Political Science and Public Administration within the Latin American Faculty of Social Sciences (FLACSO) in Santiago, Chile. The general orientation of the school, according to a recent expression of purposes by the institution, is

to establish the foundations for the development of a scientific activity in the field of teaching as well as in the field of research which will permit the use of the most modern means and methods which are being employed in the most advanced institutes of political studies.

The importance assigned to the methods of research and analysis, with an interdisciplinary approach and in a spirit both critical and empirical, is explained by the same publication not only in terms of the need to follow the new trends in the corresponding disciplines but also in terms of "the need to redirect the way in which the intellect of the Latin American works in social and political matters." The school will try to combine a "rationalist, dogmatic, deductive, idealist, metaphysical, and frequently romantic" way of thinking, in which the Latin American intellect would seem to have demonstrated its intuitive capacity, with "a more modern approach, more empirical, pragmatic, critical, inductive, precise, and systematic."

Apart from other considerations this institution's announced purposes reveal the emerging "scientific" pattern of Latin American political thought. And this can serve as an indication of the basic political options in Latin America today considered in their cultural implications, because between political thought and political reality the relationship is one of mutual reference and even implication. This is so particularly in Latin America, where the Weberian "objectivity" and "neutrality" of the social scientist is considered an attitude as politically significant as any form of active involvement on his part.

A North American political scientist, Vernon van Dyke, has suggested that the tendency of North American political scientists to avoid philosophical, ideological, and, in general, what we might call value-thought positions and to prefer, instead, a sober and restrained empirical and pragmatic approach, is related to a conservative political attitude with the desire to maintain the security which this system offers by not raising the question of its fundamental operative ideals, which are in fact transempirical and metapragmatic. If this is so, then we can say that the scientific pattern of North American political thought has, or at least can have, a quite different political significance.

To explain this we should first point to the fact that the emergence of this pattern is generally accompanied in Latin America by a demand for a primary autonomous status for political thought, and particularly for political science, as a discipline different from law and public administration, with which it has been generally associated as a subordinate discipline in our universities and academic institutions. This subordinate association of political thought with law and public administration reveals the relatively static political context which has prevailed. For, in truth, in a rather static situation the established order is an accepted fact and the major concern is the way it functions, either through the application of its rules, which constitutes a legal problem, or through the formation of public servants, which constitutes an administrative problem. Specifically political problems, such as the genesis of consensus and legitimacy and the displacement of centers of power, were relegated to a secondary consideration, if considered at all. But in an explosively dynamic situation these are the very problems which predominate, and because of this a need is felt to seek a primary autonomous status for political thought and science, which would permit them to play a directive role with respect to other social disciplines and to the social reality they study.

In other words, the demand for a primary autonomous status for political thought—which accompanies the emergence of a scientific pattern within this thought—is to my mind another indication of the explosively dynamic political reality of present-day Latin America. Our societies are subject to a process of profound, total, and rapid change. And this is not just a change from a given "state" to another "state," both imposed on men by the so-called circumstances, but rather an entering into a "state of change" which men promote, direct, and sustain. This means, therefore, that we are dealing with revolution, rather than with evolution, a fact which requires of us Latin Americans a new understanding of our changing society and its politics in order that we might understand and direct the process of change.

Thus the new pattern of political thought in Latin America corresponds to the revolutionary option which characterizes our political reality. And it corresponds or can correspond to the developmental option of this same reality. In this respect we should point out that the present Latin American revolutionary process may be the first with a specific and explicit developmental perspective, in the sense that the term "development" has acquired in recent times. This means that from the point of view of its values the process is directed from the traditional society to modern society. And however we may characterize these terms, it is clear that the second type of society involves the appearance of theoretical and practical rationality in the form of science and technology, not only in the field of the natural disciplines but very particularly in the field of the anthropological and social disciplines. It is this appearance which permits modern man to affirm himself as the creator of his world and of his history by planning his projects and organizing his realizations. And it is thus that man can generate the production which makes possible the increasing well-being of all members of the society and can structure life in such a way as to offer all a growing participation in social responsibility.

The developmental perspective of our revolutionary process requires therefore that our social and political consciousness acquire a scientific and technological dimension, with particular attention to analytical and projective methods. And this in turn implies that besides its primary autonomy from law and public administration, social and political science gain what I would call a complementary autonomy from such classic disciplines as ethics, metaphysics, and theology.

The acquisition of this new scientific and technological dimension, with all that it implies, is now felt as a need within political thought in Latin America, after this dimension was felt first in economics and later in social thought. This sequence in the emergence of the scientific pattern of thought—economics, sociology, and political science, in that order—is itself significant with respect to the unfolding of our process of development. The succeeding reports of the United Nations Economic Commission for Latin

America (CEPAL) reveal the progressive discovery and planning, first, of economic development, followed by what was called the social aspects of economic development, then of social development considered as "the other face" of economic development, and, finally, of political development as the axis of social development and, in consequence, of economic development also. The sequence to which I have alluded in the emergence of a scientific pattern of thought corresponds to a sequence in the strategies of the process of global development in our region as it unfolds, meets with obstacles, and requires new energies for it to reach its fullness.

The sequence serves as an indication of what has been accomplished thus far and of what is yet to be done if it is true, as has been suggested, that one of the characteristics of modern developed societies lies in the inversion of the classic relationship between economics and politics. In such a society, K. Silvert convincingly argues, "the political and social function of man, instead of depending on other presumably more fundamental circumstances, acquires importance as a mechanism of fundamental choice."

The demand for a scientific dimension in Latin American political thought is indicative of the developmental option which is also typical of our political reality and of the fact that this option is being faced in all its full meaning.

The emergence of the "scientific" pattern within our political thought must also be related to the integration option. The movement toward integration within the different societies and toward Latin American unity is not merely a means to make our revolution and development feasible but also through this a way to discover and to forge our own identity. Integration is, therefore, not merely an object for the consideration of Latin American political science; it is its manner of approach and its methodological style. It is interesting in this respect to note that the new School of Political Science and Public Administration to which I have referred is precisely an integrated Latin American center.

One cannot deny the importance of political science studies on Latin America undertaken by foreign experts, particularly by North Americans, and their influence in the emergence of the scientific pattern within Latin American thought. But this influence has been exercised through the characteristic channels of intercommunication between, on the one hand, integrated and developed societies, and, on the other hand, nonintegrated and underdeveloped societies. It is not surprising, therefore, that certain aspects of value predominance have been involved. This value predominance has been stronger because of the methodological "objectivity" and "neutrality" which has served as its vehicle. But such methodological "objectivity" and "neutrality" do, in fact, carry with them the values proper to a society—the United States, for example, which seems devoid of ideology in the very measure that within it a given ideology has been generally accepted and has become a so-called "way of life." And thus one can understand that in certain cases such a predominance could turn into what has been designated as "an unconscious scientific colonialism."

Some results of this value predominance can be pointed out. In studies on the Latin American revolution, as well as in attitudes with respect to it, the presupposition is sometimes made that it should follow either the model of diffuse violence and exploitation characteristic of the Industrial Revolution in capitalist countries or the model of the concentrated violence and exploitation characteristic of the French, and particularly of the Soviet, Revolution, and that any process of change which would not follow these molds could not possibly succeed or be called a revolution. At other times it is presupposed that Latin American development, identified as fundamentally similar to that of other Third World areas, must lead to a modern society similar to one of the types already existing in the contemporary world. This development would turn us, at best, from an exploited producer of the primary stuff of which contemporary history is made into an active consumer of the finished goods which other societies elaborate as autonomous producers of contemporary history. But we would never become creative agents of this and of future history.

Finally, the value predominance which accompanies the influence of foreign political science studies in Latin America often results in an understanding of our movement toward integration either in terms of the emergence of national states in Europe and North America during the past two centuries or in terms of the regional unification of already existing national states such as has occurred in Western Europe since 1945. But our movement toward integration is, in fact, original in the sense that it fosters the unity of preexisting independent states, which sociologically constitute nations only in an incipient manner.

Thus the movement toward integration, considered at its roots and in its aims, as a will to invent the identity of Latin America, has inspired and required an effort by Latin American political thought to overcome the distance between an alienated intellectual conscience and an unthought-of and unvalued vital reality. Because of this, Latin American political thought begins to foster not only our own studies but our own reality, and also and more deeply an epistemological reflection on itself as knowledge and conscience, with reference to approaches, methods, concepts, laws, theories, and so on. "We are less interested," someone has said, "in the study of our problems by North American social scientists than in general discussion on social science with our colleagues. There is in Latin America a crisis with respect to research carried out by foreigners."

The scientific pattern which emerges in Latin American political thought has or can have a threefold political significance. It corresponds, first, to a revolutionary process of change, which requires a new political conscience, with primary autonomy vis-à-vis legal and administrative disciplines and considerations, in order that this conscience may encompass rather than serve these disciplines and considerations. It gives rise, secondly, to a developmental perspective, in accordance with which our political conscience must acquire a scientific dimension, with a complementary autonomy vis-à-vis ethics, metaphysics, and theology, in order that it can promote more efficaciously the decision processes leading to full modernization. And it involves, finally, the movement of integration, requiring a political conscience with scientific dimension which can overcome its alienation and be capable of thinking and communicating our own reality.

Now, I have been careful to say that the emerging scientific pattern within Latin American political thought has, or rather *can have*, this reference to our basic political options. I underline this as a possibility, because in my mind the emergence of this pattern could also have a different reference to these options—let us say a conservative, nondevelopmental, alienating reference. This could happen if the scientific pattern in political thought is considered as a simple substitute for what I have called the value-thought pattern, or even if the scientific pattern is considered as capable of coexisting with the value-thought pattern as this latter expressed itself before the emergence of the former. In the first case the emergence of the scientific pattern would have a conservative, nondevelopmental, and alienating reference to our political options by reason of its apparent noninvolvement with a value-thought pattern, and in the second case it would have this type of reference by reason of its syncretic involvement with a previous traditional value-thought pattern.

In order for the emergence of the scientific pattern in Latin American political thought to have a revolutionary, developmental, and integrating reference to our political options, it is necessary that it be viewed as a pattern to be incorporated, together with a renovated value-thought pattern, within an integral political knowledge and awareness. Without this joint incorporation, political thought in Latin America will not respond to the needs of a revolutionary change, which because it is revolutionary involves man in his most intimate being and so requires renewed ideological perspectives as well as new scientific technology. Without these complementary dimensions, political thought in Latin America will also not respond to the needs of the process of development, since modernization implies the emergence of a renovated vision of man, in his relationship to the world, to other men, to himself, and to God. This is in contrast with a pseudomodernization (or modernized traditionalism) which would consist in the introduction of new procedures within the context of an older vision of man or without any vision of man at all if this latter possibility were feasible. Finally, without the joint incorporation of a scientific pattern and a renewed value-thought pattern within an integral political reflection, this reflection will not respond to the needs of integration. To invent one's own identity, it is necessary to actualize authentic values capable of inspiring one's conscience and action and not just to apply the values inspiring someone else.

In this respect the role of Christians in fostering political thought in Latin America and in guaranteeing that it relate positively to revolution, development, and integration is of primary importance. For Christians should be in a most favorable situation to promote the joint incorporation of which I have spoken, particularly under the impulse of the Second Vatican Council, which called for a recognition of the autonomy of secular realities and disciplines, while at the same time it recalled the need for maintaining their relationship to the religious dimension of life and thought. What is particularly suggestive and promising with respect to this role of Christians in fostering the political thought required in Latin America is that it has rendered necessary the Christian vocation as it is being lived by Latin Americans and by the actual demands of this thought and of the reality to which it refers as they unfold in Latin America.

PART THREE

EDUCATION AND CULTURE

EDUCATIONAL NEEDS IN
A DEVELOPING SOCIETY

PAULO DE TARSO

In this essay I should like to provide some themes for thought about the educational target of the Alliance for Progress and its achievements to this moment. We shall particularly examine the role of education as an institution serving a policy of social transformation within an inter-American framework of cooperation. To do this, it will be necessary not only to mention those characteristics proper to present-day Latin American development but also to describe the interaction between education and development in historical perspective. We will then try to indicate values applicable to a new Latin American society which can define new ways to an education dedicated to social change.

Other topics to be considered are the potential influence of Christian schools in education, their impact on Latin America's development, and the North American influence on Latin American education.

The Present Situation

In recent years and increasingly since the Alliance, Latin America has made great efforts to increase its education programs. There has, for instance, been an increase in the percent of resources allotted to assist education. Data gathered by UNESCO indicate that between 1962 and 1964 the percentage of expenditures on education vis-à-vis public expenditures amounted to 16.6 and 17.9 percent respectively.[1] With regard to the number of enrolled students an extraordinary increase was recorded in secondary and university education between 1955 and 1965. At the end of the decade 12 percent more students were enrolled in secondary schools, and 114 percent more in higher levels of education. In 1965 the total percentage of the population enrolled in Latin American education programs was 17 percent as against a world average of 14.6 percent.[2] Latin America was thus making definite progress toward meeting some of the quantitative goals set by the Alliance for Progress in promoting the use of human resources for development.

But the Charter calls for qualitative change as well, to make education a true instrument of change in the deeply imbedded existing social structure. It asks for programs that will eliminate illiteracy among adults in the hemisphere by 1970 and ensure a minimum of six years of primary school for all children. This program is intended to modernize and increase educational means at secondary, vocational, technical, and superior levels, to multiply the facilities for pure and applied research, and to provide qualified personnel for those societies undergoing rapid development.

It is clear that there was concern to aid educational programs that would assist economic development. But specific changes in the objectives, contents, methods, and structure of education were not considered. The only way to make education confront traditional society in a process of cultural change is to prepare the educated person to play a role in the nation-building dynamics of a new society. Thus, among Latin American nations there is still a need for reform in education as an integral part of a policy aimed at social transformation.

Some countries seem to have achieved impressive quantitative goals. Chile, for example, presently has 23 percent of the total population attending schools. In reality, however, a high increase in the projected demographic growth rate (2.8 percent annually between 1965 and 1970 according to figures published by CELADE) must warn us not to see meaningful educational gains in terms of absolute numbers. Table I shows that, despite a reduction of the percentage of people who are illiterate in recent years, the number of illiterates tends to increase in many Latin American countries. This is the case in Bolivia, Brazil, Colombia, Honduras, and Mexico. This faltering progress in eliminating illiteracy is due to rapid population growth and difficulties of a financial order.

With regard to this problem the recommendations of the World Congress of Ministers of Education for the liquidation of illiteracy, held at Teheran in 1965, should be mentioned. At that conference some of the delegations insisted that adult literacy programs, as short-term investments, should have as much priority as the education of children, a long-term investment. Yet even if it were recognized that total mass education on a primary level works for the "elimination of evil" at its foundation, such a program would not succeed in removing illiteracy from the major portion of the population.[3]

In fact, the slow elimination of illiteracy that characterizes so many Latin American countries is partly a result of the lack of motivation on the part of the illiterate adults. To overcome this, modern methods of adult education like the psychosocial approach that is being used in Chile endeavor to relate literacy to the life experiences of the illiterate. In this way we endeavor to bring about a modification of the relations of the illiterate to his environment by showing him that literacy is a key to the solution of his vital problems.[4]

TABLE I

NUMBER AND PERCENTAGE OF ILLITERATES IN
POPULATION 15 YEARS AND OLDER IN SOME
LATIN AMERICAN COUNTRIES

COUNTRY	CENSUS OF THE YEAR	NUMBER ILLITERATE (in thousands)	PERCENTAGE
Argentina	1895	1.305.7	53.3
	1914	1.765.9	35.1
	1947	1.541.7	13.6
	1960	1.221.4	8.6
Bolivia	1900	1.086.6	86.3
	1950	1.570.0	68.9
	1960	1.278.0	29.5
Brazil	1900	6.371.7	65.3
	1920	11.461.7	64.9
	1940	13.269.4	56.1
	1950	15.272.6	50.5
	1960	15.815.0	39.5
Colombia	1918	2.215.6	57.6
	1928	2.717.6	48.4
	1938	2.699.4	44.2
	1960	3.130.0	37.5
Chile	1907	1.202.2	49.9
	1920	1.024.0	36.9
	1930	746.2	24.4
	1940	971.4	26.4
	1952	868.4	20.0
	1960	717.4	16.2
Honduras	1930	327.0	66.6
	1935	394.8	67.4

	1940	415.3	65.3
	1945	445.6	63.7
	1960	639.4	53.1
Mexico	1900	7.631.5	77.7
	1910	7.817.1	72.3
	1921	6.973.9	66.2
	1930	7.223.9	61.5
	1940	7.544.0	54.0
	1960	10.573.2	37.8

Sources: *The Education Situation in Latin America* (Paris: UNESCO, 1960), Table No. 20, p. 263. Tomas Amadeo Vasconi *Education and Underdevelopment* (Santiago: ILPES, April, 1967).

Another factor worth emphasizing is that the effort to promote literacy should especially be concentrated in rural areas. As Table II shows, the rate of illiteracy in the countryside is very much greater than that of the urban areas. In Panama, for example, with 31 percent illiteracy in the whole country, urban illiteracy is only 7.2 percent, while rural illiteracy is 42.9 percent, nearly six times as great as in urban areas.

Important studies and projects relating to elementary education have also been made. UNESCO, with the cooperation of the Economic Commission for Latin America (CEPAL), the Organization of American States (OAS), and several United States organizations, drew up plans for a major elementary education program at meetings in Peru in 1965. The goals of the project, enlarged and clarified several times, were as follows:

adequate education facilities by 1968 for all the Latin American population of school age;

revision of plans of study to adapt them to the regional peculiarities of each country;

improvement of the systems of teacher training;

training of a group of leaders for each country, especially in education.

An evaluation of the project made in 1966 indicates that between 1957 and 1965 the increase in the number of children between 7 and 14 years of age was 11.6 million, while the increase in primary enrollment in the same period was 11.7 million. We see that student enrollment is barely keeping up with the increase of the school-age population. The report concluded that the 14.7

TABLE II
ILLITERACY PER COUNTRY 1950
(population 15 years or older)

COUNTRY	TOTAL	URBAN	RURAL
Central America			
Costa Rica	20.6	8.1	27.9
Guatemala	70.6	—	—
Honduras	64.8	43.6	74.7
Nicaragua	61.6	—	—
Panama	30.1	7.2	42.9
El Salvador	60.6	34.7	77.1
Caribbean			
Cuba	22.1	11.1	40.0
Haiti	89.5	—	—
Dominican Rep.	57.1	29.5	67.3
South America			
Argentina	13.6	8.8	23.2
Bolivia	67.9	—	—
Brazil	50.6	21.7	66.9
Chile	19.9	10.4	36.0
Colombia	37.6	—	—
Ecuador	44.3	—	—
Paraguay	34.2	—	—
Venezuela	47.8	29.5	72.0

Source: Main Project of Education, UNESCO Bulletin X, 1960/1961.

million children of primary school age who were not in school in 1957 had been only slightly reduced in numbers to 14.6 million in 1965. In percentage terms the improvement appears more notable, rising from 59 percent of children ages 7 to 14 in school in 1957 to 69 percent in 1965.

Secondary-school enrollment increases during the same period were still more impressive. In 1955 the enrollment at the middle level represented 10 percent of the population of school age; in 1960 this percentage rose to 15 percent, and in 1965 to 23 percent, an increase during the decade of more than 100 percent.[5] As it can be seen in Table III, the proportion of those registered in general secondary learning (university preparation) continues very high. Argentina alone, as Solari points out, has a well-differentiated system of secondary education.[6]

The relative improvement in enrollment is also evident at the third level of education (university). In fact, a comparative study reveals that while the percentage of those registered in primary education decreased slowly (from 88 percent of all those in school in 1950 to 82 percent in 1965) and rose somewhat at the secondary level (from 11 percent in 1950 to 16 percent in 1965), the percentage at the university level doubled (from 1 percent in 1950 to 2 percent in 1965). Despite this increase, only 5 percent of the young adults between the ages of 19 and 22 were enrolled in higher education in 1965.[7] Only one out of every twenty were thus able to receive the specialized training that is so vital to the building and maintenance of an advanced society. The Latin American educational pyramid continues to have an enormous predominance of students in the primary grades (more than 80 percent of the total enrollment) and a tragically truncated top. There is urgent need for an effort of great magnitude to increase the number of professionals required by the demands of Latin American development.

It is interesting to compare the formulation of the goals of agrarian and educational reforms in the Punta del Este meetings

TABLE III

PERCENTAGE OF STUDENTS IN SECONDARY SCHOOL, 1961

COUNTRY	SECONDARY EDUCATION	VOCATIONAL	TEACHER TRAINING
Argentina	25.3	50.5	24.3
Bolivia[1]	70.6	19.9	9.5
Brazil	73.4	18.9	7.7
Chile	70.1	27.3	2.6
Colombia	63.4	33.1	3.5
Costa Rica	80.2	15.3	4.5
Cuba	61.5	33.7	4.8
Dominican Rep.	60.6	38.7	.7
Ecuador	58.2	31.4	10.4
El Salvador	62.8	25.5	11.7
Guatemala	77.9	11.7	10.4
Haiti[1]	77.6	21.4	1.0
Honduras	78.7	14.0	7.3
Mexico[1]	54.3	32.7	13.0
Nicaragua[2]	53.5	27.4	19.1
Panama	67.4	30.4	2.2
Paraguay	55.9	15.5	28.6
Peru[1]	80.1	19.9	—
Uruguay	76.3	20.3	3.4
Venezuela	59.2	25.0	15.8

Source: UNESCO, *Statistical Yearbook, 1963.*
[1] 1960
[2] 1959
See Aldo E. Solari, "Secondary Education and the Development of
   Elites," *op. cit.*

of 1961 to 1967. As for the agrarian goal the 1967 meeting was
careful to avoid any repetition of the emphatic declarations of
1961. At the earlier conference the delegates spoke of integral
agrarian reform, of "transforming the unjust system of tenure,"
of "substituting a just system of property for the rule of the

latifundio." In the 1967 meeting there was visible retrogression in the refusal to accept the idea of an integral agrarian reform conceived as a medium to achieve an effective social transformation. There is talk, instead, of "the modernization of rural life" and of "colonization," so that no land need be taken from existing large estates. The previous direct reference to the change of traditional rules of tenancy is omitted.

As to education, analysis of the 1961 and 1967 meetings shows that the essential concern is still formal rationality, that is, the extension and perfecting of the traditional education system. There is rhetoric about the need for more basic change, but no real effort or intention to achieve it. The declaration of 1967, it is true, does speak of "education's role in the economic, social, and cultural development of Latin America," and it alludes to the need for "educational innovations." But major educational reform programs, like the one now in progress in Chile, are left to be carried out by the countries involved.

Aspects of Latin American Development

Analysis of the Latin American reality, with its culture of poverty and vicious circles in education, agriculture, industry, and politics, leads us to the conviction that our underdevelopment is not just a phase which will be followed by a repetition of the experiences of the developed countries. Needed scientific and technological innovations in our countries will not come about automatically as a result of a laissez-faire system. They must be introduced with a critical spirit and in line with the proper individuality of each country. After examining the stagnation of Latin America, Celso Furtado rightly concludes that the advance of each underdeveloped nation on the road to development is related to its capacity "to create itself in history." "The way in which techniques are brought in," he notes, "creates problems with great social consequences. [Development] tends to generate social instability and aggravate the antagonism of a society structured in classes."[8] Analysts at the Latin American Institute of Economy and Social Planning came to the same conclusion:

> Economic development and social transformation in Latin America are in a structural frame in which the peculiar peripheral conditions, the behavior of groups and social classes, and the movement constituted by them, assume individual characteristics. These affect the forms of organization, the ideologies, the normative systems, and the operative possibilities of the social agents of change and persistence.[9]

Latin America's economic problems, with their interlocking relationships, have often been described. Our countries suffer from low per-capita income (as little as one-tenth the per-capita income of developed nations) and an excessive concentration of income in the higher levels. Our backward agriculture retards the development of industry, commerce, and public services. The lack of internal markets and the resulting dependency on foreign trade results in a loss of economic independence. Insufficient growth in the economy and an inadequate politics of investment cause persistent deterioration in the terms of exchange. To all these economic problems must be added the absence or insufficiency of social mobility, the high rate of demographic increase, and the high rates of unemployment that result from economic stagnation. As a cause and result of these factors there is the situation of "social marginality" that affects wide sectors of our people, whose lives are characterized by the absence or insufficiency of organized participation in development. Politically, economically, and socially the marginalized people do not count.[10] The existing structure of Latin American society thus imposes severe limitations on any developmental program. What is urgently needed is change in these structures.

Education and Development

To determine the educational needs of a developing society we are obliged to consider not only the rate of its economic growth but also the transformation that is taking place in its social structure and institutional framework. When an economy begins to alter the means of production through the introduction of technological innovations, education becomes an essential part of the process. Man in the exercise of his liberty, relating himself to other men, transforms nature and assumes better control of the world through work to put it at the service of his needs. But education should not merely aim at increased productivity and personal advancement. It must, at the service of the whole man and of all men, emphasize the instrumental value of economic growth and put it at the service of human growth. Thus the free man affirms himself as a subject of development, achieves mastery of the world, and recognizes his solidarity with the rest of mankind.

In present-day Latin America, in contrast, the social structures and institutions were created for a dual society of rulers and ruled. It will not be enough to consider development as simply a process of technological change to increase the availability of goods and services, while an unjust social order is maintained. It is, moreover, clear that without social integration economic growth will be frustrated. In a society like Latin America's with wide sectors of the population cut off from decision-making and the money economy, a mass-production, mass-consumption advanced economy cannot be developed.

If we therefore consider education as a means to the social communication of culture and a preparation of man for his fulfillment in development, the process has a double aspect. It must prepare man for technical change, that is, for an increase of production and of productivity. But it must also prepare him for social change, to play a part in the transformation of the social structure. Technological change and social change are, of course, interrelated, the one as a positive catalyst of the development of the other. But the demands they make on education are different and should be analyzed separately.

As a social institution, historically determined and in union with other institutions, our educational systems tend to act in a conservative manner. They impede the process of social integration and seldom act as innovators with regard to technological change. Those who are familiar with the efforts at educational reform in Latin America know that there is active resistance to attempts at modernization in the social and natural sciences. Education has not attempted to lead us out of the maze of underdevelopment, but is instead part of the problem.

Literacy for example, looked at from the traditional point of view, is just a mechanism of learning to read and write. It is taught through spelling books, mechanical exercises having no relation to the interests and vital problems of the child or adult illiterate. It must instead be turned into a creative search that the illiterate makes with his own words into an expression of his culture. In this way the adult, as he becomes literate, grows conscious of the reality in which he lives, transforms it, and takes part in the development process. Method and message are fused; life and literacy are joined. This is the essence of the psychosocial method that is being applied in Chile.

In a society on the road to development, education should thus dedicate itself to preparing in a rational and planned manner the human resources necessary for economic growth. At the same time it acts on the social order, by either communicating the moral values needed to promote a breaking down of the duality of participants versus nonparticipants or, by omission, denying those that are at the margin of social life the conditions for cultural development.

We may turn next to consider briefly the historical evolution of Latin American education.[11] During the five-hundred-odd years of the colonial period in Latin America there was a dual society of conquistadores versus natives and a corresponding dual educational system. Higher education was reserved for a tiny minority, while the masses were denied any education at all except for primitive agricultural methods and a few simple crafts. This system was in perfect harmony with the characteristics of colonial society. Its aim was to provide Western culture for Spaniards and Creoles, and to preserve the colonial structure. The local indigenous masses were denied literacy. This was due, among other factors, to the fact that Castilian, the only language of instruction, was alien to the native peoples, some of whom continued to speak their ancient languages.

Then during the first quarter of the nineteenth century, through the influence of the French and American revolutions, the Latin American countries achieved independence. They tried to reorient their educational systems by nationalizing the confessional (parochial) schools and endeavoring to assure their democratization and freedom. In Brazil, for example, the first universities were created only after independence. Everywhere there was much rhetoric and legislation about free, equal, and universal education. But in reality there was little change in the dual structure inherited from the colonial period. Throughout the nineteenth century there continued to exist special establishments for the old and new agrarian aristocracy and for the emerging urban classes, while the common laborers remained illiterate.

After World War I the process of import substitution, accelerated by the world crisis of 1929, brought about an alteration of the productive forces in our countries. The period of industrial development thus initiated would demand qualified and literate personnel to staff the new factories. There was also stepped-up migration from the country to the city, with far-reaching impact on the school system.[12] By the middle of the twentieth century various international agencies for the study of Latin American education were created, and meetings on a regional and inter-American level were regularly held. It was hoped that integral educational planning could achieve the objectives of education. Yet the planners were generally trying to preserve the traditional ways of thinking and acting, while endeavoring to fit the "offer" of human resources to the "demand" of development, but without considering any major change of the social structures.

We have at least come to understand that Latin American education will have to be changed drastically if it is to aid in the process of social change. And while there are important differences between one Latin American country and another, we believe there are common aspects and a certain cultural originality revealed by our history that can guide the process of change. We find a common vision of man and the world, for example, in the fight for independence achieved in all the countries at about the same time. We see, at the present time, a similar generalized aspiration toward the transformation of our socio-economic structures.[13] Our plans, therefore, go deeper than the mere formal rationality mentioned above. We want to use education to help transform our world.

The University Department of the Latin American Episcopal Council (CELAM), meeting in Buga, Colombia, in February, 1967, published a document in which it referred to three stages of educational development.

First, in the nineteenth century there was aristocratic education, individualistic and humanist, utterly unconcerned with economics and society. By the 1930's there was developmental education, one adjusted to the existing social order and seeking only to prepare technicians for it. And, finally, in our own time there is the growing call for liberating education, one designed to enable man to participate freely and creatively in the transformation of traditional structures. All three stages still exist today, sometimes side by side, in the complicated reality of our societies.[14]

Technological innovations, which change the forms of work, gave to education the task of preparing man for the fulfillment of new functions. Economists have demonstrated that education, as compared with other long-term capital investments, is closely connected with productivity and yields a high rate of return. We may take as an example the studies by Salomon Fabricant of the North American economy between 1889 and 1957. The average growth of that economy over seven decades was 3.5 percent per year. The increase in capital investment and hours of work was 1.7 percent, which left an unexplained difference of 1.8 percent. Fabricant analyzed this "unknown factor" and concluded that it was a product of research, the assimilation of new techniques, the capacity to organize, the instinct of discovery, the sense of discipline, and the pleasure of work.[15]

In the developed countries from 75 to 90 percent of the increase in annual production is due to improved efficiency in the use of general technical progress. In the United States, for example, there are nearly fifty thousand technical newspapers, which publish yearly about 1,200,000 articles, enormously widening the field of knowledge. Specialization has developed to the point that there are nine thousand different categories of scientists and technical personnel in the United States.[16] These statistics give us some idea of the task that the Latin American countries have to face in trying to prepare the necessary human resources for their own economic growth. The secretariat of CEPAL estimates that by 1980 Latin America will require more than 5 million middle-level technicians, more than double the number available in 1965.[17] By 1980, the same source informs us, 1.2 million higher-level professionals will be needed, again almost double the 660,000 of 1965.

To emphasize in another way the importance of education for technological change, we may mention our negative index of per-capita agricultural production for the period 1938/1939 to 1963/1964. As Table IV shows, productivity in Latin America actually *fell* 11 percent per capita in that quarter of a century, the worst record of any region in the world, while the world average was rising 11 percent. Lack of knowledge and lack of capital went hand in hand in producing this retrogression, with all its tragic consequences for our people. And it is education that must end the marginality of our rural people through literacy programs and agricultural training.

Faced with the existing traditional society, the Latin American educational system can either play a conservative role or carry out a revolutionary mission. It is conservative when it functions as a process of "socialization" oriented toward training new generations in the traditional ways of thinking and acting. It is revolutionary when it helps to promote rapid cultural change by preparing educated men for their role in the dynamic construction of a new society. Our schools today, oriented toward social cohesion, tend to function as "agents of conformism, mainly because they have to be financed by the state or by the society that they serve."[18]

In a dual society (domineering-dominated) like ours education

TABLE IV

INDEX FOR AGRICULTURAL PRODUCTION PER INHABITANT AND PER REGION
(1952–1957 = 100)

REGIONS	PRE-WAR AVER-AGE	1952/53	1958/59	1962/63	1963/64 PRELIMI-NARY	VARI-ATION
Eastern Europe & USSR	83	96	122	124	121	38
Western Europe	93	102	106	115	115	23
North America	88	101	98	97	100	+12
Latin America	110	98	106	101	99	−11
Africa	92	100	99	100	98	+ 6
Far East	109	100	108	104	104	− 5
Near East	96	102	107	107	110	14
Oceania	103	99	107	110	110	+ 7
World	95	100	105	106	105	+11

Source: Food and Agriculture Organization (FAO), Regional Office for Latin America, "FAO's Work in Latin America," 1965.

incorporates values, habits, and attitudes that are compatible with that duality. Social inequality and injustice appear to the educated man to be something inevitable, something that man cannot change. To educate for the construction of a new society, we must give man a new conscience and a new sense of the world. Education can thus free man from his cultural inhibitions, make him more than the mere "cash register" described by Eric Fromm. We must not, on the other hand, impose our own absolute definitions of the good society; that would reduce education to an absurd process of indoctrination, of cultural domination. It is instead a question of formulating a tentative interpretation of the actual moment in history, and of projecting this interpretation toward the future by presenting to the educated the problem of overcoming traditional society. We offer the student ideas, suggestions, hypotheses, themes for reflection, and analyses of the existing situation so that he himself will be encouraged to look for his own solutions. Thus we replace the traditional pedagogy of adjustment to the world by the pedagogy of building a new one, a pedagogy founded on the attitude which Eric Fromm in his study of the pathology of social normality call "normative humanism."[19] We impose no dogmas, no ideologies, but seek to develop such qualities in our students as a critical vision of reality, confidence in liberty and in the capacity of ordinary persons, cooperation, solidarity, generosity, the spirit of achievement, social discipline, a capacity to sacrifice, dedication to work, acceptance of the risk and insecurity that accompanies the process of change, efficiency, rationality in the assigning of roles and benefits, personal autonomy, respect for plurality, promotion of the common good, and integrated international development. The long-range goal would be an open society with room for personal achievement and social justice.

To achieve this goal we require an integral reform of education, a change in its objectives, its structure, its contents, and its methods. Middle-level agricultural education, for example, cannot be purely technical and concerned with seeds, fertilizer, irrigation, and farm machinery. It must help promote the agrarian reform: increase in the number of owners with managerial capacity, increase in production and productivity through integration of the *campesino,* a change in the rural social structure. In Chile we are attempting to alter the entire educational system along similar lines. There has been a massive increase in enrollments at all levels, emergency preparation of teachers through accelerated courses, an attempt to combine a new emphasis on technical education with a breaking down of the old attitudes that separated the practical and the liberal, humanistic disciplines. We feel that the modernization process should not be limited to natural science and technology. It should extend also to the social sciences, which are able to address themselves directly to the politics of change.

As for methods, it is a question of overcoming the vertical system of professor-student relationships and avoiding all that involves cultural prescription or paternalism. We want to make education a dynamic, a dialogue in which the participants inter-communicate their consciences and reshape the world. Teachers and students alike should concentrate on an orderly search for the means of bringing about cultural change. They should, for example, examine new plans in the social sciences, the education of adults, university reform, the methods of social communication, social education, the educational action of the family and the churches, the suitability of existing pedagogic institutions to the new objectives, educational integration in the context of economic and political integration, and so on.

At a time when values are in crises, when the American man asks himself what he should do and what goals he should seek, the Christian Churches have a special role to play. If they identify with man's values and with his new concept of himself and the world, they can develop a pedagogic labor of real importance and fulfill their historic mission.

No one can ignore, for example, the importance that the Catholic Church has had in educational activities in Latin America. Its first schools were built at the time of the Conquest, and the rare tentative effort to educate the masses came shortly after. These Catholic schools of the colonial period essentially had religious preoccupation, and were run by Franciscans, Dominicans, Augustinians, Carmelites, and Jesuits. The tension between the educational work of the religious orders and the interests of the civil authorities was often sharp and resulted, for example, in the expulsion of the Jesuits.

But what the CELAM document, previously cited, says about Latin American education in general applies as well to present-day Catholic education. Within it coexist the "aristocratic" orientation, the "developing" orientation, and the "liberator" orientation. Any national plan for education aimed at social transformation cannot disregard the Catholic schools, which are so numerous in Latin America, especially at the secondary level. In Chile, for example, private (usually Catholic) schools represent close to one-third of the total enrollment. In 1962, according to official data of the superintendent of education, the private schools (including the universities) represented 33.4 percent of the total system. The exact percentages of private-school enrollment by levels were preschool, 18 percent; primary, 30 percent; secondary, 42 percent; commercial, 35 percent; industrial, 32 percent; female instruction, 36 percent; agricultural, 50 percent; normal school, 17 percent; university, 40 percent.

In Brazil, to take another country and a different angle of vision, a recent inquiry reveals less than 10 percent of the secondary schoolteachers profess no religion. The overwhelming majority of the 100,000 secondary schoolteachers are Christian and Catholic.[20] We hardly need more data to prove the significance of Christianity in Latin American education. If schools could put themselves at the service of social transformation in the context of a "liberating" education, they could make a decisive contribution to the achievement of a decent level of life for all our people.

In the case of the Catholic schools, acceptance of new values is facilitated by the latest papal documents concerning the Catholic Church and the world, development, and education. The Pastoral Constitution on the Church in the Modern World, pointing out the intimate solidarity of the Church "with humanity and with its history," tells us that "every day more profound changes are produced in the traditional local communities" and in the "relations established by social convenience." Similarly, the encyclical *Populorum Progressio,* characterizing the process of development, shows how it is not simply a matter of economic growth, but it should be integral, that is, concerned with the promotion of "all men and all of man." Galvanizing Christian humanity, the Pope endeavors to evoke the dynamic sense of human existence by the affirmation that man is the measure of development, and his growth its key.

When talking of the aspirations and values that should orient human growth, Pope Paul VI points out the meaning of "having more" and "being more," and presents authentic human growth as involving limits to the exaggerated anxiety for possessions. Man is not merely an acquisitive animal; he seeks to participate in cultural creation, he longs to love and be loved. Such an integral development, the encyclical adds, "cannot be achieved without the unified development of mankind." We need not only large numbers of technicians but also "thinkers of profound reflection who will look for a new humanism." The Catholic schools of Latin America must accept this invitation as a real challenge. They must form men and women capable of creating this "new humanism."

As an example of Catholic educational innovation, we may mention the experience of the Basic Education Movement (MEB). Supported by the Catholic bishops of Northeast Brazil, and directed by laymen, MEB has realized through its radio schools an important task oriented toward literacy and the cultural and economic integration of rural communities. In Colombia, also, the Church has taken part in shaping an effective new educational instrument. The Popular Cultural Action (ACPO) radio schools of Sutatenza are contributions of the Colombian Catholic Church to "the integral Christian education of the people, especially the adult peasants, with a system that includes basic culture and a preparation for social and economic life." In 1964 these radio schools had 68,000 enrolled and active pupils, and reached 865 of the 1,100 towns in Colombia.[21]

These brief references to the role of the Christian Churches in education oriented toward social change would be incomplete if we did not mention the growing importance of the role of the Evangelical Churches in our educational programs. As one example of many, we may cite a recently signed agreement between the Evangelical Audiovisual Center and the Ministry of Education of Chile to use Evangelical churches to make literate fifteen thousand adults. The plan will embrace literacy and general education, and will be in effect in various zones throughout the country. In Mexico, similarly, there existed in 1961 nearly 2,700 Protestant educational centers: 125 primary schools, 27 secondary, 14 preparatory, 13 technical, 4 normal schools, 3 nursing, 8 agricultural, 2,470 Sunday Schools, 1 school for the blind, 24 student houses, 13 social centers, and 5 YMCA-YWCA centers.[22] In Brazil a Protestant educational institution, the Mackenzie Institute, has close to seven thousand students at all levels, from kindergarten to the university.[23]

We turn next to consider the North American influence on our schools. As it was indicated above, there is a contradiction in the Charter of Punta del Este that helps to explain some of the problems of the Alliance for Progress. Since the Latin American countries are not internally integrated, the Alliance has to work with one or several of the disintegrated social sectors whose interests are generally in conflict with one another. If a politics of change of the socioeconomic structure is decided upon, one must work with the social groups who will benefit from the change. If, on the other hand, only economic growth without social change is sought, then the traditional alliance with the conservative forces can be maintained.

At Punta del Este the policy of social change entered into conflict with the traditional dominant groups that wish to preserve the status quo and defend existing interests. The Center for Social and Economic Development in Latin America (DESAL), in its critical study of the Alliance for Progress, focused upon this conflict and demonstrated that without the realization of major reforms it would not be possible to have meaningful economic growth. The DESAL report goes on to argue that the North American collaboration "serves to consolidate at least temporarily the situation of the governing minority, to make it richer and therefore to impoverish the sectors of the population that it sought to help."[24] This kind of contradiction is what Senator Eugene McCarthy is referring to when he compares the "myth" of the Alliance to the "reality" of its politics in Latin America.[25]

But in the case of education we cannot speak of the failure to carry out an agreed-upon reform. As we have seen, no definition was reached in the Charter of Punta del Este as to the necessity of such a reform unless we consider that the vague rhetoric of the "Declaration to the Peoples of America" implies a call for revolutionary changes in educational objectives and methods. Those in positions of power must eventually make a choice: either they sacrifice the Alliance, with its ideology of social transformation, or they sacrifice traditional allies of the status quo. We can hardly expect to convert those traditional allies to a policy of social change that would be contrary to their interests in a direct and irreversible way.

All policies of social change have their ideological "moment" which constitutes the point of reference from which existing social forces and the impulse to development can be studied.

To be effective, this ideological formulation must integrate its values and reality. It cannot, therefore, be an imported nor alien stereotype. It should be an original formulation, liberally conceived and based upon an honest assessment of the national reality. The formulation of such a revolutionary theory would clear up some of the doubts that have always made difficult the dialogue between us and liberal sectors of North American public opinion.

Arthur Schlesinger, Jr., observes that the men of the New Frontier had a natural sympathy with what he calls the "democratic left" in Latin America, but he questions whether their policies "were really effective." Let us attempt, then, to analyze the presence of the United States in Latin American education from the perspective of those actively working toward autonomous development. We may begin with the affirmation that no country can delegate the task of educating its people to another. If one country should abandon the task of defining its educational policies, it would mean an alienation of its true interests and an abdication of its national individuality. Such a country would be demonstrating a total lack of national consciousness and an inability to express its own essential characteristics.

When speaking of an education "that would conform to the culture and native traditions," Pope Paul VI asks that education "be open to fraternal relations with other peoples to the end of fomenting true unity and peace on earth." But we must not forget that culture, as a projection of man, is reflected in the forms of personal and collective life, and that habits, attitudes, customs, dynamisms, and inhibitions develop in accord with a vision of the world and of human life.

What we wish for, then, is an intercultural dialogue, the meeting of two cultures on a plane of mutual respect, with the desire to contribute and to receive, with the humility to recognize that the contributions of the other can mean a genuine cultural enrichment. As Robert Alexander has observed, both cultures, the

North American and the Latin American, tend to misunderstand
and to underestimate the cultural contributions of the one to the
other. The Latin Americans, Alexander points out, stress so-called
Yankee materialism. They consider North Americans to be semi-
barbarian, very capable in the production and manipulation of
artifacts, but without any soul and with little or no interest in
the finer things of life. For their part, North Americans tend to
look at their Latin American neighbors as "romantics," rather
incompetent and totally "unsophisticated."[26]

In the United States the war in Vietnam and racial difficulties
at home caused many to ask if the values and attitudes of today
are in accord with the fundamental historic characteristics of
their society. In Latin America the contemporary crisis is related
to our eagerness to do away with certain traditional values. In
the United States, as Senator Fulbright points out, the effort
is to find a role in the world that will be compatible with the
nation's traditional values:

> those upon which the Republic was founded: the feeling of the people,
> the optimism, a rudimentary quality, friendliness, good humor, ingeniosity
> (or ingenuity), the pleasure of life, the preoccupation of the people, the
> idea that maybe they could give to the world an example of democracy and
> human dignity.[27]

In resisting the dream of an imperial destiny the American people are trying out the solidity of the American Dream, Senator
Fulbright goes on, and adds that American society "cannot
be defended with methods that are violent without destroying
the same thing which we are trying to build." Are the technical
education programs of the Alliance for Progress part of the "imperial destiny," or are they a worthy expression of the American
Dream?

In reality American technical assistance assumes different
characteristics and provokes acceptance or rejection according
to the grade of respect that is revealed to the cultural individuality and autonomy of each country. Education, let us remember,

is one of the most essential aspects of national sovereignty. Foreign assistance to education, therefore, should limit itself to helping carry out a given education policy. Foreigners may not decide what is to be done, what values are to be communicated. If this is not the case, foreign aid becomes paternalism and cultural domination.

In Brazil, for example, between 1964 and 1966 the military regime and various North American organizations, without public debate, signed far-reaching agreements concerning higher education, middle education, and primary education, training of teachers, adult literacy programs, graduate training in economics and engineering, leadership training, technical publications, planning, educational pedagogy and the sciences, and modernization of university administration. Such agreements, said to be in accord with the "obligation by the Brazilian government, assumed in the Charter of Punta del Este as a member of the Alliance for Progress," give the United States an inordinate voice in planning the education of Brazil. As Dom Helder Camara, the Archbishop of Olinda and Recife, told the Deputies of Brazil:

To accept a cultural model prefabricated in any foreign country or to surrender half the national education to foreign technicians is to realize education for antidevelopment."[28]

As an example of a more praiseworthy form of technical and financial assistance, we may cite the one that the North American organizations have adopted in Chile. Here, the Ministry of Education and the Agrarian Reform Corporation (CORA) have made agreements with the Inter-American Bank to finance educational aspects of the agrarian reform. These agreements involve more than 30 million dollars destined to finance fundamental reforms. But these loans, unlike those in Brazil, are made according to plans discussed and drawn up in advance by the government of Chile in the context of its policy of social transformation.

Other aspects of United States educational cooperation with

Latin America should be mentioned. There is, first of all, the program of scholarships, whose problem is to train people to suit the needs of Latin America, not to add to the "brain drain" discussed elsewhere in this book. American commercial instruments—the movie industry, television programs, comic books, and teen-age magazines, and so on—have a profound and often disquieting effect upon our peoples. The rapid development of communications satellites will also affect Latin American society. All to often we find the media materials which deluge us to be steeped in alienation and violence. We need a change in our diet, to become acquainted with the traditional values of American civilization mentioned above. The epic poem of the conquest of the West, for instance, can be restudied as an example of the domination of nature by man, with emphasis on creative work and sacrifice, and not, as at present, on violence.

Existing vested interests in the United States and Latin America make such fruitful collaboration difficult, if not impossible. Perhaps we should begin by informal discussions with the most open groups in the United States, dialogues over what ought to be done. We must make every effort to see that North Americans, as long as they are active in Latin American education, instill, not the contingent contents of their present military, economic, and racial crisis, but the basic human values of their civilization.

NOTES

1. Information by the Evaluation Commission Main Project, Conference of the Ministers of Education and Ministers Charged with Economic Planning in Latin America and the Caribbean Nations. UNESCO-MINEDECAL, May 5, 1966.

2. See Education and Development in Latin America, Basis for Educational Policy. UNESCO-MINEDECAL /7, Santiago, Chile, April, 1966.

3. Final Report of the Teheran Conference (September 8–19, 1965), UNESCO.

4. Lauro de Oliveira, *The Paulo Freire Method* and *Democracy, Technology, and Education* (Rio de Janeiro).

5. Aldo E. Solari, "Secondary Education and the Development of Elites," in Seymour Lipset and Aldo Solari, eds., *Elites in Latin America* (New York: Oxford University Press, 1967); Tomas Amadeo Vasconi, *Education and Social Change in Latin America* (Santiago: ILPES, 1967).

6. Solari, *op. cit.*, pp. 467–468.

7. Vasconi, *op. cit.*

8. Celso Furtado, *Underdevelopment and Stagnation in Latin America* (Rio de Janeiro: Civilizacao Publishers, 1966).

9. Fernando H. Cardoso, *The Social Agents of Change and Conservation in Latin America* (Santiago: ILPES, 1964).

10. See DESAL, *Latin America and Social Development* (Santiago: Herder, 1966).

11. See the author's "Feasibility of Agrarian Reform," address delivered to the Second Meeting of Executives of the Agrarian Reform (II CA-OAS).

12. Until 1925 the rural areas contained close to 85 percent of the total population of Latin America. See C. A. Miro, "Population of Latin America in the 20th. Century" (mimeographed), CELADE Internal Distribution Publication.

13. Paulo de Tarso, "Latin American Cultural Integration" (mimeographed). Introduction to the basic document of the Chilean delegation to the First Meeting of the Permanent Commission of Cultural Integration and Education of the Latin American Parliament.

14. See University Pastoral, Buga, 1967; series 1, doc. 4, CELAM Documentation Service.

15. Salomon Fabricant, "Basic Facts on Productivity Change," National Bureau of Economic Research, Occasional Paper, no. 3 (New York, 1959). Cited in Pablo Latapí, *Economy and Education* (Mexico, 1964).

16. Eli Simberg, *Technology and Social Change* (Mexico City: Editorial Uteha, 1965).

17. CEPAL, UNESCO/MINEDECAL. See note 9 above.

18. Lima Oliverira, *To Educate for the Community* (Rio de Janeiro: Editores Vozes, 1966).

19. Eric Fromm, *Psychoanalysis of Contemporary Society* (Mexico City: Fondo de Cultura Economica, 1964).

20. See Aparecida Joly Gouveia, "Education and Development:

Opinions of Secondary Schoolteachers," in Seymour Lipset and Aldo Solari, eds., *Elites in Latin America*.

21. Herman Troncoso, "Report on Popular Cultural Action" (mimeographed), Center for Social and Economic Development in Latin America (DESAL), 1964.

22. Pedro Rivera, R.S.J., *Protestant Institutions in Mexico* (Mexico City: Editorial Jus, 1962).

23. Stanley N. Rycroft, *A Factual Study of Latin America* (New York, 1963).

24. DESAL, *The Alliance for Progress, A Critical Study* (Santiago: Edicións DESAL/CLASS, 1967).

25. Eugene J. McCarthy, *The Limits of Power; America's Role in the World* (New York: Holt, Rinehart and Winston, 1967).

26. Robert J. Alexander, *Today's Latin America* (New York: Anchor Books, 1962).

27. J. W. Fulbright, "United States, A Sick Society," *Mensaje* (Santiago, Chile), 163 (October, 1967).

28. See Dom Helder Camara, "Education for Development," Panel Promoted by the Institute of Inquiry and Studies of Brazilian Reality, Chamber of Deputies, June 21, 1967; *Brazilian Business*, XLVII, 8 (August, 1967).

MIGRATION OF TALENT
FROM LATIN AMERICA
TO THE UNITED STATES

FRANK MARINO HERNANDEZ

Our country is lucky enough in having a strong power of attraction over foreign scientists. Well-administered migration is one of our main sources of national wealth.

Dean Rusk

Introduction

The study of the causes and effects of the emigration of Latin American scientists and technicians is difficult. Although this problem has begun to be discussed in our countries, it has come to light owing to studies being carried on elsewhere, with results which are then brought to our America by mass communication media. The discussion of the "brain drain" is considered of vital interest in Great Britain. It is likewise being discussed and studied in Germany and other countries of the European Common Market. In the United States, scientific curiosity and the honesty of professional researchers have also brought this problem into prominence. It has been examined under two major aspects: the favorable effect on the United States and the negative force it represents for the nations of the Third World.

In my country, the Dominican Republic, it is especially difficult to evaluate the significance of the "brain drain" because of our insularity, the lack of a national library, the lack of modern university libraries (although these are now in the process of formation), and the lack of private or official archives from which data regarding the results of current research in scientific matters can be retrieved. Because of these limitations the scope of this paper will be severely limited. The data offered is obtained chiefly from magazines and newspapers, both Latin American and European.

Higher Education and Economic Development

The programming of economic and social development in recent decades has emphasized the acute need and the painful lack of trained human resources formed in the universities or equivalent institutions. Scientists and technicians are the creators and adapters of the discoveries which have made possible innovation in the design and production of consumer goods and services in demand in an emerging society or in one that has high levels of consumption. The developing nations of the Third World, because of the "demonstration effect," have tried to copy the consumer patterns of the rich nations and in this way have established the basis for the existence of a group of professionals in the field of engineering and related areas, as well as in economics and the social sciences.

In the early stages of development the small demand for sophisticated goods is satisfied by means of imports from the industrial nations. Widening aspiration to participate in the enjoyment of wealth then creates the need for these new markets to have the human resources which can produce the same goods and services at home. But in many rural areas the production patterns are still pre-Columbian. Their sudden confrontation with the consumption patterns of North America represents a challenge to the stability and growth of these developing societies. The urgent need arises, then, to form experts in those fields which enable man to enrich nature through the application of Western science and technology. As control of the death rate through imported technology leads to rapid population growth, the very health and life of our people demand the rapid modernization of our agriculture and industry.

Universities and institutions of learning have attempted to satisfy these needs in part. But most universities in Latin America hold tightly to traditional studies in the humanities. Their devotion to the liberal professions still follows medieval scholastic patterns. In order to complement the narrow scope of the traditional universities, new institutions, with new ideas and new aspirations, are emerging. But the size, competence, and professional diversity of the new universities of the Third World are so limited that many poor countries practically have a university abroad if the number of students who are pursuing higher studies outside their country of origin is taken into account.

These professionals, formed in what we will call the "exterior university," grow accustomed to a new life style. They admire the new level of instruction, the higher standard of living, the political, social, and economic stability of the developed countries. This stability, accompanied by a real demand for professionals, tempts them to ignore the great need for their new skills at home, to turn their backs on the problems of underdevelopment, and to become part of the advanced society which has trained them and can give full scope and rich rewards to their talents.

It is necessary to go back to the years immediately after World War II to understand how concern about the emigration of professionals was born. The significance for the United States of the migration of German scientists who worked in war industry and related fields during the struggle against the Third Reich was obvious. The war gave rise in the United States to new ideas about the strategy of defense and the role of this nation as a world power. Foreign scientists and technicians—Enrico Fermi, Leo Szilard, Lise Meitner, and Werner von Braun the best known among them—brought the ideas adopted and enlarged by North

American scientists through research and development projects. And these projects have been the main source of demand for well-paid engineers and scientists, and they also provide facilities which could hardly be found in countries relatively less developed than the United States.

Besides the number of professionals absorbed by institutions and projects of the government dedicated to research and development, one has to consider the large number of professionals in North American industry and in the universities, which are even more interested in attracting the best talent in the world. American society offers these men the door to the teaching profession or to research under exceedingly favorable conditions. The attractions of the great North American market thus turn it into the main point of convergence of professionals in the world today. Even the developed nations of Western Europe are affected. This can be observed by examining the number of losses which Great Britain suffers from its annual production of scientists, engineers, and technicians, of which it is estimated that one-third go to the United States to live permanently, or at least for one-year periods. For the year 1966 the loss of scientists and engineers suffered by Great Britain has been estimated to be more than six thousand. In the same period only about half as many foreign engineers and scientists came to Great Britain. The extraordinary movement of Britons to the United States can be explained not only in terms of salary and institutional facilities for research but also by the common language and other equally significant cultural factors. Other European contributors to the North American market for professionals are the Germans and the Dutch, with France trailing far behind. This last fact can be attributed, perhaps somewhat superficially, to cultural differences and to a difference in technological development.

The causes and the magnitude of the migration of talent from Latin America cannot be determined with the same precision that it can be done in Europe. The frequent internal convulsions in the nations south of the Río Bravo are unstable factors which surely have a profound effect on the social behavior of professional men as regards their residence. But there does not exist in these countries a clear awareness of this problem, and therefore effective measures have not been taken to determine the net number of professionals who migrate to complete their studies or with the intention to reside in the United States. The best source of information on this subject is the Immigration and Naturalization Service of the Department of Justice of the United States, which registers the professional qualifications of persons who enter the country under a resident visa. There are, however, no records pertaining to the number of resident professionals who eventually leave this country to return to their country of origin or another.

Let us look at some estimates of the migration to the United States of professionals from the whole world, from a group of Latin American countries, and, in more specific detail, from Argentina and the Dominican Republic.

Between 1948 and 1961 a total of 44,430 foreign scientists and technicians entered the United States. Of these, 26,883 were aeronautical, chemical, civil, electrical, industrial, mechanical, metalurgic, and mining engineers. Another 17,547 qualified under fields other than engineering. A study by David Greenwood of the National Science Foundation gives us the following information about the emigration of trained specialists from Latin America:

TABLE I

LATIN AMERICAN SPECIALISTS ENTERING
THE UNITED STATES

YEAR	ENGINEERS	SCIENTISTS
1957	402	186
1958	450	190
1959	325	101
1960	386	124
1961	455	119
Total	2,018	720
Annual Average	404	144

Latin America thus lost two scientists every five days, and more than one engineer a day. These numbers, significant enough in themselves, are cause for further alarm when we realize the critical shortage of trained persons in Latin America. And the pattern of emigration of other professional groups such as doctors, dentists, economists, agronomists, accountants, sociologists, librarians, and others is doubtless similar. Dr. Morris Horowitz, chairman of the Department of Economics at Northeastern University, in a study of human resources carried out under the auspices of the Ford Foundation, offers the following numbers of professionals in eighteen different occupations who entered the United States from Argentina between 1951 and 1964:

TABLE II

EMIGRATION OF PROFESSIONALS FROM ARGENTINA
TO THE UNITED STATES

YEAR	NUMBER	YEAR	NUMBER
1951	48	1958	628
1952	80	1959	413
1953	124	1960	418
1954	162	1961	443
1955	182	1962	404
1956	296	1963	639
1957	490	1964	912
		Total	5,239
		Annual Average	373

These numbers show that Argentina loses an average of more than one professional a day.

From *El Mercurio* (Santiago, Chile) we take the data given in a letter from Dr. Julio Rivera in which he states that between 1958 and 1965 a total of 45,868 Latin American professionals and technicians were absorbed by the United States. The data offered by Dr. Rivera for some individual countries is as follows:

TABLE III

MIGRATION OF LATIN AMERICAN PROFESSIONALS
TO THE UNITED STATES, 1958–1965

Argentina	5,020
Brazil	1,523
Colombia	4,025
Cuba	12,141
Ecuador	1,543
Atiti	1,828
Dominican Republic	1,364

We have no way to confirm the accuracy of this information and merely offer it to give an idea of what may be happening and what is being divulged in Latin American periodicals regarding the "brain drain."

Finally, we offer some data regarding the Dominican Republic:

TABLE IV

MIGRATION OF PROFESSIONALS FROM THE DOMINICAN
REPUBLIC TO THE UNITED STATES, 1961–1965

	1961	1962	1963	1964	1965	TOTAL
Accountants and auditors	15	35	42	14	13	119
Agricultural sciences	2	2	2	3	—	9
Architects	3	8	—	2	2	15
Dentists	4	4	7	—	4	19
Engineers	47	43	34	17	16	147
Doctors and surgeons	76	67	65	39	32	279
Veterinarians	—	1	1	1	1	4

These numbers show that during these five years migration to the United States reached more than 10 percent of the total graduates from selected fields, which is higher than the 8 percent of migrants computed from the studies of Greenwood and Horowitz for the migration of engineers from Latin America in relation to

the annual number of graduates. We may urge those interested
in this problem to read the study entitled "The Migration of High-
Level Chilean Human Resources to the United States" by Sergio
Gutierrez Olivos.

Significance of Migration

When the meaning of the "brain drain" is discussed in England,
they emphasize the effect it will have on technological progress,
because professional contribution to the building of the nation is
recognized. This is not the case in Latin America. In many countries the use of professionals in positions where they would be
taken for granted in developed nations is still not recognized as
having priority. Important posts go to relatives, to military men, to
persons with political influence. Hence the seriousness of the loss
of trained people is not recognized; they are not so badly missed.

Let us try then to analyze other effects of it. The investment in
higher education is high wherever there is a large student population, because it is expensive to form a professional. In the
Dominican Republic, for example, it can be estimated that it
costs around one thousand dollars a year to support a student
going to the university, and a graduate represents total investment of ten thousand dollars. This means that every one hundred
professionals who have completed a five-year course of study and
come to live in the United States represent one million dollars in
an informal program of foreign aid from the poor countries to the
rich ones. The aggregated riches represented by one hundred
Latin American professionals residing in the United States with
a minimum salary of 500 dollars a month each can be estimated
at more than 600,000 dollars a year. If we estimate that there are
currently thirty thousand Latin American professionals living in
the United States, a reduction of 30 percent in Professor Rivera's
figures, and if we consider that each professional earns 500 dollars
monthly, we would come up with an annual amount of at least
180 million dollars. This example is nothing more than a mental

exercise, and we use.it only to show the size of the problem.

If one wished to make a more serious study, one would have to consult the sources of information mentioned above, estimate the actual per-capita income of each professional, and subtract the contribution that North American technicians and scientists living in that area are making to development in Latin America. Moreover, aside from the waste of money that an investment in lost higher education represents for a poor nation, we must allow for the contribution toward development that is made by the Latin American professionals who finish their education in the United States and then go home. Others, contributing to North American development as permanent residents, are a kind of unofficial and generally overlooked form of foreign aid. Their migration, when it becomes permanent, deprives the poor countries of trained personnel needed at home and also constitutes a deterring factor for future professionals, who orient themselves toward the achievements and living standards of their countrymen abroad. The quality of higher education in their home country likewise suffers.

Factors Promoting Migration

In Europe, until recently, the causes most frequently mentioned as attracting professionals to the United States were high wages and the facilities for research and creative work. Less important factors have been the greater ease with which university positions can be obtained, the supposed facilities afforded women by mechanical devices to perform many domestic tasks, and the greater esteem in which the scientist is held in this country.

As Latin Americans, we must add other considerations that are the counterpart of the "pull" of the United States, factors that operate as a "push" in the majority of our countries. The professional at home must accept a very low salary, the lack of real demand for professional services, the absence of good libraries and laboratories, political instability, and a rigid social structure that often hampers the vertical mobility of the trained man. Lack of predictability in our countries, the product of *golpes,* inflation, assassination, expropriation, dictatorship, and so on, is another factor that can contribute to the search for a proper atmosphere for continuous and quiet work. Strikes, budgetary troubles, deficient public services, the lack of consistency in laws and institutions—these destroy the favorable atmosphere for technical and scientific work. The physicist, the medical doctor, the economist, goes to a country where he can forget politics for a while and do his work efficiently. The result of all these factors is that of the 100,000 foreign students in the United States, some 30 percent have expressed some interest in remaining in the States. In regard to some countries (Formosa and South Korea, for example) almost all the expatriate students wish to remain in the United States.

Possible Ways of Solution to the Problem

Among the possible solutions that have been advanced to deal with the problem of professional migration we can distinguish two groups, or categories. On the one hand there are possibilities that are desirable and effective but that cannot be adopted; on the other are minor palliatives which national governments might be persuaded to implement. Avoiding subjective judgments in this difficult area, I shall simply suggest some ways in which we might slow down the loss of Latin America's invaluable talent:

a. Revision of salary levels and structures.

b. Establishment of systems of promotion and ascent that convey prestige and payment according to the quality and kind of services, not according to kinship and influence.

c. Increased investment in research and the creation of national and inter-American research centers.

d. Providing incentives to promote the return of professionals presently out of the country.

e. Acceleration of the political and economic integration of Latin America to promote the free movement of production factors, including human resources.

f. Ideological orientation at the university level with regard to the commitment of future professionals to the destiny of their nation and of Latin America.

g. Exploration of the idea of cultural relativity regarding the desirable adaptation to different ways of life, thus to avoid exaggerated expectations that lead to a frustration or to desertion of the national environment.

h. Promotion of social mobility and fluidity of relations between different social classes.

i. Explanation of the differences between real needs and the apparent absent demand for professional services. (Take, for example, the medical doctors. Many sick people, with little or no income, never consult a doctor because of the lack of ability to pay. Then we are told that we have a surplus of doctors because they cannot make a living.)

j. Laws to recover part or all of the investment in higher education of the professionals who go to live as residents outside their own country.

k. Organization of institutions to aid returning expatriates.

l. Permanent communication with students registered in foreign universities to avoid loss of contact with their nations and to make them feel more favorably inclined to return.

m. Exchange programs of teachers and students to promote the cross-fertilization that is so necessary to scientific and technological growth.

I would like to close this paper by pointing out that the problem of migration of talents takes us back to the ancient Aristotelian discussion of the "good man" and the "good citizen." Must man first fulfill his duties toward society? Or should he first attend to the necessities of his family and his personal improvement? There is no final answer to these questions. For the Christian, however, there is no choice. We must be where love and justice demand us to be, where we can contribute to enlarge the hope of man. The hour has come to develop consciousness and to act in an effective way to avoid the frustration of the aspirations of poor countries, frustrations which will be caused by the lack of professionals able and willing to give their knowledge and skill to the integral growth and greatness of Latin America.

If immediate action along the lines above is not taken, Latin American development will be crippled and our investment in higher education will be a sinful waste.

BIBLIOGRAPHY

Benn, Wedgwood. "No Simple Short-term Solution." *The Financial Times* (London), October 11, 1967.

Consejo Universitario, Universidad Autonoma de Santo Domingo. "Realidades que nos Obligan a Luchar Activamente por la Nivelación del Presupuesto de la UASD." *Listin Diario* (Santo Domingo), January 19, 1968.

Davidson, Andrew. "La Austeridad Empuja Ingleses hacia Australia." *El Caribe* (Santo Domingo), October 8, 1966.

"El Desarrolla Humano y una Universidad en Marcha hacia el Futuro" (mimeographed). Universidad Católica Madre y Maestra (Santiago), 1967.

"El Drenaje Intelectual Afecta Muchos Paises." *El Caribe* (Santo Domingo), June 22, 1967.

"Emigración de Científicos Latinoamericanos." *Mensaje* (Santiago), XV, 148 (May, 1966).

"Fuga de Talentos." *Excelsior* (Mexico), November 10, 1966.

"El Exodo de Cerebros." *Listin Diario* (Santo Domingo), December 30, 1967.

Hernandez-Reyes, Frank Mario. "Informe del Estudio de Evaluación de Recursos Humanos de Nivel Superior en la Republica Dominicana." Comite de Estudios Dominicanos (Santiago), 1967.

Lernous, Penny. "See Sometera a un Estudio el Drenaje de Cerebros." *El Caribe* (Santo Domingo), August 26, 1967.

Once Anos de Estadistica. Departamento de Estadisticas, Universidad

Autonoma de Santo Domingo (Santo Domingo), 1967.

Shanks, Michael. *The Innovators*. London: Penguin Books, 1967.

Sherman, Gene. "Plan Ingles de Austeridad Provoca Exodo del Talento." *El Caribe* (Santo Domingo), January 7, 1967.

"When The Young Men Go West It Is Time To Think Again." *The Financial Times* (London), October 17, 1967.

Van der Eyken, Willem. "Insufficient Rewards and Opportunities." *The Financial Times* (London), October 11, 1967.

BASIC EDUCATION AND
CULTURAL TRANSFORMATION

MARINA BANDEIRA

I have been asked to examine basic education and cultural transformation with particular reference to literacy programs, specialized elementary schooling, radio schools, vocational training,
religious instruction, and other educational services available
to the masses. We are especially interested in knowing how
these programs affect cultural transformation and what Christian
values should underlie mass education in a rapidly changing
society.

Individual Catholic Inter-American Cooperation Program (CI-
COP) committee members have suggested that many of these
means are "old hat" and that I should set forth the philosophy,
the *raison d'être*, for them and describe how the people, the
users and beneficiaries, evaluate them in practice. It is these
points that I wish to emphasize—the reasoning behind basic
education and what people think of it.

Let us begin with the expression "basic education" itself.
Basic education, fundamental education, integral education,

functional literacy—these are expressions coined during the more recent decades and officially accepted by UNESCO. Very often these expressions merely represent a set of subjects such as reading and writing, hygiene, agricultural information, the elementary workings of a cooperative. According to this traditional, conservative, point of view, the "have nots" have nothing because they do not have the knowledge accumulated by Western civilization. Therefore, this ignorance places these "ignorant" in a state of marginality with regard to the economic and social benefits that the modern world puts at their disposal. The expression "basic education" and its synonyms, according to this concept, stand exclusively for the basic tools which, once acquired, incorporate the "ignorant" population into a society which is well organized and perfect, and ready and even eager to receive them.

The role of the marginalized, then, is to accept, without argument, without asking questions, the efforts which are carried out for their benefit. They are to adapt themselves to the patterns of behavior, the set of values, the techniques established by the existing society. When they have had the necessary training, they will have jobs waiting for them, and doctors and hospitals to attend to them. Their salaries will be raised as they contribute to the improved productivity of industry and agriculture. Each backward nation will, inevitably, reach the level of the progress and prosperity already enjoyed by the countries which were the immediate beneficiaries of the Industrial Revolution.

The history of Latin America, of Africa, of Asia, comprising the majority of the population of the world, demonstrates that enough money and energy has been spent on behalf of this utopia without any valid results. Experience has shown that liberal capitalism, with its individualistic philosophy and related educational concepts, is not a magic formula which gives positive results everywhere. The efforts, some of them very well intentioned, to apply to the problems of the Third World solutions which were successful in other cultures and at other times, have met with dismal failure.

Let us admit world society as a whole, and Western society in particular, is at fault.

Let us admit the prevailing concepts about education may be questioned.

No one of good faith can deny the relationship that exists between education and society. The disagreement arises with regard to the type of education which will better contribute to a given type of society. In 1965 UNESCO, during a world congress held in Teheran, declared in very clear terms that functional literacy cannot limit itself to the mere transmission of information. The education of adults must bear in mind man's commitment to life, man's opinions, his experience and knowledge, his family, his social responsibilities. The conclusions of the congress of Teheran stress that education must encourage man to participate in his own education. It must emancipate man from the limitations of an unfavorable milieu not adequate to his development. Education for adults, far from being an end in itself, must consciously prepare man for the social and economic role he must have in society.

Starting from the UNESCO statement, we may go further and affirm that, in order to demarginalize the marginalized, society itself must be destratified. And this destratification can only be achieved by the marginalized themselves. Basic education, therefore, must attempt to make all men capable of participating consciously in the transformation of the culture.

If we are Christians, we must admit that "God *alone* exists of himself, and is infinite in all perfections." Therefore, society, created by man, is subject to improvement. And education is one of the essential tools that can help make society more just. This modern concept of society and of education, however, is in opposition to the traditional concept of education which states, or unconsciously thinks, that man must be integrated into an existing social order.

In some Catholic countries these ideas would be targets for

criticism, and we would hear arguments saying that we are placing too great an emphasis on man and that we run the risk of leading man into materialism, into some form of atheistic humanism, or even of seeing man as a new "God." Let us have a closer look at these arguments.

We are told by the Bible, in the very beginning of Genesis, that God created man to his image and likeness and entrusted to him the mission of dominating nature and completing creation. To fulfill this human mission, Christ gave us very clear instructions: "Thou shalt love the Lord thy God with thy whole heart and thy whole soul and thy whole mind. This is the greatest of the commandments, and the first. And the second, its like, is this, Thou shalt love thy neighbor as thyself. On these two commandments, all the law and the prophets depend" (Matt 22:37–40).

We can never recall this too often. We must never forget that economic, social, and political organizations, or other accidental conditions, do not alter the central nucleus of our doctrine: that the measure of man is his dimension as image and likeness of God. The old catechisms used to stress the first part of Christ's commandment. But they did not emphasize the second part so much: that man was ordered to love other men, also, and that all men were made in the image and likeness of God.

We cannot be satisfied with the effort to save ourselves alone. It is part of the mission of Christians to proclaim that each man is a son of God and must find in his daily life the opportunity to develop fully and responsibly according to the plans of God.

All this has become very clear in the documents of the Second Vatican Council and, with regard to Latin America, in the statement of the Latin American Episcopal Council (CELAM) at Mar del Plata, in the chapter where the theology of earthly values is sketched and where man is described as a cocreator. The meeting held at Buga (Colombia) by the Department of Education of CELAM that studied the role of Catholic universities in Latin America came to similar conclusions. Throughout all these documents runs the feeling that if the faithful are consciously committed, if religion for them is not a mere repetition of rites or a series of acquired habits, if their religion is based upon an intellectual contact with the Gospel and the sacraments, it is legitimate to expect that it will open their eyes to a sense of social justice and to a morality aiming at the advancement of all human beings.

The Christian can no longer limit his interest to his own salvation or to his own "ghetto." Tradition, the Scriptures, social demands—all lead us to understand the need to live in an organized structure where responsibilities are defined and each member has its place. It is clearer each day that the behavior of the people of God is subject to evolution, and that this evolution projects itself upon the history of man. Although pastoral work is the direct mission of the hierarchy, the planning and application of projects are the responsibility of the whole Church, of the whole People of God. The papacy, the episcopate, the clergy, and the laity have specific tasks as part of one whole effort to impregnate all human structures with Christian values.

While we are at this point, we may discuss some inheritances of the past that we simply must overcome. One of them is the old concept of elitism. To hear some people talk, we might think we were having a nightmare in which we are at the Palace of Versailles or at the Escorial of Philip II. We must stop perpetuating an aristocratic notion of a static, permanent "elite" ruling the "masses" who are forever down below.

The "masses" can become the "people" if every individual, every family, every local community, ceases to be a mere object or a mere integer recorded by statistics and becomes a person. We should rapidly forget about an "elite," permanently better educated than the "masses," forever holding positions of leadership, forever handing out alms in the form of jobs, or information, or make-believe positions in local governments. God never said that He had stepchildren, be they Negroes, Quechuas, Aymaras,

Tupi-Guaranis, or plain *campesinos*.

Let us beware, also, of a new aristocracy that is developing: the aristocracy of the technocrats. The knowledge of some developed techniques does not give any man the right to decide the destiny of the others. And if some social or economic structures are a hindrance to human development, why not scrap them? Let us be honest. We do not have the right to baptize, or beautify, or try to mask unjust social structures with new forms of face-lifting.

Sometimes we are told that no civilization that is not religious has ever existed. In the contemporary age we can say Yes, such does exist. The first really atheistic civilization began, not in Russia in 1917, but in the so-called Christian Western world.

Another concept that must be scrapped refers to poverty. Poverty will always exist. But misery is another thing. We can talk about the misery of the rich as well as about material hunger. But we cannot forget that Christ multiplied wine, bread, and fish, nor can we forget all the words of Christ condemning the rich.

These examples of negative concepts can serve as warnings to us all, as red lights to show us the perils of new forms of the negation of the spirit of poverty.

From all that has been said so far it becomes obvious that the educational effort can no longer be directed only to children and adolescents. It is reaching all human groups; we see the emergence of permanent education. Today, even in the developed countries, the new generations refuse to accept the mere transmission of old values. They feel the urge to discuss, reject, or accept values on a level of quality with the older generation. Persons, groups of persons, countries, now refuse to be classified as immature or dependent. Instead of teachers versus students, we are coming to the new concept of permanent education for all, young and old. All, together, striving for improvement.

Our times have also reached the stage when brain cramming can be classified as vicious. We have reached the point when we think in terms of learning something by doing it effectively, not by listening to masters who speak *ex cathedra* and do not accept being contradicted by their pupils.

It is very clear, also, that human progress can be meaningful only if man assumes the responsibility for his own advancement. The general objective of education, therefore, should be to cooperate in the formation of man by offering him the basic information which will allow him to assume the role of agent of his own advancement. And here the creative capacity of man must be stressed. Man has the capacity to distinguish and choose one object from another, to choose values. By the communication of these values man participates in the creation of the cultural world.

Education should strive to permit the participation of all in changing existing values, in adapting to new situations, new behavior, new relationships, new attitudes. Education must lead to the discovery by all of the bottlenecks in society, to an understanding of the political mechanism and the power structure, to the finding and implementation of new and better solutions to problems.

If education is the process which aims at forming an integrated man, it is necessary that it offers him the elements which will allow him to reach a clear vision of his dignity as a human being. Thus he will come to see the dignity of other human beings. And it is this vision of his own dignity, and of the dignity of others, that will render him capable of a critical analysis of the situation in which he is placed, will lead to the discovery in himself of his potential as an agent playing an active role in the creation of culture, a subject of history capable of transforming the natural world into a humanized world.

All we have said about education in general applies, of course, to basic education. As we indicated above, basic education can be understood as the minimum elements needed to rise above the level of ignorance and poverty. Or, in more polite words, to lead a human life. Basic education is also what comes first, what is fundamental, what reaches man at his core. Basic education is that which can offer

elements enabling man to understand what he is (consciousness of self), what other men are (communication of persons as subjects), what the world is;

elements enabling man to assert himself as a human person, a participant in the transformation of the world, a creator of culture;

elements capable of enabling man to satisfy the basic material needs without which he cannot live on a human level;

elements which will lead to a communitarian action aimed at transforming the social structure of competition into structures of cooperation.

The synthesis of these concepts is expressed for us from the Brazilian Basic Education Movement (MEB) by the expression "conscientização," which I may translate roughly as "the awakening of historical consciousness," or "creating an awareness of man's active role in the historical process."

Let me say a few words about MEB as an example of an organization that tries to work according to the principles described here. The origin of MEB may be traced to the experience of radio education conducted by some Catholic bishops in the Northeast of Brazil. At the present time it also operates in the Amazon and in the west-central part of Brazil. Seven years of practice have shown us how to transform the radio schools into nuclei of "popular animation" where men can exercise their creative capacity, their capacity to communicate with other human beings on equal terms whereby they can discover their full dignity as persons and develop their critical capacity to analyze their situation.

MEB is a service to the local community and takes upon itself the role of "starter," of catalyst for the emergence of the marginalized. MEB's methods are the result of an effort to give value to man's dominion and to render evident man's development as an intelligent and conscious human being. This means

stressing the importance of elementary manifestations and also
of self-expression through popular art. This means to understand
the transformation that takes place when man cuts down a tree,
makes a hut, invents a song, creates conditions to integrate himself in the society in which he lives, without running the risk
of alienating himself in the process. He neither submits to the
"wisdom" of his "betters" nor accepts as superior the culture of
any dominating group.

MEB tries to make the best possible use of many methods of
group-dynamics, such as panel discussions, sociodrama, debating
groups, circular discussions, and others. These techniques are
used in the community by the local-level teams and by the community leaders, who are not always experts in reading and writing
and in some cases may even be illiterate.

At the grass-roots level the real aim of the work, normally
initiated in sessions of two or three days, is to lead to the discovery by the communities of a motivation for a joint effort based
upon common interests. One of the results of the discussions is
the analysis, by the group itself, of the characteristics of the
community, the possibilities of action, the planning of improvements in the local situation. The initial motivation might be the
decision to organize a school for the children of the community.
It might be building a football field, a cemetery, a pharmacy, a
chapel. Of course I am not talking about building a large chapel.
I am talking about a hut, where the community would like to
gather to pray together.

Those responsible for MEB do not consider themselves gen-
iuses who have all the answers. The secret of MEB was the feed-
back that it received from the population of the underdeveloped
areas, and the constant communication on all levels. But today,
January, 1968, MEB is only a ghost of what it has been and of
what it could be. MEB has been about to stop operations time
and again. The level of efficiency has deteriorated. MEB suffers
the fate of so many other organizations that provoke the fear

of those in power. But although MEB is only a pallid shadow of what it used to be, we believe that it is better to do something, while we may, rather than do nothing at all. The struggle of MEB is now staunchly supported by the Brazilian hierarchy. In spite of this, it is still possible that our day of reckoning will come and that we will be crushed by the government. What we will not do is become another literacy campaign trying to mold the people to the requirements of the powerful. We refuse to act as a buffer between the aspirations of the people and the present unjust social structures.

All of us know, at the present crucial stage of our history, that there are countless efforts of education in Latin America under the control of Christians. There are radio schools, elementary schools, vocational training centers, secondary schools, universities. It is needless to describe the quality of some of the buildings, the high level of some of the equipment, the dedication of many of the teachers. Many make use of very modern and elaborate methods of transmission of information.

But I should like to ask how many of them, consciously or unconsciously, are aiming at the maintenance of a dual society, with an elite versus the masses? And how many are aiming at a healthy cultural transformation and a society centered on man and based upon Truth?

LATIN AMERICAN CULTURE
AND ITS TRANSFORMATION

HORACIO H. GODOY

The first concept that should be clarified is this, To what extent can we speak about Latin America as a whole? In other words, in what ways can we speak about Latin America in general and in what other ways must we distinguish among twenty separate republics? There are, as we know, many and great differences among these nations in size, climate, population, degree of development, gross national product, and so on. At the same time there are some characteristics common to all Latin Americans. All of them share similar notions about life, wealth, power, family, love. We can speak about Latin America in general only on the assumption that everybody knows the differences among these countries. Therefore, I am going to assume here that my readers know the difference between Brazil and El Salvador, Argentina and Nicaragua, Mexico and Haiti, Chile and Paraguay, Bolivia and Costa Rica.

Another introductory remark I would like to make is one concerning the problem of understanding between North and

Latin America. One cannot understand things that one does not love. And one cannot love things that one does not know. Therefore, knowledge, and knowledge alone, is the source of love and understanding. In the same way love is the source of respect. Unless you know Latin America, and you respect Latin America, there will be no real understanding. What does this mean in practical terms? First, Latin America's way of life, its own set of values, cannot and should not be compared in a negative way with the North American way of life and the North American set of values. And second, we must realize that Latin America is undergoing a painful process of change and modernization which affects every country in the area. At the same time Latin America is awakening to the process of economic, cultural, and political integration. Latin America, with all its special history and idiosyncrasies, is striving to express itself, defining its objectives, its ideals, its aims. In Chile and in Brazil, in Argentina and Mexico and Bolivia, questioning, conflict over the national destiny, rapid economic change, are all taking place together, and North Americans must be aware of this.

A final introductory remark deals with the difference between the Latin American continent and the rest of the underdeveloped world. Some countries or parts of countries in Latin America may have per-capita incomes as low as any in Africa or Asia. But Latin America differs from them in that its basic social, political, and economic values come from the European tradition. Three hundred years of colonization by Spain and Portugal, more than one hundred and fifty years of independent life inspired by European and American ideals, and the important contributions by European immigrants, have produced a continent of many races unified by a common set of values inspired by Western Christian culture. These factors—differences among Latin American nations, the process of rapid change, and the European heritage—form the basis for our remarks in the rest of this essay.

A major characteristic of Latin America's present situation is the coexistence at different levels and in different regions of traditional patterns of culture and modern technical societies. Latin America has eight metropolises with populations larger than one million, and seventy cities with more than 100,000 inhabitants. The great urban centers—Buenos Aires, Mexico City, Rio de Janeiro, São Paulo, Santiago, Caracas, Bogotá, Havana—are expressions of a dynamic and progressive class. The role of the more than two hundred universities as instruments of social and economic progress is largely centered in these important urban concentrations. The growth of industry in the largest cities attracts people from the rural areas. These migrants cannot be assimilated rapidly and flock to slums on the outskirts of the cities, the *villas miseria* in Argentina, the *favelas* in Brazil, the *callampas* in Chile. These marginal groups give to Latin American cities an indigenous quasi-rural element that coexists simultaneously with the modern, highly urbanized population. This explains the violent contrasts we find within the largest cities of Latin America.

A distinguished American political scientist has remarked that because this region is a part of the Western cultural continuum, its social underdevelopment is less pronounced than its economic underdevelopment. Much of our value structure and our knowledge is gained as a kind of unearned income from our European ties. As a corollary, when we cast about for methods to modernizing our economies, we display less resistance to European models than most other parts of the underdeveloped world.

Let us compare Latin America with other underdeveloped areas like India and Africa with regard to the following factors: class structure, politics, cultural values, wealth, education and technology, and race relations. Except for a few small countries we do not find in Latin America any examples of a two-class society, one in which a small ruling group makes all the important decisions for the rest of the population. The old Iberian tradition of government and administration has changed as a modern, industrial society has developed. The middle sectors, particularly in Mexico and in Argentina, have become significant. The presence of a class structure differentiates typical under-developed societies from Latin America. Here and there we do find groups of Indians, no more than 16 million among 200 million Latin Americans, who live in a rather primitive way. But these groups are not nearly so numerous as in Africa or Asia.

Americans, in considering our political life, are impressed by the news of coups d'etat, military uprisings, revolutions, and the like. We Latin Americans have a long tradition of battles for freedom that never completely succeed but never completely fail either. The present process of profound change in social, economic, and political matters helps explain the political insta-bility of governments in Latin America today. Nevertheless, we have good examples of stable governments in Mexico, Costa Rica, Chile, and Uruguay. And in general the increasing importance of the middle sector creates the sociological base for political democracy. The way to democracy is not easy, of course, espe-cially if we think of democracy not only as a system of periodic elections but also as social and racial justice, economic progress, and effective government.

European cultural values, as we have indicated, are dominant everywhere in Latin America. This is the result, not of a colonial imposition, but the expression of a historical and ethnic link with Europe. Nobody should be surprised to find European ways of life in Chile, Argentina, Uruguay, or Brazil, since the people living there in large part come from European ancestors. The millions of descendants of Italians or Spanish living in Buenos Aires, although recognizing themselves as Argentines, kept in touch with their relatives in Europe, and in education and family relations often followed cultural patterns of their ancestors. We find some important contributions from Indian culture, as in Mexico, Bolivia, and Guatemala. But Latin American language, religion, and way of life reflect the basic values of European culture. It is true that social and economic development are changing the distribution of the national income. The best indicator of a process of income distribution is the growing importance of the middle sectors in urban Latin America.

Professional training through high schools and universities is another important characteristic of modern Latin America. Education has increasingly made possible the participation of Latin American women in public administration and professional work. The existence of important industrial centers in Mexico, Argentina, Brazil, and other countries emphasizes the ongoing process of modernization of Latin America. Another fact on which we can pride ourselves is the relatively good state of race relations. We do not find racial conflicts in Latin America on the scale that exists in the United States, South Africa, England, or other areas of the world.

The characteristics briefly noted above are not typical of a colonial, underdeveloped society. We have no two-class societies in Latin America, no small groups of Europeans or Americans who dominate the natives. Occupational skills are obviously growing; there are no racial distinctions or caste ranking; and there are basic European cultural values firmly rooted in our society and supported by the great majority of the Latin Americans. We are not Europeans, of course. But we are not Africans or Asians, either. North Americans are mistaken when they lump the underdeveloped countries of Asia, Africa, and Latin America all together, without recognizing the tremendous differences between people and continents.

What are the basic values and social institutions characteristic of our Latin American way of life? It is not possible to describe the values and institutions that define our culture in a brief essay. But we can select some examples that may give us a preliminary understanding. Let us take, for example, the attitude of Latin Americans toward *work*. Latin Americans work only to improve their situation; they work just enough to get what they think they need to enjoy life. For Latin Americans life is much more important than work, and leisure will generally be valued more than overtime pay. In the so-called industrialized societies, on the contrary, the aim of life seems to be working, not living. People seem to live for their work, and not vice versa. We cannot teach you North Americans how to work, but perhaps we have some good suggestions about how to relax!

From this point of view the coming years will be exciting ones. Automation will take over the jobs of many, many people. Leisure, not work, will be the main sociological problem. And to leisure the Latin American way of life has a great contribution to make. The spiritual approach to material things, a flexible attitude vis-à-vis time, are some of the important elements in the leisure society of the future, elements you can learn from us.

Our attitude toward money is another basic factor in our way of life. I believe that Latin Americans are less dependent, less concerned, less involved with money. Latin Americans like to invite a friend to dinner or the theater and pay the bill. I once asked a Mexican taxi driver what were the differences he recognized between a Latin American and a North American. He said that one day he was driving a young American couple in his cab. Apparently, he said, they were something more than just friends. When she arrived at her home, she asked the boy how much the fare was, the boy divided it in half, and asked the girl to pay her share. The taxi driver said, "Imagine senor! We Mexicans would never do a thing like that!" And, indeed, while we cannot teach you how to make money, perhaps we may give you some ideas about how to spend it.

The attitude toward the family is also a crucial factor in the Latin American way of life. The authority of the father is still alive with us, despite the fact that Latin American women are becoming more independent because more and more of them work and contribute to the maintenance of the family. The relationship between father and children is strongly based on paternal authority. The Latin American family is also still composed not only of husband, wife, and children but also of the grandparents, uncles, aunts, and cousins. The conception of the family is more traditional, and I believe it also much more human. What I want to say is that the Latin American way of life is idealistic. We are more ready than you to accept racial equality and, in general, egalitarian philosophies. At the same time this idealistic approach is the explanation of the extreme individualism that we find in Latin America and of our inability to organize a common effort within our countries or among them. That is why we frequently say that one Latin American plus one Latin American equals zero. Everybody opposes everybody. We lack the capacity to unify our efforts, and, therefore, all of us like to start everything as if we were the founders of the idea.

Our way of life is based on subjectivity rather than on objectivity, which is another expression of the individualistic approach. A typical example of this subjective, individualistic attitude is the way we attend church. If one goes to a church in Germany or in the United States, one sees a highly organized participation of the people during Mass. Everybody stand up, everybody sits, everybody sings, everybody kneels, everybody leaves together after the priest has concluded the service. In Latin America, on the other hand, most of the people arrive late, some stand when the rest are seated, few people sing, and many leave before the priest does.

Let me conclude with a final example of the Latin American way of life: the popular fiesta. In Bahia, Brazil, a few years ago a North American economist was invited to a fiesta and started to watch carefully how the people enjoyed the party. He made an evaluation of the fiesta in economic terms and said that for him the institution was a sign of underdevelopment. If the people did not stop singing and dancing, the community would never progress. A Brazilian economist answered that this fiesta was, on the contrary, an example of the perfect application of economic principles. The cost of the party for the people participating was almost nothing. Everybody made a small contribution, but the benefit to all was great. For a very small investment a large return in happiness was received. And the Brazilian argued that in the United States one invests a lot of money in parties without getting the enjoyment expected. Tedious cocktail parties, with a great deal of money spent on clothing, food, and drink, give very poor returns.

Let me conclude by repeating what I said at first: there is no understanding without respect, there is no respect without love, and there is no love without knowledge. We must constantly insist on more and better teaching about Latin America in the United States. There should not be a high school or university in the United States without a program of teaching about Latin America. The American people must be made to know the real situation of modern Latin America, to understand the efforts we are making to improve our situation. They must learn to respect our differences, to realize that their concerns are not ours, to recognize that Latin America has great possibilities of making a contribution to world history. Americans must resist the temptation to try to change Latin Americans according to the North American model of development. You must stop trying to give us what you think we need. If you really understand Latin Americans, and want to help us, you will agree with me that aid is for us to receive from you what we think we need according to our own definition of what we need.

CULTURAL ISSUES AND
TECHNICAL ASSISTANCE

GUSTAVO PEREZ-RAMIREZ

Technical assistance is an unfortunate expression for what French-speaking scholars and development experts more adequately call *coopération technique*. Father Lebret, a Dominican priest famous for his dedication to integral humanism as far back as 1960 and for his contribution to the Encyclical *Populorum Progressio*, proposed that we use the word "cooperation" instead of "assistance" in order to preserve the dignity of those who receive it. According to him

assistance supposes that one provides and the other receives. It is an act of the better-off to the worse-off, of the wealthier to the poorer, of the better educated to the more ignorant, of the more efficient to the less efficient. Hence, in any act of assistance there is the danger of a secret and increasing conflict between the one who assists, who behaves like the one who has, and the assisted, who suffers the feeling of being dependent, if not of being dominated or scorned.[1]

At a time when "technical assistance" or *"coopération technique"* are magic words, and when technicians and experts are traveling around the world as saviors or, so often, as bringers of a new form of colonialism from the West or the East, it is essential to keep alive, as a major cultural issue, the consciousness that technical society is a fearful threat against the *person*. I do not deny that the growth of technology and mechanization is one of the three axes "without which it is mere self-delusion to suppose that we can conceive or undertake any re-ordering or development of the Earth," as stated by Teilhard de Chardin.² Technology is undoubtedly an essential element in contemporary society. It is inevitable that the mechanical equipment of society will become all-pervading. This is, no doubt, an advantageous phenomenon since "it both facilitates and indefinitely multiplies our activities. Not only does it relieve us mechanically of a crushing weight of physical and mental labour," as explained by Teilhard, "but by the miraculous enhancing of our senses, through its powers of enlargement, penetration and exact measurement, it constantly increases the scope and clarity of our perceptions."³

Yet, technology is also a destructive force. With the discoveries of recent decades the predictions of George Orwell are rapidly becoming reality. The year 1984 seems close and horrifying:

Do you begin to see, then, what kind of world we are creating? It is the exact opposite of the stupid hedonistic Utopias that the old reformers imagined. A world of fear and treachery and torment, a world of trampling and being trampled upon, a world which will grow not less but *more* merciless as it refines itself. . . . The old civilizations claimed that they were founded on love and justice. Ours is founded upon hatred. In our world there will be no emotions except fear, rage, triumph, and self-abasement. Everything else we shall destroy—everything. . . . There will be no love, except the love of Big Brother. There will be no laughter, except the laugh of triumph over a defeated enemy. There will be no art, no literature, no science. When we are omnipotent we shall have no more need of science.⁴

Thus spoke O'Brien to Winston in George Orwell's novel.

The destructive forces of technology are challenges to the underdeveloped areas of the world in which man is striving for a better living. The trap would be to have more—thanks to

technology—and yet not "to be more," to become a victim of
one's own inventions. I consider this cultural issue as the most
relevant among the many others implied by technical cooperation.

Many contemporary thinkers have indicated the dangers of
advancing technology. Friedrich Junger, who wrote *The Failure
of Technology*,[5] and Paul Tillich, the existentialist theologian,
coincide in pointing out that depersonalization in our mass society
is strongly linked with technology and large-scale organization.
Tillich, for instance, in his essay "The Person in a Technical
Society"[6] explains that the movement called existentialism, in
his understanding, rebels in the name of personality against the
depersonalizing forces of technical society. This rebellion is rooted
in the protests of the lonely prophets of the nineteenth century
against the threatened destruction of humanity and personality
by technical society. In this new society the person is menaced,
being transformed into a thing, an object of scientific calculation
and political management.

Against this chaos, Tillich explains, Kierkegaard raised the
existentialist protest. He did it on the basis of faith by asking
the individual to break away from technical society in order to
save his existence as a person. The existing person can only be
saved by Kierkegaard's metaphor of a "leap."

Marx, the sociologist, saw much more clearly than Kierkegaard,
says Tillich, that it is not a system of thought but the reality
of modern society which is responsible for the reduction of the
person to a commodity. Marx did not think that it is the technical
method of production as such which destroys personal freedom,
but that the social structure of class society is responsible for it.
He believed in the possibility of humanizing the technical process,
but he did not believe that this could happen within the framework of a class society. Therefore, he became a political rebel
against this society.

Tillich analyzes also how the fight against the dangers of the
technical society was waged at the same time on a third front:

by Nietzsche, in the name of life, against the "nihilism" of the technical culture. His message was that technical society destroys the creative power of life; he therefore denounced technical mass civilization and the system of values accepted by this civilization, including those Christian values which were amalgamated with the ideals of modern society. Nietzsche and his followers wanted to restore the integrity of creative life by looking for some unity below the split into subject and object.

Recent existentialists carry on the same protest. Sartre asks that we break the power of technical civilization by isolating the individual from its embracing structure. He tries to save the person by asking him "to create himself, without the aid of norms, laws, and principles, without anybody else or anything else." For Sartre the individual's creation of himself is the aim of true humanism.

All these different appeals appear to be ambiguous and contradictory. Yet they help to face with realism the dangerous challenges of technical society. It is with this cultural background and with apprehension that the man of the Third World faces technology, as a necessary but ambiguous and dangerous tool for development. Technical "assistance," he feels, should be provided and accepted with a strong dose of humanism.

This cautious attitude is that of the Ecumenical Council, which provides us with guidelines to enable men of good will to promote the necessary renewal and restructuring of society. The Pastoral Constitution on the Church in the Modern World is quite specific:

A man is more precious for what he is than for what he has. Similarly, all that men do to obtain greater justice, wider brotherhood, and more humane ordering of social relationships has greater worth than technical advances. For these advances can supply the material for human progress, but of themselves alone they can never actually bring it about (no. 35).

Humanism is then the key to an adequate use of technology, since human activity is ordered toward man. Technical "cooperation" should thus be the witness of

the birth of a new humanism, one in which man is defined first of all by his responsibility toward his brothers and toward history (no. 55). This truth grows clearer if we consider how the world is becoming unified and how we have the duty to build a better world based upon truth and justice (no. 55).

This is the goal to be pursued by technical cooperation in all underdeveloped areas of the world in order to help in creating societies in which every human being has the goods and services which enable him to be a person and to gradually "be more." If we do not embrace this path of humanism, technical cooperation would simply be a question of following, by parody, the path of one or the other of two contradictory systems which claim to struggle against depersonalization. Capitalism, as Tillich suggests, pretends to save the person within the framework of a market economy in a bourgeois society. But the free enterprise it espouses often ends in destroying the person by reducing him to a commodity. Communism, the other system, pretends to save the person within the framework of centralized planning. Salvation will be achieved in a future state by suppressing the person in the present for the sake of the expected citizen of the future.

Fortunately there is already a tendency in the Third World to follow a new path toward development, independent of both Communism or capitalism. This tendency, which could turn out to be the major historical event of our age, was in evidence at the Bandung Conference in 1955, when for the first time the countries of the Third World united in a collective protest against imposed economic and political systems.

I do not wish to deny the value and necessity of technical cooperation and of all other kinds of foreign aid in an increasingly interdependent world. But I have my doubts as to whether salvation for the man of the Third World is simply a question of "imports," whether they be capital goods, technology, human

resources, or expertise in how to succeed in business or in guerilla warfare. What I question about foreign aid is its frequent
lack of humanism, its political ambiguities, its imperialistic drives,
its cultural approach, leading it so often to be wasted by isolated
and ineffective measures.

Many failures of technical cooperation derive from this lack
of humanism, which prevents technicians and experts from really
becoming incarnated in the underdeveloped areas of the world.
Knowing only technique, unable to act in solidarity and authen-
ticity, their commitment to modernization rings hollow, and they
accomplish little. The challenge they have to face is the necessity
of radical changes in all the underdeveloped countries. Without
it their cooperation is a farce or a reinforcement of obsolete
structures, and therefore an obstacle rather than a contribution
toward progress and development.

The fact is that the countries of the underdeveloped world
are becoming progressively poorer, getting less and less for their
products, and becoming increasingly dependent of financial
foreign aid and technical "assistance" when the need is for trade.
In 1966, at the midpoint of the "decade of development," imports
were only a fraction of what the underdeveloped countries were
able to buy at the beginning of the decade. Because of price
declines in raw material exports they were losing 2.5 billion
dollars a year in purchasing power.

Since the conference of 1967 in Algeria there is an increasing
awareness among underdeveloped countries that they can no
longer wait and rely on paternalistic "assistance." They feel
that they can get together and go on strike, demanding better
terms and not being satisfied with simply presenting their list
of grievances and expecting answers.

This question of justice in the terms of trade has deep relations
to technical "assistance." It will be brought up for discussion at
all future gatherings which discuss such questions. The Third

World will no longer wait, hat in hand, at the doors of the "wealthy men's club," as happened at the Geneva Trade Conference a few years ago.

The central issue of technical cooperation, to sum up, is a problem of humanism. What finally counts for us is man, man as an actor and master of his own destiny, not a passive recipient of alms or an object of a political or economic system. That explains why we insist on the word "cooperation" instead of "assistance." We feel that aid should be an operation of interchange in which both parties are enriched. Then the process of modernization with the aid of technical "assistance" could be accomplished without the loss of values of the recipient culture, and without a subordination of human and social values to technical aims. Such a process would favor the progress of social man toward greater interdependence and cohesion. Only then would technology and mechanization be one of the constructive bases of human development as conceived by Teilhard. And no person, no political or economic system, could prevent mankind from achieving planetary dimensions in his struggle for true unity.

NOTES

1. Louis J. Lebret, O.P., "Alerte a l'assistance technique," *Développement et Civilisations* (Paris), 2 (June, 1960), 15.

2. Pierre Teilhard de Chardin, *The Future of Man* (New York: Harper & Row, 1964), p. 228.

3. *Ibid.*, p. 229.

4. George Orwell, *1984* (21st ed., Signet Book, 1960), p. 220.

5. Friedrich Georg Junger, *The Failure of Technology* (Chicago: Gateway, 1956).

6. Paul J. Tillich, "The Person in a Technical Society," in *Varieties of Modern Social Theory* (New York: Dutton, 1963), pp. 287–303.

PART FOUR

THE ROLE
OF THE CHURCH

THEOLOGICAL REFLECTIONS
ON INTER-AMERICAN RELATIONS

MARCOS G. McGRATH, C.S.C.

In our time there is quite a reaction against religious structures and institutions. This reaction often goes too far, because we cannot in fact live in society without institutions to serve our needs. But undoubtedly the reaction does force us to reexamine many of our Church institutions. To what degree have they come to exist for themselves rather than for our needs? To that degree they must be reformed, suppressed, or replaced. In the same way there is quite a reaction against theology. Some would even suppress the word "God." This recalls Abe Lincoln's remark in Sherwood Anderson's play of thirty years ago. Speaking of his fiancee, Mary Todd, he said that she really had to be something, because even God spelled his name with one "d," but Mary spelled hers with two. Much of our theologizing about God has been really something—abstract, couched in scholastic terms, and a view of the cosmos hardly acceptable or relevant to many today, and, above all, with little relation to the depth and thrust of the new phase of history which is opening around us.

This has been a problem in the whole of our theology. As the Second Vatican Council pointed out, one of the greatest defects among Christians today is the lack of connection between what we believe and what we do. From the "good tidings" of a new life, absorbing and illuminating our whole existence, the Gospel has often become but a set of commandments to be fulfilled at certain hours, religious acts apart from and with no significance for the important matters of business or pleasure which really make up our lives.

Yet there is today a great search for the fundamental values which can illuminate and give direction to our lives. Marxism and various other ideologies attract many precisely because they offer absolute values. Others reject absolutes, but pick and choose where they can find meaning. As one young agnostic said on television the other day, "You have to believe in something." It is interesting that while some theologians talk about "the death of God," many sociologists are bringing him to life again in their studies and in their search for values in man beyond man.

For a subject as complex as inter-American relations we must not attempt to spin out a theology that would attempt to answer so much that it would really answer nothing. This would again be a theology separated from life, or, rather, one not integrated with the other aspects of life. Arend Th. van Leeuwen has put it well. Our modern secularized society, he says, is trying to build its own tower of Babel with which to reach the heavens. But the "tower of Babel has *no* top" on earth. Only God can complete it.

. . . and it is not the business of Christian theology to fill that vacuum, either by providing the unfinished tower with a Christian top or by showing that the top which the non-Christian religions [and secular forces] are trying to build in fact largely resembles the Christian one, so that the most it could require would be a Christian 'finishing touch.' No: the point of encounter between the Christian faith and the non-Christian religions [and secular forces] does not lie at the top, but at the base; or rather, it lies in co-operation of Christians with non-Christians in a concerted effort to 'build ourselves a city and a tower. . . .'[1]

We do not forget that the kingdom of God's grace and love is already within us and among us, that the Church is the "universal sign of salvation" meant by God to unite all men among themselves and in him. We recognize the fact that both creation and redemption are from God, that the two are mysteriously intertwined, that

Earthly progress must be carefully distinguished from the growth of Christ's kingdom. Nevertheless, to the extent that the former can contribute to the better ordering of human society, it is of vital concern to the kingdom of God.[2] Hence it is clear that men are not deterred by the Christian message from building up the world, or impelled to neglect the welfare of their fellows. They are, rather, more stringently bound to do these very things.[3]

These reflections bring us to the heart of our matter. We do not pretend to spell out a detailed theology of inter-American relations. Rather we propose to stress a few simple affirmations of Christian faith recalled to us in our days by the Council, upon which we must reflect if we are to act as Christians, indeed, if we are to act as brothers at all and be some kind of a sign rather than a scandal to the rest of men. We are talking as Christians, among Christians, but aware of the fact that many of the human values brought to the world by Our Lord are now part and parcel of our culture and are often lived more faithfully by others than by ourselves who profess to follow the Lord.

It is interesting to note the gradual emergence of a more living theology in the Catholic Church, and in the other Christian Churches, since the end of the nineteenth century. The Council is the fruit of this growth and the seed of future growth. Many movements—biblical, ecumenical, lay apostolic, and others—contributed to this development, but nowhere is the growth more obvious than in the social sphere. Calvez and Perrin trace it admirably in their volume *The Church and the Economic Society*. They point out a transition from Leo XIII and Pius XI, who used somewhat casuistic moral agruments to buttress our obligations for social justice, to Pius XII, who insisted more on an existential sense of the full value of the human person, as man and son of God, called to a social living of his vocation. This stress on the basic Christian view of man in society, with a growing emphasis on the free determination of the Christian conscience, grew greater with John XXIII, the Council, and Paul VI. Let us recall a few Christian values applicable to our subject and offer a few of the more striking and more obvious examples of their significance.

Following the example of the Council, we should first look at the "signs of our times." Each generation will certainly be judged on how it understood and answered its own times in its adventurous walk across the chasms of time toward eternity. It may be trite to repeat, with the Council, that we have already entered into a new period of world history. Trite but important. It may be trite to say that, thanks to the atom, we are now capable of blowing ourselves into kingdom come, in biblical parlance, into the *parusia*. Trite but important. Important in what we should do about it.

The Church in the Modern World, in its provocative description of the world today, stresses several key phenomena that characterize the new age in which we live. First of all, there is the factor of change, more rapid, profound, and extensive than ever before. Second is the scientific and technological mentality behind this change, which looks upon the world now as something to be known rather than placated, something to be controlled and turned to our service. This science and this technology, developing alone, imply an unspoken ideology of endless possibilities, of the *parusia* here below, of a secularism which would refer to nothing beyond what man himself can know and do. Third is this very secularism, a rediscovery of the intrinsic value of things at the service of man and a forgetting of all else. Fourth is our growing interdependence as we populate the world more densely, need one another so much more for the whole socioeconomic and political process typified by urban culture, and are so much more intimately informed and united by lightning communications and ever-swifter means of travel. Finally there are the immense contrasts developing between what we believe this great modern civilization can do for all men and what it really does, which is typified in the growing tension between the haves and the have-nots, within nations and between nations. All of which builds up a tremendous challenge to further peaceful, balanced development on the world plane, a message announced in *Pacem in Terris* and spelled out in anguishing terms in *Populorum Progressio.*

How does the Church respond to these challenges of a new age? The Council is its most dramatic response. In it have converged and fused into a clearer and brighter guiding light all the sparks of response kindled over past generations in the various areas of a Church which for the first time is geographically catholic, as broad as the world, and native, even if a minority, in every part of the world. This Council is the first to address itself to the problems of the entire world and to speak with the sense of the world, through the voices of churchmen identified with each of its areas.

But the Council, drawing from the living movements of the past generations, would be quite sterile if it were not projected forward, applied, and developed in these succeeding years, and in every part of the world. The Council above all faced up to change. We have to realize what this means. A Church which had fixed firmly its liturgy, its ecclesiastical structures, and the expression of its doctrines suddenly embraced the principle of change and variety in the liturgy. It accepted the principle of reform at all levels of ecclesiastical structure, the principle of progress in the understanding of revelation, and the need for more individual responsibility in its moral applications. This concept of a changing Church is part of a newly dynamic sense of tradition, enriched by the centuries, pushing onto new applications, true in the essentials, growing in the essentials, free and anxious to serve the present and the future. The biblical sense of the history of our salvation comes sharply forward in the Council. Theologians begin to recast all of theology in this dynamic pattern, in which essences and concepts are viewed in their existential context and comprehension. Judaeo-Christianity introduced into Western culture the notion of history as a dynamic, ongoing process, with a beginning and a striving toward a fulfillment. The Council has recaptured that vision now by meditating upon the relation of temporal progress to the history of salvation.[4]

The process of secularization was almost the central preoccupation of the Council. Openly lamenting the Church's mistakes in the past vis-à-vis the legitimate autonomy of science, the Council now stresses this autonomy as the will of the Creator. It interprets the biblical description of man as "image of God" in the Hebraic and early patristic sense, and sees man as the practical continuer of God's work, as "lord of the entire visible creation" placed over it by God "to govern it and use it to the glory of God." In this use the Council recognizes the divisive presence of sin, the need for the cross and redemption, the duality which divides the heart of each man and distinguishes the kingdom of Christ from the world itself, however mysteriously they compenetrate one another through the course of history. As the sign and cause of unity, of elevation and of completion in the new man, it recognizes Christ and his Church. It sees a closed "autonomy of earthly affairs," a secularization converted into radical secularism, as the atheistic temptation of the day. "Today's civilization, not of itself but because of its excessive concentration on temporal things, can often make more difficult man's access to God." This dichotomy of secularization and salvation is not yet fully worked out in the Council. But the question and the principles are well posed. They have a great deal to do with the specific roles of priests, religious, and laity in the Church and in the world.

The growing unity and interdependence of mankind force us

to reflect more intensely upon the social nature of man. The Council did so. In its description of secularization it stressed that material things should be at the service of man. Here it stresses that social ties are to be at the service of the human person. The consequences of this principle are many. Respect for each man's fundamental rights demands equality, dignity, and opportunity for all, irrespective of racial, national, or other differences. The greater socialization required by the multiplication of services in today's society is a process by which the individual ethic gives way to an ethic of service to each of society's members. And to serve each it must respect the basic liberty of each and assist all to participate actively and responsibly in social decisions. The great fact of our time is that social interdependence and social obligation go beyond local limits and national frontiers. Each citizen must cultivate a great loyalty to his country but at the same time remember his obligations to the entire human family.[5] The consequences of these international obligations are spelled out with urgency in an entire chapter of The Church in the Modern World on "The Fostering of Peace and the Promotion of a Community of Nations" and, of course, in *Populorum Progressio.*

All of these obligations take on their inner meaning only in the full evangelical Gospel vision of God's will for mankind, which the Council freshly outlines for us. The dawn of a new age has permitted us to return to the dawn of the Christian message. Living tradition has added to our understanding of that message, and, according to the Council, we must go on striving continually toward "the fullness of divine truth."[6] To do so, the return to sources helps us to renew our vision of faith in view of the new circumstances of our time. It is this renewal which profits from the growing faith of the Church over the centuries, while it refreshes it in its origins for our times, which is the heart of the conciliar renewal.

There can be no doubt that the historical necessities of defense

over the past centuries imprinted upon the Church a character
which was more defensive than expansive. The Church found
itself embattled during the past three centuries because so many
of the dynamic tendencies of this period, even though arising
from the energy the Church had released in Western civilization,
ran contrary to its structure, to the static medieval concept of
one Christian world in which there was little real distinction
between the religious and temporal order. The struggle of Catholics to retain the identity of Christian society against forces
which would dissolve it placed the Church in a defensive and
isolated posture. The universal mission of the Church to serve
all mankind was overshadowed by the Church's defense of her
identity in doctrine and in life against insistent attack, and the
Catholics of individual nations became so identified with the task
of struggling for the Church at home that they often lost the
sense of their unity with Catholics everywhere. Thus the missionary effort of the Church, while outstandingly vital during the
nineteenth and twentieth centuries, became in large measure
the work of professional Catholic missionaries, while Catholics
themselves, even the missionaries, were much more identified
with their individual nations. The negative effects of secularism
were also felt in the separation into distinct categories of religious
duty on the one hand and the normal pursuits of life on the other,
so that religion would have little to say about the latter. In the
West this took the pervasive form of doctrinaire economic liberalism, the individualistic ethic, almost impervious to the simplest
of social obligations in the economic domain.

By tightening her sense of internal unity during the last century
the Church prepared for the expansiveness of the present. A
sense of historical dynamism and purpose, a universal identification with the whole of the human race, a deep sense of the
value of God's creation as the material theater and instrument
in the history of man's development within God's plan for his
salvation: these are values freshly restated, values of the Christian

message, values deeply embedded in Western culture and seeking their expression, often quite deformed, in various modern forms, often openly opposed to Christianity.

This entire vision is summed up in the vision of the Church at the service of the world. It is the divine vision of creation and redemption which is the beginning and the end of all. The Church is not the end, but the means: "the sign and the instrument of the union of all men among themselves and in God." The Church is a communion in which all of its members are fundamentally equal in the common glory of the people of God.[7] All ministries in the Church are ministries of service; indeed this is the sense of authority in the Church.[8] The Church is meant for all men, and stresses all that is common to all Christians, with whom communion is not yet complete, and to all other men of good will in their striving for a better world. This is possible because the task of constructing a better temporal order is somehow a part of the whole process of salvation.[9] In the chapter on the eschatological character of the Church this truth was expressed in one of the versions of the text when the Church was described as the "sign (or sacrament) of the salvation of the entire world." Later this phrase was changed to read "a sign (or sacrament) of universal salvation." But the broad cosmic sense remains latent in the text.

Much of this universal sense of the Church's mission has been expressed through the emphasis upon collegiality, the collective responsibility of the bishops everywhere for the Church. But this must be taken in a sense of service. The bishops are the builders of the local communities, and of the broader sense of community. But the missionary obligation of the Church rests not merely on the bishops, nor on a few full-time missionaries, but on every Christian. The apostolate of all Christians embraces both their religious action and their leavening Christian presence in the building of the world.[10]

Obviously this paper has become disproportionate. I have

dwelt so long upon the theological vision that I will hardly have space to enter upon its application to inter-American relations. But I have done this deliberately. We have before us this wonderful vision of community in the Church, seeking not to dominate but to serve the world. But it is not only before us; it is way ahead of us. We Catholics, everywhere, are among the most individualistic and the most provincial of men. Instead of being ourselves a "sign" to the world of community and service, in the name of God and Christ, we are often a countersign which drives sincere people away from God and Christ and the Church.

This may sound unfair, perhaps exaggerated. But before we turn to inter-American relations, let each of us think of his own local and national community. Can Catholics in the United States pride themselves on their leadership in racial integration? True there is a sincere awakening. Much is now being written; much is being done. But how much has the Church here gone out to the Negro in the past? Is it not true that until very recently few of our Catholic universities or religious communities had Negroes in their ranks? Is it not true now that many of the worst racial conflicts take place in Catholic areas of the big cities? I remember a pastor who told me with sorrow of watching one of his Catholic parishioners throw a stone at a nun of the parish, who had been working for years in the parish school, because she was walking in an integration march. He told me of his discussion that night in the rectory with the other priests of the parish, which ended with the question What have we been teaching our people?

I can be bold in mentioning this dolorous situation because we Catholics in Latin America are just as lacking in a sense of community rooted in the conviction of the brotherhood in Christ, in the People of God, to which we are called at the service of all men. We and our people who are materially well-off have tolerated as a normal thing the grinding, dehumanizing poverty of the masses in many of our countries. We have conveniently forgotten the dignity of each human person, comfortably writing off the poor as unredeemable, thieves, drunkards, and worse, when we know in our hearts that placed in their situation of chronic malnutrition, illiteracy, promiscuity, and worse, we would not be as good as they are. Where are the Catholics among our people to give the drive of service to the common good which must be the very definition and purpose of political action? Where are the Catholics willing to make sacrifices to help bring on the radical reforms which all our modern Church documents call for? True, there are some. True, there is an awakening among us, on all levels. But there is much, much more to awaken to and to do. We must admit that we are still far behind the Council and the recent encyclicals, that we are still terribly individualistic and provincial, that we are often countersign, keeping many from finding the fullness of Christ's live in the life of his Church.

The confession of these things does us good. We need not try to hide our shortcomings. They are too obvious anyway. Far better to profess our ideals and at the same time our short-comings. In that way we render service to the ideal and stir ourselves to incarnate it in our lives. Perhaps this frankness and humility is the greatest service we can render one another. I am not speaking here about the awakening to a vision of the Church in the realm of faith, liturgy, and religious apostolate. This is not the area of application in this talk. That is why I chose social examples of our shortcomings, yours and ours, though we could point out others in the strictly ecclesial domain. We are speaking of our presence as Christians in the temporal order, in what we call the world.

Looking at the inter-American dimension, we must back up a bit before we can apply ourselves to some concrete examples. Here I might insert the entire fifth chapter of the second part of The Church in the Modern World, entitled "The Fostering of Peace and the Promotion of a Community of Nations," and con-tinue with *Pacem in Terris* and *Populorum Progressio*. It is not only what these documents say; it is why they say it. Their urgency springs from the vision of Church and world we have described at some length above. It is time that we all compare our practice with this vision and what it implies.

There is particular reason for doing so between the Americas. There is, first of all, our geographical proximity. We are neighbors, for better or for worse. We depend heavily upon one another. Latin America is the greatest single importer of United States goods and in turn sells more to the United States than to any other area. The United States has more of her private foreign investments in Latin America than in any other area except Europe and Canada. There are close to twenty thousand university students from Latin America presently studying in the United States. Our industries, our businesses, many of our educational and social programs, and even our attempted reforms, are introduced by these students on their return, frequently working with and often under persons from the United States. We live under the shadow of United States world politics; we feel her presence, sometimes her armed presence, whenever any serious political crisis develops in our countries.

But there is another consideration. In *Rich Nations and Poor Nations* Barbara Ward has pointed out that the major changes affecting the underdeveloped nations are due to the impact of colonialism and technology brought to them from abroad. Latin America is continually under the fire of United States technocracy, commerce, and mass media. We are in the position of a boy on his bicycle who is trying to balance it so it will not topple over, but is continually receiving spasmodic pushes from an older man in an automobile behind him.

Most of what comes to us in our magazines, newspapers, movies, and television is prepared in the United States. I remember in January, 1964, reading in Panama about the riots occurring all around us in Panama City over the canal issue—reading about them in our Panamanian newspapers, but in news releases from the AP and UPI.

It is the medical revolution of Europe, and more recently of the United States, which has provoked our geometric population growth. Thanks be to God for lives that are saved and prolonged. But these living people must also work and eat and have a place to sleep and receive an education that will enable them to live like the human beings they are. In Europe and North America the population explosion came after the industrial revolution was well under way. In Latin America it has come before. This means that our population increases at a far greater rate than job opportunities.

We could go into other aspects of the impact upon Latin America of all that is done, produced, or written in the United States. The turmoil of our growing populations, pressing into the cities, clustered about the new industries, demanding a better material standard of life, or restive on the land, unguided, unprepared, lacking in technical know-how and social organization, divorced from an old structure and a familiar cultural pattern, unstructured now for living the democratic process—all this has been said by others, and better.

I would make one particular point regarding our mutual relations. If it is true that underdeveloped areas by definition require assistance to come out of their frustrating and vicious circle of poverty, and if Latin America depends so heavily on its economic and social cycle upon the United States, which in large measure has provoked and continues to provoke constant change, then it is to the United States that Latin America is entitled to look for much of the assistance it needs in this hour.

Poverty, of course, is a global problem. The whole of developed Europe and North America, as single nations and through international organizations, must assist the developing nations toward some form of equality and equilibrium with them, as the requisite of justice and the condition of world peace. Some of the European nations are actively and effectively assisting Latin America. But obviously their connections with us in this sphere are neither as massive nor as immediate as those of North America.

Furthermore, there should be with regard to Latin America a special kind of dialogue. The technology which now sweeps the world was born in the West. Many see in it, and in the scientific attitudes behind it, an outgrowth of the biblically inspired approach to nature and its conquest.[11] We have seen that this technology in Europe and North America, where not infused with a concomitant ideology, tends to develop its own implicit ideology, a highly pragmatic and this-worldly one. This is creating deep cultural and spiritual crises in the advanced nations. But its impact upon the underdeveloped nations is even more dramatic. The difference in this impact on Latin America from that experienced on Asia and Africa is quite simply that the former has been formed for four centuries in a Western European religious and cultural pattern, whereas the latter have not. This creates a special kind of dialogue within more recognizable limits. This provides a fundamentally more common religious approach. We have spoken in recent years of the sharp cultural contrasts between the United States and Latin America; and we do not intend to minimize them. But we must not forget the common Christian heritage which is still ours. Latin America, in other words, is the only large sector of the underdeveloped world which is predominantly of Western culture and of Christian faith. Without neglecting our obligations to the rest of the world, we may fairly say that if Christians do not understand and live up to their social and international obligations in this area (of European-Latin American, and especially of inter-American, relations), we cannot expect to have much to say to the rest of the world. As Pope Paul VI put it, brotherhood throughout the world is on trial. It is particularly on trial between us, because we so especially claim to be brothers.

Our relations are many and complicated. We need not go into such matters as economic aid, international price determination, or mutual respect for different cultural attitudes. These are specialized problems. But they are too important to be left to specialists alone. I have heard economists explain that United States investors should keep away from Latin American markets because they are not a good risk, owing to inflation or political instability, and they do not offer as good a return as home or European markets. I have heard foreign-owned company leaders in Latin America expound on their economic rights with little or no reference to the social situation of the countries they operate in. I have heard United States diplomats laugh at the ineffective efforts of small nations to insist on their political rights. If we are to build up a good case and a good program for effective international, inter-American action for justice and for peace, it will not be done out of short-term personal economic or political interest, whether of individuals or of nations. It will come from the conviction that only thus can more war and strife be avoided, that only thus can peaceful economic development be assured for all; fundamentally, as Barbara Ward said in closing a brilliant address given to the Catholic Inter-American Cooperation Program (CICOP) two years ago, it can only come if we genuinely hold to the conviction that we are brothers. Certainly some leadership must be expected from Christians of this Western world in advancing and acting upon this conviction.

Perhaps this simple conclusion may seem a tremendous comedown from the doctrinal vision of the Church in the world we have set forth above. It is merely a coming down to earth. The Council points out that our great ideals of love and union of all men in Christ must be lived in our daily round of activities, in the most ordinary relations. In a generous land of great possibilities the conscience of the United States is now riven by the uprising of the Negro minority. In Latin America our conscience is riven by the oppressed situation of what in some countries is a majority. This oppression leads sometimes to desperation, sometimes to violence. Our violence, our struggles with conscience, can help us to understand yours, and vice versa. If we cannot develop brotherhood at home, it is hopeless to expect it to stretch over the oceans. But we have to work at it on all levels. There is perhaps very little time for us to do so.

Let us realize, at last, how much we have to do. Our responsibility as bishops is great. The bishops of the United States in their recently published pastoral letter spell the matter out clearly.[12] Our Latin American hierarchy has done the same in many documents, above all in the declarations of Mar del Plata, Argentina, prepared by ninety bishops and some sixty experts in November, 1966. In doing so we give echo to the Council, to the encyclicals, to the Gospel, and to our own Christian consciences. But the task is an enduring one. CICOP is a generous move in the right direction. Every pulpit must carry it on, every classroom, and every home. Christians of the United States are still terribly provincial, not at all aware of their tremendous individual and collective responsibilities for the entire world at this crucial hour. The United States as a nation continues to ignore Latin America, with a foreign-aid program declining year by year—preparing new conflicts and violence for the future— because the Christian and human conscience of a generous nation is not aware of and not aroused to the task which history assigns it at this hour. Christians of Latin America, especially those who can do most for their brothers, are still terribly individualistic, not at all aware of their social obligations to their neighbors, their communities, their nations, to the integration of Latin America and the world. They also, if not informed and aroused, will continue to sow the seeds of violence.

The Church today, we have said so often, is a Church of service to the world. We are the Church. We wish to work with all good men for a more peaceful world, in the dynamic sense of justice and human progress for all. If we live these values on the human level, we will truly share in The Church in the Modern World, the hope and the joy of all men. It is what is expected of us; it is what is demanded of us. If we do so in the full dimension of God's life in us and his plan for the union of all men in his love, then it is the kingdom of God which we are living as a "sign raised up to all the nations," the great and necessary sign of our times.

NOTES

1. Arend Th. van Leeuwen, *Christianity in World History* (London: Edinburgh House Press, 1964), pp. 417–418.

2. Pastoral Constitution on the Church in the Modern World, no. 39.

3. Ibid., no. 34.

4. See ibid., nos. 39 and 40.

5. Ibid., no. 75.

6. Dogmatic Constitution on Divine Revelation, no. 8.

7. Dogmatic Constitution on the Church, Chapter II.

8. Ibid., Chapter III.

9. Pastoral Constitution on the Church in the Modern World, Part I, Chapter III.

10. Decree on the Apostolate of the Laity, no. 2.

11. See Harvey Cox, "The Responsibility of the Christian in a World of Technology," and Paul Abrecht, "Issues for Christians," in Denys Munby, ed., *Economic Growth in World Perspective* (New York: Association Press, 1966).

12. National Conference of Catholic Bishops, *The Church in Our Day* (Washington, D.C.: U. S. Catholic Conference, 1968), pp. 23–24.

THE TASK OF THE CHURCH IN INTER-AMERICAN RELATIONSHIPS

JOSEPH GREMILLION

Other contributions in this volume deal with economic, cultural, and political aspects of inter-American relations. Our subject is the role of the Church, and its relevance to present-day reality. Because the Church is Christ continuing his Incarnation in history and society, the Church must know and love the created reality by which the Whole Christ "takes on flesh." Consequently, the Church must constantly seek to understand and give proper value to the economic, political, social, and cultural institutions and movements among which it exercises its apostolate. The Church's apostolate must indeed be directed to the transformation of these institutions themselves, because the integral apostolate, proclaiming and seeking to continue and complete the Incarnation, embraces man and all his works and ways.

The Word, the Good News that God cares for us and calls us to share his life, is preached, and grace, God's light and strength, is given, to man-in-society. Everything human concerns the People of God, we who are becoming the Whole Christ, "the joys and hopes, the sorrows and anxieties" of all.

We see, then, that the secular institutions of the Americas come within the scope of the Church's task. The economic and political structures of our hemisphere, social and cultural relations, intellectual cross-fertilization, the communications media— all of these things of this world, even those things which are Caesar's—must concern us who continue Christ, the People of God, because these inter-American creations are also creatures of God, who wills them to exist, who calls us to continue some and to create others, who sees that they are good.

We focus next on the task of the Church of the Americas by looking toward the *future*. We need not dissect once again the past to uncover the historical reasons and cultural causes of our current situation. We will not analyze the present state of affairs, North and South. This has already been done, and very well done indeed.

Rather, we now ask these questions: What is the role of the Church in the immediate future? during this coming year and decade? and even into the next generation and century? Our emphasis is on perspective, the forward thrust toward what is coming, what, in the Lord, we must bring about in order to be the Church, in order to become truly the whole People of God, joined together to continue the God-Man here on earth. Bishop McGrath has shown in his historical analysis how the Church has been cramped by theological concepts which were wedded to past cultures, and by the static sociopolitical structures and geographic egotism of the medieval era. All of us have been stunted by time-space narrowness as well as by dogmatic myopia and moral faintheartedness.

The Second Vatican Council, with its openness and stress on eschatology, gives new value and impetus to the future, and gives new stature to the virtue of hope. And hope above all is sorely needed in building inter-American relations and solidarity. How the theological virture of hope in the pleroma, in the coming of Christ and his kingdom, is transmuted into secular hope is a theological-psychological problem I will not go into here. But I am convinced that Christ's gift of hope to his People imparts also through Christians-as-citizens-in-the-world an infusion of courage and determination for continuing creation, for promoting justice and development and peace. In some way St. John's apocalyptic vision of "a new heaven and a new earth" inspires us, energizes us, today and tomorrow for building a better world.

From this we see another of the major tasks of the Church. It must impart hope to secular society. It must scorn mental and moral fatigue. Defying defeatism, it must generate courage, the vision of a beckoning future, determination, the will to act. It must project the solidarity of the American hemisphere as an attainable goal, worth the creative work and sacrifice this will require. This means planning and coordination for joint operations among conferences of bishops, religious orders, and lay movements, with the plans of secular society, with governments, inter-American bodies, business, labor, universities, and others. Planning is the new ascetics of modern life.

Third, as the Church brings hope and courage for the future into the time dimension, it must bring a vision that is universal into the dimension of space. What other body but the Church is endowed by its constitution, its attributes, its goals, to embrace the whole family of man? What other body is mandated by God to penetrate national boundaries, ethnic difference, and cultural diversity? Who besides Christ truly embraces the whole of mankind? Since Pentecost, who but his Spirit reaches out his Love for all the human race? The Church *is* Christ uniting us in his Spirit of love, a love that serves others.

What a betrayal of our churchly task, then, if we concentrate too exclusively on our particular nation or ethnic group, if we value too highly our own culture or "way of life," if we despise those of others. Exaggerated nationalism or cultural particularism go directly opposite to the call of Christ. To the extent that we open ourselves to others we are more open and apt to "put on Christ," to live in him, as St. Paul says. Just as the theological virtue of hope, in ways we know not how, energizes the secular society toward the future, so the universality of Christ in us extends the vision and will of man for widening solidarity in space. The Church must open Americans to each other by cutting across national, racial, and cultural lines to beget a consciousness of being one as men and nations, because we are one in Christ, all sons of the same Father to whom we must render an account of our works. Two more conclusions that we can make are very briefly: first, that our task must involve all the People of God, not only clergy, and religious, and laymen directly involved in the apostolate. Christians-as-citizens must fill their role, as voters, as taxpayers, as businessmen and workers, in universities and mass media. And, finally, the task must be conceived ecumenically. All the Christian Churches and the Hebrew synogogues of the Western Hemisphere must find their role together with all men of good will. The Catholic Inter-American Cooperation Program (CICOP) from its very beginning has understood this, and Protestant, Orthodox, and Jewish leaders have participated in our annual meetings in increasing numbers. We must especially seek to cooperate with the Pentecostal and Holiness Churches, both North and South, with whom as Catholics our differences are greatest.

To summarize what we have said so far, the Church's apostolate throughout the Americas must

be incarnational, embracing the secular institutions of society; impart hope and determination for the future;

generate openness and universality among nations and cultures; involve all Christians-as-citizens-of-this-world;

work ecumenically, with all Christians, Jews, and men of good will.

Let us turn now to an examination of the process of renewal within the Church in Latin America. In October, 1966, the Latin

American Episcopal Council (CELAM) held an extraordinary assembly at Mar del Plata, Argentina. Following the leadership of CELAM's Social Action Department, the sixty bishops who are responsible for the social apostolate in Latin America asked sociologists, economists, theologians, and civic leaders to help them spell out the role of the Church in the development and integration of Latin America.

The conclusions of Mar del Plata are of great significance. They set forth the task of the Church as perceived by the Church of Latin America itself. It is fitting that I quote from a text of the recommendations published, not by CELAM, not by the Church itself, but one printed by the Organization of American States in Washington. This is truly "a sign of the times." Let us examine the six principal recommendations, with their implications for us as North Americans working with or in Latin America.

The Integration of Latin America

Integration means the joining together of the respective nations, for example, into common markets, for regional advance, and the incorporation of peasants, proletariat, the Indian peoples, and other ethnic groups into the mainstream of society. Integration has become an indispensable instrument for harmonious regional development and a notable step toward the unification of the human family. It is, also, an essential contribution toward world peace.

In his message to the Mar del Plata meeting Pope Paul stated clearly the Church's role:

In the name of the Gospel, the Church can offer valuable assistance in spreading the ideal of integration by awakening in Christians the conviction that individual national destinies can be achieved only through international solidarity, thus creating a supranational consciousness. (Message to CELAM, September 29, 1966)

The Church of Latin America formally committed itself at Mar del Plata "to participate actively in this historical process . . . and to offer her services toward this . . . noble undertaking." The Mar del Plata conclusions then provided practical indications for carrying this out. Through the written and spoken word, addressed to the general public or to the formation of elite groups, "the signs of the times" should be interpreted in such a way as to diffuse the doctrine of integration. To this end, it is necessary to insist upon the brotherhood of man, which finds its most noble expression in our common creation by God the Father and our common universal redemption in Christ, but a brotherhood which is continually sought by many men in diverse ways. Attention is called to the difficulties to be encountered:

individualistic nationalism that is indifferent to the common good of Latin America;

the egotism of groups and classes that subordinate the development of the continent of their own interests;

economic power groups which can exercise a negative influence by subordinating spiritual values to their material interests.

The Church must proceed with its own integration at the parochial, diocesan, national, and continental levels. A pastoral plan on the continental level should be worked out, one using the experiences already acquired in individual nations. Structures and services should be created or adapted to assist Church movements which promote integration. The Church must make known its support to all organizations dedicated to Latin American integration. The Church's educational institutions must spread the idea of integration and development. They must go beyond nationalism by defining and strengthening a regional consciousness which will promote solidarity and an awareness of Christian unity. Finally, Mar del Plata pledges its support to the Pontifical Commission for Justice and Peace, created by Pope Paul a year ago to promote world justice and development, integration, and peace.

Basic Reforms for the Transformation of Structures

The second major conclusion of Mar del Plata calls for a transformation of social structures so that they "have as their purpose the development of the whole man and of all men." The report stresses three of these structures: property, economic organization, and the state. While maintaining the right to private ownership, the report insists that "the fundamental right of all to the use of the material goods of the earth precedes the right to private property." It is necessary, firmly and wisely, to correct the accumulation of property in the hands of the few. The state, in the name of social justice and the common good, has the right to determine the limits "within which owners can freely administer their goods."

With regard to economic structures it is imperative to promote a system in business enterprise which would contribute to a just distribution of the product and lead to joint responsibility among the participants of the enterprise. The organization of labor unions should be free from external pressures; employer and worker organizations should participate in the management of the enterprise. Cooperative organizations should assist workers in augmenting their productivity.

The bishops and other Church leaders at Mar del Plata recognized clearly that "the role of the state is every day greater; circumstances demand this in Latin America." But to achieve the common good, the economy must be planned with the cooperation of the whole community. The structures of democratic authority and public administration must be modified to fulfill their social and economic function more effectively, a condition which requires a greater participation of the people through their own organizations.

Agrarian Reform

Mar del Plata gives agrarian reform a special place among necessary structural reforms:

The Church should expend every effort so that programs of authentic and integral agrarian reform can be put into effect. This involves the social and personal formation of those who are going to receive and utilize the land, for example, through cooperatives.

To achieve these ends, it is necessary to give Church property an effective social function. The Church must contribute to the creation of a rural middle class capable of participating in the social, economic, cultural, and political life of the country. It must help introduce modern techniques of production and promote fundamental education. It should seek to provide technical assistance and financial credit through appropriate organisms.

Charity, Leadership Training, and Integral Development

Besides addressing itself to reform and to the creation of new secular institutions, the Church in Latin America reaffirms its role of loving service to those in need, especially through charity. But Mar del Plata makes clear that:

Social service has a new spirit. The charity of Catholics must renew itself in order to face up to the new dimensions of social needs. *Caritas* can do a great service to the effort of development of infusing this new spirit into all works of social assistance.

Pastoral Action

Pope Paul wrote as follows to the leaders of CELAM at Mar del Plata:

Because the problems of today are general ones, they require common solutions. No one can solve them alone. . . . The union and common effort of the bishops does not take away the liberty and personal responsibility of each one, but eliminates the harmful effects provoked by internal division. . . . Wise planning can offer to the Church an efficacious means and an incentive to work. The work of evangelization could never be limited to a few groups, but takes in the whole community in all its diversity.

The Church, the house of all and not only of a few privileged ones, is destined to insert in the human mass the leaven capable of keeping the whole world united.

The pastoral plan of CELAM has two major goals: to reach

the abandoned masses of the people in rural villages and urban slums, and to form apostolic Christians in order to raise the mass of the people with the leaven of the Gospel; raising them at the same time toward higher human development.

To fulfill these tasks, Mar del Plata calls for

courses to update the clergy according to the reforms of the Second Vatican Council and courses in effective social action;

purification of the songs and devotional acts of popular religion, while retaining all that gives genuine expression of faith;

multiplication of small communities of the faithful and a corresponding decentralization of traditional institutions;

the use of religious, lay people, and deacons as animators of these communities;

full use of communications media to foster the Christian presence;

preparation of apostolic leaders with creative initiative.

The Lay Apostolate, Youth, and University Students

Mar del Plata asserts that

The building up of the developing world is for the Church the specific task of the laity, whose proper vocation consists in establishing the Kingdom of God through the exercise of their daily tasks in the world. . . . Youth in Latin America constitutes an enormous percentage of the population. Moreover, they must assume adult responsibilities and must shape the Latin American world of tomorrow.

With these principles in mind the following concepts and values should be especially cultivated:

"Consciousness of the process of development, consciousness of commitment as a member of the People of God moving toward the house of the Father";

"Respect for the human person and a sense of the common good (dimensions of the Incarnation and of charity)";

"Openness to dialogue in a pluralist society (consciousness of the mission as leaven)."

Such are the six principal conclusions of the Mar del Plata meeting. Each national conference of bishops is asked to set up a commission to apply these conclusions in their respective countries. To further this, Bishop Eugenio Sales of Salvador, Brazil, president of CELAM's Department of Social Action, or another CELAM officer has visited each of the countries. Meetings of the presidents of the social action commissions of each country have been held in order to coordinate and push forward this continental undertaking.

I have centered this paper on the conclusions of Mar del Plata because they provide the charter and platform to which the Church commits itself in the present drive for integration, reform, and development. The task of the Church is clear—to promote this process, to devote itself to the aims of Mar del Plata.

The Pontifical Commission for Justice and Peace sees this social program of CELAM as a faithful projection of its own mandate on a continental scale. Pope Paul, in response to the call of the Vatican Council, has given this commission, of which I am secretary, the mandate to arouse the whole People of God to a full awareness of their mission in the world today, and particularly to foster development of the poorer regions, to promote social justice among nations, to build world peace.

Appropriately, the Holy Father named Bishop Sales to the Commission for Justice and Peace. All regional and national conferences of bishops are asked to set up corresponding bodies through and with which the People of God everywhere can promote justice, development, and peace in the mainstream of the Church. Following a schedule set up by Bishop Sales, Cardinal Roy of Quebec, president of the Pontifical Commission, has visited all the national conferences of bishops of Latin America during 1968 to carry forward the goals of Mar del Plata.

North-South Interplay and Inter-American Consequences

The concerted initiative of Mar del Plata for reform and

renewal by the Church in Latin America is of major significance for inter-American relationships. In the act of carrying out this program of social reform and renewal the Church reforms and renews itself. Latin American society and the Latin American Church can relate to the North on an improved basis to the degree the reforms succeed. The Church of North America, as a junior partner, can take part in this CELAM program, through personnel and funds, intellectual and research effort, sacrifice, and prayer. Such a program of social reform and renewal is attractive to the great majority in North American society. A main task of the Church is to communicate to the North American secular society and Church the fact, method, and meaning of the reform initiatives of the Church in Latin American society. This is one of the principal purposes of CICOP.

The example of Latin openness and creativity will spur reform and renewal in North America, both in the Church and in secular society. The formation of lay leaders and deacons, Christian living in vigorous small communities, the struggle for racial equality, the renewal of the inner city, community organization, peace movements, and so on, can be usefully influenced and guided by the Latin American example. Northern initiative in these matters also spurs the South. A deeper commonality of interests results from knowledge of comparable problems and approaches. The feeling develops that we, North and South, are doing a job *together*, in witness to Christ, at the service of the world.

This inter-American consciousness, in Christ and at the service of all men, begotten of joint reform and renewal, prepares for the hard task of establishing more equitable relationships in the economic and political field. The old structures of nationalism and cultural superiority are creaking and falling apart. The convergence of interests within the hemisphere become clearer, not only for world peace in the near future but also for the longer-term reasons of raw materials, technology and capital, abundant manpower, and larger markets. The Church must seek out these converging interests, in which economic and political motives coincide with human goals and moral imperatives. This should be a major goal of the newly established United States bishops' Committee for World Justice and Peace, in closest collaboration with CICOP and the whole Latin American apostolate of the United States Church.

That is the meaning of continuing the Incarnation in today's world in the American hemisphere. And above all, the task of the Church is to continue the Incarnation; even if the body's bone and sinew are the worldly stuff of economics and finance, of aid, trade, and development, toward which the Pope urges us in *Populorum Progressio*.

CHURCH AND CULTURE IN
LATIN AMERICA

JORGE MEJIA

The topic under discussion might more properly be the subject of a book rather than of an essay. For the interrelation of Church and culture is one of the major factors in the history of all Latin America over the past four and a half centuries. If I attempted to explain in detail, and with scholarly thoroughness, the content, limits, vicissitudes, problems, and crises of this relationship, I should have to write an entire series of articles on the subject. For it is, indeed, a very complex one, a very broad one, and a perfect example of a topic that calls for interdisciplinary treatment.

Let me instead, in the brief space available, examine the major elements in the Church-culture relationship. I shall endeavor to analyze rather schematically what the Church's contribution to culture has been, what it is or is not at the present time, and how, according to my view of things, it ought to develop in the future. In speaking of the Church I adopt the definition of the Second Vatican Council (Dogmatic Constitution on the

Church, Chapter I). In the case of culture I refer to the Pastoral Constitution on the Church in the Modern World (Part II, Chapter II, no. 53).

Church and Culture in the Latin American Past

In the sixteenth century the Church brought to the Americas a particular form of culture which was alien to the existing Indian societies. This was, of course, the culture of Iberia and of the Latin renaissance. It was, to describe it briefly, a culture which taught and thought in Latin; which was grounded on the Mediterranean version of Christianity; which had very firm ideas about the symbiosis between state and Church, king and priesthood, with a certain slant toward the king; which was committed to the defense and propagation of certain ideals, shaped and hammered out in opposition to the Reformation.

Conquistadores and clergymen could not, and would not, come to the new continent with open minds, to learn new ways and find new means of cultural adaptation. They came to plant the Church, and to plant Spain or Portugal, and it was through Spain and through Portugal that the faith of Jesus Christ came to the New World. It was, let us remember, a bull of Pope Alexander VI which divided Latin America between Spain and Portugal, and subsequent bulls of Julius II (1508) and Leo X (1515) which conferred upon the Spanish and Portuguese kings the rights of patronage. The borderline between temporal and spiritual, between religion and culture, was not an easy one to draw at the time of the Catholic Kings and Charles V.

This situation had several consequences. On the one hand, there was no form of Christian life known on the continent other than the Spanish (or Portuguese) post-Tridentine one. On the other hand, all the seeds of trouble which were alive in this combination were to give abundant fruits in the following centuries, down indeed to our own day.

One cannot, in all honesty, say that the situation thus summarily described was an altogether unfortunate one. In historical perspective we must admit that there was no alternative to it. And it did, in fact, carry real cultural and civil and religious values which were able to create a powerful local version of the original Spanish and Portuguese cultural complex. This culture was, however, much more Spanish and Portuguese than Christian, and in this sense the necessary distinction between it and the Church was quite impossible to make. For this time, therefore, we cannot speak of a real contribution of the Church to the culture. The one practically engulfed the other.

The cultures which the Iberians found *in situ* did not, seemingly, have the strength to provide the conditions for a local version of Christianity. This is a very difficult and important point, and one which still seems somewhat obscure. It is quite true, of course, that with the exception of the two great Aztec and Inca Empires the American continents were void of what we would call a higher culture. In these vast regions there was almost no choice but simply to transplant the religious and cultural situation back home. The Church was not to be modified by the few and dispersed Indians living in what is now Argentina, Chile, or the greater part of Brazil. The Jesuits, indeed, made a real effort toward a special solution of the cultural problem in what is now Paraguay and northeastern Argentina with their *reducciónes,* or almost independent centers for Indian administration, what we would now call a development. But this remarkable experiment was terminated in the late eighteenth century with the suppression of the society.

As regards the Aztecs and the Incas, one can still wonder what would have happened if these two empires had not been overwhelmed by the Spanish invasion. They might have provided some cultural elements for the Church to use and to incorporate. This, of course, from a modern viewpoint would have been the ideal situation. That such a development was not theoretically impossible, even back in the sixteenth and seventeenth centuries, is demonstrated by the fact that the Jesuits and other missionaries were able on the Malabar coast and in China to develop a local version of Christianity which nearly severed its cultural ties with the West. Father de Nobili and Father Ricci really became Indians with the Indians and Chinese with the Chinese. This just did not happen in Mexico or Peru. The major reason seems to have been the military conquest of both empires, which threw them into complete confusion. The consequence was that Church and culture and Latin America were almost indistinguishable, and that they were thoroughly Spanish or Portuguese.

Having said this, it is necessary to add that some kind of adaptation of the Church to the newly found cultures did exist. A new product developed, bred from the encounter between imported Western European Christian culture and the local populations. This did not happen, at least with the same scope and permanence anywhere else, once the experiments of Chinese and Indian adaptation died, or was killed. In Africa the marriage between Christianity and culture is a very recent one. What we see there is principally the unfortunate transposition of European forms of religious expression to a foreign environment, where they remain foreign. And the same has happened, as far as I can see, in Protestant North America. It really speaks much for the Iberian Church of that imperial day that its churchmen were able to admit a kind of blending of Western and local forms of expression which can be seen across the continent, as far south as Jujuy and Catamarca in Argentina, and sometimes as far north as Sonora, Mexico. Especially in painting and in certain liturgical (or paraliturgical) ceremonies the accent is much more local than Spanish. When one considers these facts against the background of what was then, and for many centuries after, a kind of dogma—that there were Christian cultures and pagan cultures, and these last had to be baptized, which meant more or less Westernized—one cannot help but wonder at this partial fusion between an almost completely Spanish (or Portuguese) Church and several native cultures.

What was the explanation for this unexpected phenomenon?

Was it only the weight of history and geography? Was it a certain instinct of the Holy Spirit which makes the Church find its way even in the midst of the most unfavorable conditions? Was it a conscious decision of some of the more lucid churchmen involved? I cannot say, not having at hand the necessary historical investigations. But I am fairly sure that the process was not simply the result of blind historical forces. There were certainly men who understood that the Church, even if it spoke Spanish, or Portuguese, and Latin, could not afford to ignore what the local people had done and went on doing in the way of religious expression. They simply learned from their catechumeni, as we are told to do now.

Church and Culture in the Present

It would be misleading to leap suddenly from the sixteenth century to the twentieth. The past is not just a frozen museum of history; it is history itself. So, I cannot avoid using it to give perspective to what I shall say about the present and about the future mingling of Church and culture.

We all know that the Church has become more and more dissociated from Western culture, which was its second cradle and its almost unique means of expression for many centuries. I am talking, of course, of the Roman, or Latin, Catholic Church. This dissociation, unfortunately, did not mean that the Church became more consciously universal or that it envisaged different versions of itself in different cultures. It only means that the developing Western culture ignored the Church more and more, and that it became more closed in itself, in a kind of subculture. This was, and in part still is, very ecclesiastical, or rather clerical, timid and diffident in confronting a world that used to be Christian but is now paganized again. To describe that world the word in favor with North American theologians is "secularized."

For many centuries before this we can follow the same process in the Latin American part of the hemisphere. Shall we call it estrangement? Shall we call it involution? Curiously enough, until the period of the great revolutions of independence the divorce between Christianity and what can be called a secular culture was not a complete one. Many bishops, clergy, and of course lay Christians did understand and fully participate, actively or intellectually, in the movements of independence. Their efforts were certainly a very definite contribution from Church to culture and from culture to Church. It is not easy to know whether these men and women, these bishops and clergy, acted in the emancipation as Christians. But they certainly saw no contradiction between their religious commitment and their temporal involvement. And this occurred precisely at a time when in Europe involvement in similar movements was frowned upon, and not long after openly disapproved by ecclesiastical authority. The dividing line between those who worked and fought for independence and those who did not is extremely important to draw for our present subject. Those who favored it were for the most part criollos, Americans of Spanish or Spanish-Indian descent; those who opposed it were usually the Spaniards, the native peninsulars who were here by reason of their administrative, military, or hierarchical employment.

We have, therefore, at this moment, when the estrangement becomes sensible, a clear proof that there had been a mixing between Church and culture in Latin America. This was now producing its fruits in the form of two different commitments of Christians in the temporal field. Loyalty to the king was no longer the only possible focal point. There was another temporal solution, which seemed in fact more adapted to the degrees of development of the people involved.

The problem is, and I may here state it in all intellectual honesty because it has quite modern implications, whether this new association between Church and culture did not bring with it the same or similar trouble as the former one. Let me make my meaning clear. If formerly there was no other possible com-

mitment but to crown and cross, so to speak, now there seemed
to be no other possible loyalty but to constitution and cross. So
that at the present moment it is really difficult for people bred
in this tradition to find yet another solution for the temporal
problem, or even to accept, as Christians or Catholics, a plurality
of temporal solutions. Let us bear in mind this real difficulty
and not just skip over it as if we had found the perfect formula.
We have not. And we never will, because this difficulty is inherent in the nature of what is now called the "incarnation" of the
Church in any culture at a given moment of history.

Be this as it may, a final divorce of Church and culture was
declared just after this brilliant, although partial, reconciliation.
The Latin American independence movements and revolutions
were not officially approved of. The clergy was formed in a different tradition, that of the European reaction of the mid-nineteenth
century, and they became bishops a short time after, the hierarchy
having been disrupted by the severing of the ties with the Spanish
crown and the *patronato*. This was the time, we should remember, of the founding of the Latin American College in Rome,
from which almost all future bishops came. And this college was
founded by Pius IX and given to the Jesuits, at that time the
staunchest supporters of *Quanta Cura* and the Syllabus of Errors,
documents which called for the greatest possible dissociation between Church and modern culture. If we follow up our metaphor
of marriage and divorce, these can be considered the final documents of repudiation.

Secular society, on its side, was permeated by liberalism.
Liberalism, the French and American version, was its creative
force. When the hierarchical Church, after a moment of local,
and even universal, hesitation, sealed its connection with the
Ancien Régime, the die was cast. And indeed it must be recognized that the liberal movement of its own had enough anti-
clerical tradition and dynamism to desire the break. The Church
was seen as the house of obscurantism and witchhunting. All

enlightened Christians were on the liberal side. Those who tried
to maintain both loyalties failed scandalously and spectacularly.
What else remained but open war?

The conflict between Church and state is one of the chief
features of Latin American history throughout the nineteeth
century and deep into the twentieth, down to our own time.
This conflict exacerbated the divorce between Church and culture
of which we have spoken. I am convinced that at no time during
the long history of the Christian Church was this divorce so
complete and absolute as in parts of Latin America at this time.
Even in Roman imperial times, surrounded by a pagan culture,
the Fathers of the Church and the bishops tried with utmost
energy to express and live Christianity inside, not outside, the
Greco-Roman cultural complex. Exactly the contrary happened
in the period we are now considering. A gigantic effort was
made to remain aloof, and aside, and indeed against the temporal
culture. It is really pathetic, from our present perspective, to
recall how much energy was wasted in such an unproductive
effort.

We can see now that the result of this divorce was, not at all
the preservation of faith and the implantation of the kingdom
of God, but a very curious situation, in which women were
practicing Christians or Catholics, and were against almost everything that happened around them, while their husbands and sons
were baptized and married in the Church, and even sometimes
blessed by the Church at the time of death, but for the rest of
their lives and work were completely indifferent to, if not against,
any ecclesiastical commitment. Religion was the domain of clergy
and women. It was culturally a different world altogether.

What was the response of the official Church to this abnormal
state of affairs? In many places and for a long time the reaction
was a very militant one, backed by the Holy See, at least through
the first years of Leo XIII. And this kind of reaction produced
it effects, because here and there, in Colombia and Ecuador, for

example, Catholic people if not Catholic parties, obtained political power and revived the old intimate association between Church and state. This resulted, among other things, in the very remarkable concordat with Colombia, concluded in the 1880's, as a result of which civilly married people were publicly excommunicated and their names read in the service (I have heard of this practice continued as late as 1961). On the other hand, other countries like Argentina became still more openly, and aggressively, and officially liberal, with the expulsion of papal nuncios and the rest. Of course, we must carefully distinguish here between the official position of the government and the sentiments of the masses. Typically, during all these years, political life continued to be a question of the educated classes, while the people, workers, immigrants, and Indians, or what remained of them, went their own way, quite indifferent to the conflicts which agitated their rulers. But these lower classes were not attracted to the Church either. Lack of priests, the trauma of immigration, and perhaps the concentration of the official Church on political problems, left the masses dissatisfied with Christianity as they knew it.

Some farseeing people tried, even at this early date, to bridge the gulf which was opening between the masses and official Christian life. The Salesians in Argentina, who knew the ways of the immigrants because both were Italians, created all sorts of educational institutions for the lesser classes, including several in recently explored and still uncivilized Patagonia. But the Church normally tried to provide schools for the education of the rich and ruling-class children and youth through the conviction that if you could get to the minds and hearts of these people, you would certainly have the rest. This was, we may recall, an important category in Leo XIII's thought: the *imperita multitudo*. So we had, springing up in every city of some size, schools and colleges where the children of the leading families were educated, rather incongruously, because their fathers were not real believers anymore. Nor were the results very satisfactory.

This last fact needs some explanation. The Christian formation which was imparted in such schools and colleges was normally the very defensive one which was dominant at the time. It was the ideal milieu for the transmission of the ecclesiastical subculture of which we spoke before. The failure of this formation, a spectacular failure if one considers the amount of human effort and resources given to the task, is a remarkable proof of the divorce between Church and culture. There seemed to be no communication between both worlds, so that even spending the formative years in a closed climate could not infuse into the minds of the young the kind of broad vision which the Church cherished as its own. I am afraid this vision was already dead. And very unfortunately, religion, the true Christian commitment, went much the same way.

Let us examine the consequences of this painful situation. The most visible consequence, and one of the most grievous, was that Latin American culture arrived to its present maturity outside the Church or against her. I certainly do not believe that the Church should in any way have an imperium over culture. I think I have said enough to the contrary by now, and shall say more further on. But a healthy separation of spiritual and secular affairs is quite a different thing from the situation which confronts us now on the continent.

Our society is formed of an immense mass of baptized people. For the most part these people live in a cultural world, or, more exactly, in many different cultural worlds, where the Church is more or less absent. And, conversely, they look to the Church as to a kind of strange world in itself, one of which they do not feel themselves "citizens," as they should, according to St. Paul's teaching to the Ephesians (2:19).

Let me illustrate this fact with some examples. Latin American literature, which is so rich, so important, and at the present moment achieving worldwide fame, has very little to do with the Church. It may not be hostile. It simply ignores the Church as if it were of no real significance. Deeply rooted in the Latin American reality, it does not find the Church at the heart of that reality. And our authors, with very few exceptions, are not Christians. They are leftists, Marxists.

The urban culture in our great cities may to the superficial and foreign observer seem to be very clerical, in certain places almost Caesaropapist. But this is only the external fringe of upper-class society life. Mostly the official Church has remained at the roadside, a mere spectator of urban life. It has, sometimes, a kind of decorative function. Sometimes it is used in a way which reminds one of the "opium of the masses" of Marxist fame, although the sign is exactly the opposite. In some sense the Church is just another relic of the colonial or early independence periods. And there is, deep in the Latin American soul, a secret longing for the golden time of Hierarchical society. We may deny it with our mouths, but a great deal of sincerity and honesty is required not to change the present status of Church-culture relations into a sort of clericalism of the eleventh hour.

Some Guidelines for the Future

I am not in any sense a prophet, and I do not like making predictions which can promptly be proved inaccurate. I do not pretend to know what is going to happen in Latin America in the complex field of relations between the Church and culture. On the other hand, I do see what is happening now, the situation I have described above. As the past was and is present today, the future already begins. Thus we are witnesses to the future; we are, indeed, its authors. Something can and should be said, therefore, about likely developments in the immediate future.

The first thing I ought to say is this: I do not believe the situation just described has been entirely disastrous. There is at least one very good side to it. It is the lesson we have learned about culture and the Church. Some people, perhaps, have still to learn the lesson. But the lesson is there, and it is proclaimed in crystal-clear terms in the Second Vatican Council for everybody to read and understand: "this sacred Synod affirms the legitimate autonomy of human culture and especially of the sciences." (Pastoral Constitution on the Church in the Modern World, no. 59). And this is not an isolated affirmation.

The culture, or cultures, we live in are autonomous. Autonomy refers not to God, or human welfare, but to the tutelage of the Church, as explained in the same chapter of the Pastoral Constitution on the Church. Therefore, we are not to weep if we ascertain that the cultures mentioned above grow now on their own. We should be very glad of it and give thanks to God for it. This is the time of maturity of freedom, not of infancy and submission.

Let us, furthermore, acknowledge very expressly that we would not be up to the task of directing anybody's culture anymore. We have not the "keys of science," although we can sometimes make open, in Christ's name and through his grace, the gates of heaven. We can never cope with the phenomenon of culture anymore. Let us be very clear about this and make no effort to snatch some crumbs of power from the holocaust—if it is a holocaust. We will not rule Latin America in any sense, neither directly nor indirectly. Let us not have any illusions about this. We sometimes seem to think, as men of the official Church, that the moment has now arrived to atone for our past mistakes by engaging in a new kind of apostolic activity, with important consequences in practice, and with all the world following our lead. But this is emphatically not our role as members of the hierarchy. I must confess to a certain wariness when I hear certain ecclesiastical people talk or see them act. I am afraid of a new kind of confusion between the Church as the hierarchy and the Church as the People of God. I wonder very much whether we are always aware of the danger which menaces us because of our very clerical past.

If, then, the Church does have a role to play in the promotion of Latin American culture in the present day and in the future, it can never be in the form of a new imperium, nor even, I venture to say, a new leadership. Is the leadership for us who are constantly professing to be the servants of the servants of the Lord? I really do not see the connection. For us is the service and the sacrifice according to the example of our Lord.

Do I mean by this that there is nothing else that we can do but suffer and pray? That is a very invidious way to put things. We have certainly to suffer and to pray, but we have first of all to grow conscious of our different situation in a new historical context. We, as the Church, are the leaven. The leaven does not perform an innocent function, as it is sometimes, with great ignorance of chemistry, thought. Leaven has a revolutionary function, quite in the spirit of our times. It heaves up the dough and gives it flavor. It makes it mature. If I may allow myself a wordplay in Spanish, "dough" is *masa* in our language, and you know what "mass" means in English, so you can comprehend the metaphor I am using.

The Church should educate its members to become true and committed members of the secular society in which they live, so that they contribute to the building, maintenance, and transmission of their cultures. The Church must preach to its members that as one of their foremost Christian duties they must cooperate in the construction of the world and the countries they live in. I could almost say that her primary contribution to culture in the Latin American context ought to be this one. It is not for the hierarchy to build a culture unless they do it as citizens. It is for Christians, rank and file, to find their ways, choose them, and then follow them to the end, and I may recall that these ways may be different, not just one and the same, in the present situation of history.

We must not forget, furthermore, that there exists in Latin America a so-called culture of poverty which poses two challenges to the Church. One is the effort to raise people out of it by all legitimate means, with the Church always bearing in mind that welfare and promotion is a secular, and mostly a public, not a private, task. The other is the evangelic call to live itself in poverty, so as to be close to its people. The first challenge puts a severe burden on the educational resources of the Church, and creates a tension with regard to its traditional ties with the ruling classes, a tension which can easily go to the breaking point, a tension which will not end even if other ruling classes take the place of the present ones. The second challenge implies for the Church a real and total impoverishment not only in the field of property or finance but also in the field of culture, of power, and of social significance. You are not really poor while you cherish your own culture to the point of bringing others into it. You are not really poor while you keep in your hands the reins of power over whoever is to follow your directions.

This renunciation of any kind of cultural imperialism on the part of the Church must lead also to a very deep adaptation to Latin American culture. It implies a renunciation of the principle of the European and/or Roman formula of Christian life. Importation has been the sign of the last two decades of religious life on the continent. Now, a different period begins in which to be Christian means to become autonomous and creative. We shall not pursue this subject any longer. Anyone can see that we are thinking of many different aspects of the Church. The liturgy, the reform of canon law, the practice of ecumenism, the organization of pastoral work, the style of ecclesiastical government, religious life, and so forth, must find still their local version. They can no longer be a true copy or a faithful replica of what is being done abroad. On the contrary, it is widely hoped, even in Rome, that we will make our own original contribution to the reforms now being hammered out for the whole Church.

This is to accept plurality. If we do accept plurality, let us accept it in all its consequences. Let us not create now, as a substitute for it, a kind of theoretical Latin American culture which exists only in books and articles. Let us face the fact that the continent is varied and that many cultures live and thrive on its soil. It is ridiculous to pretend that the same liturgy should satisfy the Andean Indians and the city-dwellers of Caracas or Buenos Aires. They do not speak the same language; not even the Porteños and Caraqueños speak in the same way. Let us face the differentiation of the Church in the differentiation of cultures. Let us, all the same, maintain the close bonds of unity and cooperation which we have built. Neither the Church nor the continent will find its way outside this integration in diversity. And I venture to extend the same formula to Latin American relations with the United States.

There is a certain insistence in Scripture that we hear the voice of God today (Ps. 93:8; Hebr. 3:7 ff.). Today is always linked to the here and now. The People of God were told by Jeremiah to "be concerned with the welfare" of the realm of Babylon (Jer. 29:7). We know very well that we, as Christians, are still living in exile. All the same, we are told to help in the building of the place where we live. Precisely because we are exiles, and looking forward toward our permanent dwelling, we do not care to create a substitute for paradise in this world. We are happy to contribute to the construction of the cities and cultures of this world but do not want a city and a culture of our own. We wish to remain free, and poor. And, thus we fulfill the word of our Lord, who said: "My kingdom belongs not to this world" (John 18:36). If we keep to this principle, we shall really contribute, as a Church, to the culture of cultures of Latin America. And indeed, being a Church universal, to the culture of the world.

THE CHRISTIAN ETHOS IN
SOCIOECONOMIC DEVELOPMENT

ARÍSTIDES CALVANI

In this essay I will try to explain a difficult subject which needs an extensive vocabulary and a real mastery of language. The subject is very abstract. We need to be precise because the words we must use in dealing with it are ambiguous. We may use the same words but mean different things, because we have not clearly defined our terms. The Christian ethos. We must begin with ethos. What is ethos? For that we need to examine the word "culture." I shall be as brief as possible: ethic, ethos, and finally Christian ethos.

First ethos, the culture forming. Man has a special nature: he is a rational being. Culture is the result of the process of perfection of the man, of the human being. This man has relations with other men. He is a social being, and he has a capacity, a need, to be in contact, in relation with the others. These relations, as we distinguish among them, are subjective relations and objective relations. Subjective relations are the direct relations of man to man. But a man needs more than that. Many times it is difficult

227

to have a direct relation, and a man puts himself in contact with another through objective elements. For instance, I love, I have the ability to love. But the love must be expressed objectively, for instance, with a kiss, with a smile, or with the institution of marriage. Culture, growing from these needs, is the result of man's effort to perfect himself, to achieve himself.

In the same way, we have two kinds of culture, subjective culture and objective culture. Subjective culture is the development of the different possibilities of the human person; objective culture arises from the creations realized by our work in the world. Between subjective culture and objective culture there is a dialectic relationship. The more I can fulfill myself, the more I am able to create objective things, elements. The more I have these objective elements in my hands, the more I can perfect, fulfill myself.

Ethics is another word and also requires a definition. Ethics concern the relations between men, and the relation of human action to the good. These relations generate an obligation, the moral obligation. Ethics works on the level of the obligation. It concerns the relationship between man's acts and his rational good.

Ethos is the ethic which is becoming history, the ethical principles we apply in our personal life, to our life situation. Little by little we convert it into social habits. Let me give an elementary example. I kiss a person because I love her and I would like to express my love to her. But perhaps day by day, kissing this same person, I express not the sense of love but a habit, a formal appearance of love. This is the moment when ethics becomes ethos. A man leaving home kisses his wife. To an observer it seems an act of love, because he is maintaining the appearance of a real love. But the man is transforming a real obligation and a real expression of himself as a human being into a social habit. The conscious becomes unconscious. Ethos seems to be related to ethic, but this is only in appearance. In reality ethos is a whole composite of sentiment, attitude, habit, customs, dynamisms, and inhibitions. The difference is this: the ethic makes me free; the ethos ties me, links me. The ethic concerns the person; the ethos obligates the individual as a member of the community. The ethic pertains to the good; the ethos pertains to well-being.

The ethic, therefore, arises from an abstract conception of life. The ethos is a concrete mode of life. We may ask, Is it possible to speak about a Christian ethos? For me, strictly speaking, it is impossible to understand what a Christian ethos is, because the sense of the Christian life is absolutely opposed to a custom, a habit. The Christian must, every day and every moment, reassess his own life. He cannot act without thinking, from habit. But many times we do hear people speaking about the Christian ethos. Perhaps we may say that a Christian ethos is a social habit, a social attitude, a compulsory attitude, originally inspired by Christian principles of ethics. We have the same problem with the phrase "Christian civilization." What is a Christian civilization? Can we distinguish in our civilization that which is Christian from that which is not? For instance, when I give alms, am I expressing charity? I do not know. Perhaps it is only an old habit. I may try to transform the habit, to dress it with Christian principles. But the habit in itself has no Christian significance.

Yet another word, also confused, is "development." Politicians, economists, religious leaders tell us every day about it. And we use the word constantly ourselves. The word does, in fact, have a deep significance. What is development? Is it only economic growth? No, we are told; it is a total development. But what is total? To know what is total we need a scale of values. When we speak about development we need a pattern of development to judge, to evaluate. We see that the word is really a relative one with a historical meaning. The process of industrialization is spontaneous. This industrialization process, taking place in Europe during the eighteenth and nineteenth centuries, introduced to our world the ideas development and underdevelopment. But we do not speak of England in Chaucer's time as an underdeveloped country. We say, simply, that fifteenth century England was a traditional country. India, too, in the sixteenth century was not an underdeveloped country but a traditional society.

After the industrialization process we begin to speak not about development but about progressive areas and about backward areas. Today we are very cautious, and we do not like to offend persons. We use a euphemism and we say underdeveloped countries, or, trying to be tactful, we say sometimes the developing countries. But we are lying because in fact the developing countries are backward in comparison to the rest of the world. In what sense? In the industrialization process. We must point out these things because in a certain sense we can say that the underdeveloped countries exist because the developed countries exist. And in a certain sense the underdeveloped situation is a consequence of a frustration, the frustration of the role of the developed countries in the process of industrializing all the world. And we can see very easily what kind of problems are arising. Social medicine, public hygiene, for example, can be accepted very easily in an underdeveloped country because you do not need an active position in the face of a medical program. You are passive, pensive. And the population understands the goals of these medical programs almost immediately. They are put into effect. And very soon this population, not prepared for the consequences of medical advance, confronts a demographic explosion of massive unemployment. These two problems are caused by the application of methods that work very well in the developed countries but are distorting in underdeveloped countries.

How can we apply the Christian ethos to these problems? The Christian ethos, as I have indicated, is ambiguous. It seems to be Christian, but it is not really Christian in the religious sense of the word. It consists largely of the cultural acceptance of the word. That is, some ethical principles arising from Christianity convert themselves into social habits and insert themselves into the behavior of the culture in a specific period and in one specific country. But we can ask ourselves a different question and demand more than that. Is it possible to use Christian ethics, Christian religious principles, to reinforce, to support a development.

Generally when we speak about ethics and development, it seems we are speaking for the underdeveloped countries. It appears that they are the only ones we can ask to have certain ethical principles. And we forget a very important thing: ethics are made for the developed countries too. We ask ourselves, What is the situation of the world of today? Is that situation the result of an absence of ethical principles? I think so. I think we are in this situation because we have forgotten ethical principles. The Christian faith requires ethical principles from the developed countries and from the underdeveloped countries.

Today we are facing fact, a historical fact. We live in a world of developed countries and underdeveloped countries. Confronting this world, facing this problem, how can we use our religious principles to help the underdeveloped people themselves? We need first to understand what modernization and mechanization are. We need to know what is the real meaning of modernization. If I am going to use Christian principles to help a person, I must know where I am taking this person, where I am leading him, what kind of pattern I am pursuing: a capitalistic system, a socialistic system, a communitarian system. Under capitalism, for instance, the attitude toward profit is very specific. Business is business; time is money. If I have no gain I do not invest anything. That is the basic ideology of the capitalist system.

When we in Latin America today speak or think about free donation from one country to another, we speak about utopia. In a capitalist context we think we are dreaming, we think it is impossible. We are involved in the ideology of the system; we think it is impossible to conceive of the relations between nations in any other sense than this one of an investment for profit. That is why we must know what kind of pattern we have in mind when we speak about Christian ethical principles in development.

Let us explore the idea. We are agreed that the new world, the new society, must be a technological one. Technology requires certain attitudes, habits of mind and work. What can we do with these human attitudes? First, we require a sense of responsibility. Second, willingness to work, to work hard, to work together, to work as a team. Other essential factors are the sense of the common good, efficiency, a spirit of creativeness, a spirit of saving, a capacity to adapt ourselves to different situations, discipline.

Responsibility. What kind of virtue, of ethic, of Christian principle, can we call upon to bring forth the responsibility among people? I think we can build a pastoral base on the dignity of the human person by connecting this dignity with the love of my neighbor. With these two principles we can build a sense of responsibility, because if I love my brother (if my neighbor is my brother and I love him), I have the responsibility to work for him, to be more happy all together.

A second attribute of technological society is work, the new sense of work. Let me give an example of existing attitudes. One day a few years ago I entered a cab in Venezuela, where it is very common to have a taxi working like a bus. You pay for your seat and only your seat. If each seat costs one dollar, the five seats result in a total of five dollars. So the driver asked me, "You want to go now? Already?" "Yes, immediately." "Then I am going to ask six dollars." "And why do you ask me one dollar more? If each seat costs one dollar, why do you ask me six dollars?" And he replied: "Because I am doing you a favor. My work day is finished. I want to go home. I would like to take a bath, and then take a walk around my home." At first such a reply seems stupid, but it is a true reflection of an attitude. The man was not working for gain; he was working to live. And that is very often the approach of the lower classes in a traditional society. We want to change this mentality. We want to convert our people to work, to continuous work, because we need continuous work in a technological era. To encourage it, I think we can use the idea of serving others, the Christian sense of social service, the idea of the perfectability of man. Work of this kind would be fulfilling, give a sense of achievement. It would be, not, as in the past, a punishment, but a way to realize one's human potential. Changing the sense of work, we would change the mind of each person and prepare him to accept the technological process.

Yet another goal in modern society is efficiency. Efficiency, I think, we could obtain by perfection in details, and the common good with a sense of solidarity. The teamwork would arise through humility and the sense of the Christian community. Using the liturgical assembly, the eucharistic assembly, we are all together and we are in a real *ecclesia,* a community. This sense of community creates the possibility of working with others, accepting opinions, and creating a team.

Next comes the spirit of creativeness. To strengthen this sense, we have two commandments. We are told to fill the earth and to dominate it. By insisting on the domination of the earth as an element of Christian ethics we introduce the sense of creativeness.

We also need savings, the habit of deferring consumption. Because saving has so many psychological implications, it is difficult to explain. I think the best way to encourage it is through the family. The sense of family is very deep in Latin America, and we can teach our people to demonstrate love for their family by saving in order to protect them, to provide for their children's education, and so on.

All these things require, finally, a pastoral renewal. Our pastoral work is not up-to-date, not adequate to our world. The impact of technology on a traditional society needs to be paralleled by the impact of a new approach to religion. For this we need two things. First, a theology of the temporal society. We have a theology of the Church. The divine society, the mystical society, the Mystical Body of Christ have their theology, but we have no theology for temporal society, for a secular society made by men. And second, we need a theology of development. We have some ideas and some rules in *Populorum Progressio,* but these provide only a general outlook. We need a precise theory.

We have a long way to go in adapting ourselves to modern society. How can we, for example, use religious principles to increase civic life in an underdeveloped country through preaching about traffic? I have never heard any Venezuelan priest speak about the responsibility of drivers. And yet we have in our hands when we are in a car a machine with which we can cause much destruction and suffering, and death. When we drive in Caracas, with its great disorder, and speed even in the center of the city, we are approaching an occasion of sin, the very gravest of sins, murder. We must transform and adapt our pastoral to this new technology and prepare our people to receive its impact. To the daily situations of the new technological society we can apply Christian principles to bring forth a civic life.

Our new pastoral concern should be introduced in the schools. We can teach there the sense of saving. We can encourage the students to save money and to have prudence for the future. But I have seldom heard in a homily anything about the meaning of the different material instruments we have. The significance of man's inventions is passed over in the Church. TV, radio, the telephone, automobiles, the hours we lose in travel—all are ignored. We need a pastoral concern for leisure hours. Scriptures tell us we are going to be judged by how we use our free time, the empty moments in our life. We have found time for many things, but so far we have not found the time to prepare a pastoral about the use of leisure in a Christian sense and in a Christian way.

PASTORAL WORK AMONG
THE MASSES AND THE
RELIGIOUS ELITE

RENATO POBLETE, S.J.

Pastoral work is a complex task that must be fulfilled within
countless spatial contexts, amidst ever-changing social conditions,
in order that man might respond to God's love. Man is indeed the
center of the pastoral problem, and we may well ask, Who is
this man? In what social and cultural structures does he live?
What are the trends in his rapidly moving society?

Latin American society is rapidly moving from a predominantly
rural culture to an urban one. The movement, however, is not
homogeneous either in the speed of its realization or in the form
of its expression. New types of social relations, culture patterns,
expectations are arising everywhere. Social ties based on kinship
are disappearing, to give way to those based on social contact
and free association. There is a daily increase of specialization and
social differentiation, while new intermediary groups bridging
the gap between the upper and lower classes are being born.

This new situation is characterized by a preference for more
democratic horizontal relations. People no longer appreciate

235

traditional norms merely for their durability; they are looking, rather, for norms and regulations of a functional nature. The division of labor demanded by the advance of technology makes it impossible for a man to be an expert in many fields. This in its turn produces a mutual dependency and a necessary isolation in the face of the totality of the problem. All of these factors accelerate the process of secularization and pluralism at work in Latin America today.

In the urban scene, especially among leading groups of students, businessmen, and politicians, this process is seriously affecting their milieu. We may speak of "a secular city" in Latin America, that is to say, man is breaking away from his mythological conceptions in a sort of desacralization of his culture. He is rapidly losing the old religious mode of relating to the world. There is then a consequent ambiguity in the forms presented by the religiosity of today, already on its way to the changes of tomorrow.

The spontaneous belief held by man that both he and his world derived from and depended upon a Power deserving of his reverence has lost the strategic place it so long enjoyed in our society. It has been replaced by what Teilhard de Chardin called "a passion for the things of the earth," a concern for those things that here and now challenge man. We have no intention of describing secularization, but we do wish to point out its very real presence in Latin America. Although this data neither defines nor identifies the problem, it does provide the necessary framework for an understanding of the type of pastoral work needed among both the masses and the elite.

How deeply is secularization entrenched in Latin America? We must confess that it is difficult to assess the exact extent of its influence. However, there are visible proofs everywhere that convince us that we should by no means identify secularization with a lack of religiosity or the absence of belief. Over all the Latin American continent there are vital signs of openness to

God; we have only to recall Oscar Lewis' *The Children of Sánchez* or *Pedro Martínez*. But the Church is confronted with a dilemma. What in fact does she have to offer the masses? Are the conciliar documents and the whole spirit of renewal leading to a neglect of them in the building of a Christian elite? It is our hope in this paper to suggest a tentative answer to these problems.

We begin with a description of an ever-present problem faced by the Church. There is evident tension created by the necessity of considering two poles of thought. Should the Church give only her "pure" message that will be grasped by a relatively small group of persons and will have a definite liturgical expression, or should there also be a place for the popular devotions that are the "religion" of the masses? Of course, the tension between these poles is not a permanent one; they are not antagonistic, motionless "positions." Rather, there is a continuum that goes from one side to the other. We would like to deal first with the expression of popular religion and show its value. This answer will be sociological, not theological, in its approach.

Tertullian asserts that every man has a soul naturally Christian. All the universe has a symbolic character leading us to God, and the religious forms, even those which are non-Christian, are stepping stones to the Deity. Man is searching for a Being that is, in the expression of Rudolf Otto, a *"mysterium, tremendum and facinosum."* Without doubt, man on this path to God may develop some idols, but this danger should not make us condemn a priori the quest or the use of the sacred in popular expression and cultural values. Rather, we should try to draw these on into Christ, convert them, as it were.

Every conversion presupposes a Yes and a No. The history of the Church demonstrates a constant dialectic. In the beginning she said No to a series of pagan and Jewish rites. This was the reason why, during the first centuries (just to mention an example), the Christians did not use a system of symbols and images. However, once the originality of the religion of Christ was assured the Church began to use symbols similar to those utilized by other religions. The Church then began to say Yes to such preparations for the Gospel as we may find in the natural religions—but it was the Yes of the convert. This was the reason for the struggle against the iconoclasts and, later, for the defense of values more fully Christian against the Albigenses and Cathari, which sects or movements were trying to reduce Christianity to a single dimension. We must insist upon the values of popular devotions. We know that any popular religion is rooted in a sociological structure, and for this reason it is necessary to study these forms.

Any human group, such as a political party or religious institution, possesses different categories of people in accord with their response to the value and norms professed by the group. There are nuclear sectors that we may call "elite" and some other peripheral groups that we might term "masses." The members of the elite demonstrate greater participation and greater interest. They understand and accept the norms of the group, while their attitudes and opinions correspond to its central norms and values.

There are also passive groups in which the members are little more than spectators. Their interest is more diffused, and they do not have an intense or frequent participation. These groups— the masses—have not been deeply socialized. Nevertheless, they grasp certain values and norms superficially and possess attitudes and opinions with differing degress of intensity. These passive groups are important in any society since active groups are unable to develop all activities without some participation on the part of passive ones. The structure of any society always presents different levels of solidarity in relation to the norms and values. Although the masses do not deeply assimilate these norms and values, they do search for ways to express their solidarity *en masse*.

The attitudes of the masses are emotional and are inspired by love for an individual or a symbolic object, such as the cross. It is not uncommon to see these attitudes altered by altruistic motives of affection for a religious or political leader, or by fear, wrath, or hatred leading to aggression. Although the motivation of the masses is complex, they like slogans and stereotypes, and they are moved by simple phrases.

Let us examine this consideration further. The masses are traditionalists and suspicious of change. Any group, in order to obtain its objective, has to awaken a sense of solidarity among its members and lead them to participate little by little in the objectives of the group. When a man realizes that he shares sentiments and objectives with others, he is then conscious of belonging to a group, and this sense of mutual identification is extremely important for the group's success. These groups need massive representations and mass demonstrations to retain their solidarity. From a religious point of view the masses form what may be called "the people of God," that is to say, a sort of unity more or less organized, with a sacred character. These individuals, although not always consciously, feel related among themselves and with the organization, such as the Church for instance, and share with the others a common sentiment.

The religious experience of man and religious manifestations and motivations have a wide range of variability. A proof of this is demonstrated in the multiplicity of existing religions and by the very fact that even adherents of the same creed do not grasp their affiliations in precisely the same way. People seem to need different exterior manifestations of faith.

In an established religion the large masses show different degrees of assimilation and interiorization of cultural or religious values. The masses, as we said, are related to the organization in a different way than are the elite. They are inclined to simple and traditional values possessing characteristics of primitive religion. Popular beliefs and devotions provide instruments through which the masses are related to a higher and more universal religion. They understand and practice only part of the whole message, and sometimes mingle it with the religious patrimony of their ancestors. They are moved by instincts and unconscious sentiments. Their moral level is lower, and tradition exercises great power over them. Their tendency to fantasy is increased by their imagination. They love legends and are constantly asking for miracles because of their need of a guarantee, a visible proof of things. These elements are commonly found in all religions. The masses are bound to a routine, and accept as inviolable the sacred and hereditary forms received from their ancestors. Mensching (*La religion de type superieur*) has found a great similarity among the popular beliefs of all people through all ages. In the religion of the masses we may find magical elements and a concept of the world that has remained almost primitive.

Popular religion has at the same time a certain utilitarian character. Prosperity and personal advantage are often important motivations. Popular beliefs envision God as too distant and see a need for some mediator. Primitive religions have always had this characteristic. Devotion to "saints," who seem more accessible, is very strong. The saints give the people more confidence, since they seem more related to their daily lives and provide the needed mediation between God and man.

In the Catholic Church we also find many of these same elements. Devotion to the souls in purgatory, the use of sacramentals —holy water, relics, the recitation of the Rosary, blessed candles, and so on—have always provided the means by which people have kept in contact with the sacred and the divine. Among many people we also find the repetition of prayers and responses. These elements have always been considered worthy of being assumed, adapted, and purified within the Church.

The people attribute to the cross or holy water the power of repelling demons. Certain formulas or the repetition of certain words and prayers carry a similar connotation. Other manifestations of popular religion are processions, which are expressions of exterior adherence to God, Our Lady, or the saints. Purification rites are also old and very popular beliefs, mixed with ethnical and mystical values that help man relate himself to God.

What we are describing here are the elements of expression of the religion of the masses in Latin America. There are very few serious studies on this subject. In his books *LaVida, The Children of Sánchez,* and *Pedro Martínez* Oscar Lewis touches quite frequently the religions of the masses. He describes how deeply the sense of God is rooted among these people in the frequency with which the name of God is mentioned: "Ask God"; "My God help me"; "By the grace of God she didn't lose her mind." These expressions are part of the deep religious sentiments of the people. They may, on the other hand, be the expression of formulas that man continues to use out of custom. However, as they appear in Lewis' books, they indicate that God is felt to be the Lord of their lives and the one to whom we must go when help is needed. It is true that some fatalism is mingled with their religious sentiments; God is the "God of justice" in whose hands rests the destiny of all men. We do not find any atheism among these people, which however is common in other social strata; in the midst of their poverty they believe in God.

In a number of studies done on public opinion in several countries of Latin America the percentages representing those who believe in God are extremely high. The religions of the poor resemble the old Jewish people and their religion of pilgrimage. They too are centered around great sanctuaries like Guadalupe, Chalma, Copacabana, Andacollo y Nuestra Senora Aparecida. Each nation possesses large basilicas dedicated to Our Lady or the saints where the people go to give thanks during the important moments of their lives or for favors received. There are popular roadside shrines to Our Lady and the saints in every town where the people can be seen making the sign of the cross and pausing to pray before the image. Holy pictures are seen everywhere, in homes and buses, often accompanied by pictures of movie stars. Lewis' descriptions are applicable to all their sanctuaries.

Together with this concept of a "pilgrim Church" we find in the sanctuaries the religious dancers who dedicate their dance rituals to Our Lady. There are also the "penitents" who demonstrate the sacrificial aspect of popular devotion. No one can deny that here exists a true religious experience. Religion is for these people a complex sentiment including love, dependence, fear, and hope expressed in a deeply emotional way. It gives them a primitive world vision, although they are not seeking growth in the supernatural life of their personal perfection. God becomes for them an emotional outlet, the imposer of norms, the demanding one. Jesus appears as the God who has come to us, with whom we may talk rather than the one who imposes norms. The prayer of petition which has as its goal the solution of material problems is found everywhere. At the same time there is a need to give something to God that is concretized in offerings of money, candles, and flowers. The promises or vows so commonly made may take on the appearance of a type of trade with the divinity: "I give in order to receive." There is a curious familiarity with the dead, and All Souls Day is one of the principal feasts among these groups. Contacts with the dead through dreams, apparitions, and similar phenomena are frequently reported. The masses, in short, do not share fully in the sacramental life offered by the Catholic Church. Baptism, confirmation, and first communion are important and valued, but the other sacraments are left for the elite. Although the sacramental life is not active, love of neighbor, sacrifice, and selflessness are nevertheless part of the daily life of the people.

How much superstition is found in popular religion? What are its magical elements? We do find religious deformation and superstition in the religion of the masses, arising, as Bergson pointed out, from psychological sources. Sorcery is one type of religious deformation which is present, while spiritism, especially in Brazil, runs through all the different social strata. Nevertheless, we must insist here that popular religious beliefs are not always superstitions, nor is popular religious belief always a syncretism. It springs from deep religious sentiment. Superstitions are related to magic and show a willingness to manipulate the sacred, while syncretism presents a lack of hierarchization of the different religious elements. The Christian religion demonstrates a sense of submission to God which acknowledges his superiority while at the same time it develops a sense of trust in his power and in his help.

Every church confronts a dilemma. Because it is a church with an inclination to be universal and invites every man to conversion, it tends therefore to expand. This expansion, however, inevitably dilutes and alters the primitive message. This is the price of all institutionalization. The grasp of the total message, especially its most rational aspects, tends to be more individualistic, more personal, more spiritual, as opposed to the normal tendencies of the masses described above. The history of Catholicism has developed somewhere between these two polar tendencies. Ascetic groups have tried, as a type of protest, to regain the purity and fullness of the message. Many religious orders have their origins in such attempts. Similar protests have led people to secession, and thus gave rise to the various sects existent today.

The sociological analysis of any religious movement reveals concentric circles, each possessing a different degree of ability to grasp religious values. In the innermost circle we have the disciples who are totally consecrated to religious activities. Then come less active members, and then the broader circle of the faithful. The masses, still open to receiving the religious message, make up the outer ring. The disciples might tend to radicalism, try to separate themselves from the world, and oppose the idea of being joined to the uncomprehending masses. It is important to realize that if the masses are deprived of popular religious expressions, they will be more exposed to the process of secularization.

For a better understanding of our topic we would like to recall the classical distinction between sect and church.[1] A sect is always formed by a little group that has had a more or less homogeneous religious experience. It does not have a universal character. In order to keep this unity, the members insist that they are the only chosen ones and separate themselves from the world. They are members by voluntary adhesion. On the other hand, a church, sociologically speaking, tries to incarnate itself in the world and its culture, and accepts and assumes many of the world's values. It is not a group formed by the chosen ones only, but it aspires to a universal communication of its message. These characteristics produce a different relationship between the church and the masses.

Could a church that wishes to reach all men really achieve universality while it rejects all popular beliefs? Mensching tells us that "in the light of history it seems that the answer is negative." No universal religion can escape confrontation with this problem. Even the deeper mystical religions, based on personal factors, cannot exist indefinitely as a small circle of chosen ones. They must all attempt, sooner or later, to become a church for the multitudes by opening themselves to the masses and allowing them to join. If this church wishes to reach and to retain these masses and exercise religious influence over them, it will need to accept the assimilation of some primitive beliefs, and adapt them as much as possible whenever it may be necessary. Outright rejection of these values would only result in the masses separating themselves from the church.

The Catholic Church has always recognized that there are different levels of Catholicism. St. Thomas talks about the *majori in fide* and the *minori in fide*. Different styles of life have always been present in the Church, for the call of God is not heard by everyone in the same way, and the call to sanctity is responded to in differing degrees. God calls everyone and wants to be known by everyone, but not every man is able to respond in the same way. Mensching insists that the Church has to acknowledge these personal factors in order that she will always have a multitude within her membership and will continue to seek ways of incorporating this multitude more deeply into her organization. If the Church wants to influence the masses, she must accept the assimilation of many primitive popular beliefs and adapt them as it may be necessary.

What we have just said touches one of the central points of the pastoral work of the Catholic Church. Putting the principle into practice is not simple. It requires deep theological and sociological study. We must keep in mind that when we say that the Church wishes to be universal, it does not mean that it is looking for power in order to influence and dominate. It is universal in its desire to serve *everyone*, and not just a small elite group. It is universal in its desire to help *everyone* find the road to God.

It is very clear in the history of the evangelization of Latin America, for example, that the first missionaries accepted a series of pagan customs and rites, and used them as means of evangelization. They "baptized" many rites and beliefs of the people. Pope Gregory the Great recommended this method to the missionaries in England and Ireland when he said that the person who makes an effort to relate himself to God has to be raised little by little to a deeper knowledge of the true God. Many rites connected with the harvest, the blessing of a home, and so on were accepted. When the Church absorbed these rites, she was following the example of Christ, who assumed the total human condition, its sentiments, and its cosmos. Despite the fact that human nature fails utterly to comprehend the divine, God adapts himself to the weakness of men and communicates his revelation as to a child, gradually and patiently. God accepted the erroneous idolatrous searching of man until he was prepared to recognize Christ. Saint Irenaeus reminds us that the Incarnation cannot be taught rapidly, since man goes step by step to God.

It is evident that many images and primitive religious expressions may be purified by Christ and that the revelation of Christ may assume and adapt them. To all those who may be tempted to despise mass Catholicism and who dream of a "pure" Catholicism we may ask, What is "pure" Catholicism? Man expresses the sacredness of religion not in a vacuum but in a concrete, sociocultural context in accordance with his own personality. Is it not a religious act to attend a Benedictine ceremony even if the motivation is mingled with esthetic elements, even though a purely religious motivation is absent? The ways in which men go toward God are complex. That is why it seems prudent to respect different religious expressions and popular devotions. Is man not religious when he asks God for a good harvest, for health, or for success in love? And if this be true, why should someone despise a priori these different religious expressions? In all elements of popular religion we find an openness toward God and a preparation for hearing the Word of God in the Gospel.

The Church, as we indicated, has baptized many rites and cults by showing man how he may find God through them. Many popular devotions, and Christian rites as well, have lost the clear reference to the fullness of the Christian faith. At times the sacraments have been converted into cultural or folkloric, rather than Christian, elements. But is it not possible to reincorporate these religious signs, to enrich them again with a truly Christian meaning? We must revitalize popular devotions, processions, dances, and other practices in this way.

In the spirit of John XXIII and of the Vatican Council the Church looks for different ways to enter into an open dialogue with the atheist and the nonreligious men of today. In the same spirit would it not be incongruous to abandon the masses who have only popular devotions to assist them in their search for God? Is it not possible to find a broad basis for dialogue with them in order to help them discover the true God, precisely that God who will help them live their human lives in the fullness of freedom, the freedom of Christ?

The existence of popular religious elements is a challenge to Christianity. There is an acknowledged need that the divine Word give life to the signs used to communicate the true meaning of the Gospel. Symbols need not be suppressed because they appear to lack content. What we must do is imbue them with the Word of God, and the word must be fully Christian, with all the exigencies that this involves. These may not be diminished despite the hardships involved and the danger that many will be afraid to accept them. We do not know the future of our rural and indigenous people, but we cannot simply dedicate ourselves to fomenting popular beliefs without informing them with the fullness of the Gospel. Otherwise religion really would become the opium of the people and would in the end only increase their sense of frustration. At the present time the existence of popular religion leads many to believe that Latin America is still a Catholic continent, and allows many bishops to bask in a false security. It would be a serious mistake to think that we are dispensed from earnest efforts of searching out new formulas, or to believe that our only task is the preservation of an already existing faith. The crux of the problem is the achievement of balance in our pastoral work; any extreme position would be tantamount to suicide.

It is precisely due to these facts that we must seriously consider grass-roots work with Latin American elites. Paul VI, in his address to the bishops of our continent, pointed out a double line of action for the Latin American Church. First was the need for revitalization of the whole Christian community as such, including all the elements that would awaken the people to a consciousness of their faith, their divine vocation to be the salt of the earth, the leaven in the dough, the light that illumines and guides the whole People of God. Second, small groups or neighborhood communities, the result of parish reorganization or apostolic movements, would meet for personal formation and attempt to live as men and women conscious of their Catholicism. In them, perhaps, more than elsewhere, will be realized and experienced the concept of the universal Church, a Church formed by all men. Although the great masses would not take part in them at first, these elite groups would not live for themselves as a type of sect. They would be open to all, to those openly separated from the Church, to those united loosely to her, as well as for those wholly committed to the Gospel. All these saints, sinners, and the indifferent, all in fact belong to Christ.

Apostolic effort on behalf of these elite groups is essential today owing to the complexity of modern society. Their problems demand careful attention, and today's society requires the kind of personal interaction possible only in a small group or community that is difficult to achieve with the present number of priests. It is precisely the small number of priests which imposes upon the Church the urgent necessity to vitalize elite groups among workers, students, and intellectuals. This labor requires a presentation of the Gospel with all its exigencies in order that the members discover the authentic image of Christ. These elite groups will in their way fulfill the role exercised by priests and monks in former times. They will live the Gospel of Christ, not for themselves alone, but as apostles in the world of today.

These two lines of pastoral work called for by Paul VI should be, not parallel, but convergent. Bishops, priests, and laymen, aware of the Gospel message, should not be satisfied with an image of themselves as the only truly authentic Christians. They must recognize and respect the Christian values that are not, perhaps, expressed with complete purity and lucidity but are, nonetheless, present in many elements of popular religion. The simplicity, spontaneity, and joy of popular dances and songs possess many evangelical values which often express the desire to give oneself to God without any condition. Bishops, pastors, priests, and laymen must therefore exercise infinite respect in preaching the Gospel to the masses who, in their simplicity and unconditional love, are often like the Magdalen, closer to God than Nicodemus and his modern counterparts among the elite.

So it is that the process of elevation and purification of popular religion will have to be accomplished within a framework of respectful care. We are not the judges of what is pure or impure. It is the Lord who judges, and his spirit is present within the masses as it is among the elite. Let us hope that the Lord will open our ears that we may listen attentively to the message of the Spirit. And if we hear the voice of the Lord in this our day, may there be no hardening of our hearts against the exigencies of his demands for the Church of Latin America.

NOTES

1. R. Poblete, "Formación de Sectas," *Mensaje* (Santiago, Chile), January, 1960; Ernst Troeltsch, *The Social Teaching of the Christian Churches* (various editions).

PART FIVE

THE TWO AMERICAS

UNITED STATES CULTURE
AND ITS CAPACITY FOR
COLLABORATION

GEORGE N. SHUSTER

I am neither a social scientist nor a diplomat, at least not in the
Latin American sense of the term. Therefore I must concentrate
on what I know most about, though to be sure it is very little. My
subject is the inevitable ego, the *Ich*, as the humanistic disciplines
have caught at least a glimpse of it. The introductory words are
taken from one of Paul Weiss's books:

> To achieve civilization, we must not aim directly and fixedly at a civilized
> world, but at the attainment of beauty, of religious insight, of an under-
> standing of basic ethical principles in such a way that their outcome is
> their exemplification in this world. If we aim at civilization, what we will
> eventually attain is not civilization but people sharing in it at various degrees
> less than the optimum.

I have quoted from one of the most distinguished Jewish
thinkers of our time in order to hazard the guess that what has
robbed so many of the good deeds we North Americans have
done in Latin America of true creative effectiveness is just this:
we have presented ourselves to others as exemplars of what we

want them to be, and have not presented ourselves as men and women whose real interests lie in fact side by side with theirs beyond the area of technological civilization. This last they know is really what we most deeply revere. It is quite natural that we should do so because we are very skilled in this kind of civilization. Latin Americans relatively seldom are. Whereas the Japanese have learned from us and from Europeans all that can be taught about technology, and indeed sometimes do better than their masters, Latin America is, despite its immense natural resources, still lacking, for example, in sufficient industrial strength to make a common market possible, though this is something Simón Bolívar thought of long ago.

Let me illustrate. I have seen North Americans smuggle suitcases full of birth prevention coils into South America and distribute them at random. Looked at from the highest ethical level, they were substituting a technological device for an eminently rural recourse to abortion, which in all probability has been practiced for centuries. But as far as I have been able to tell, such devices have a strong antihumanistic implication for Latin Americans. Women have relieved themselves of unwanted growth in their wombs since time immemorial, utterly alien though this practice is to Christian moral teaching. But the proposed new way is peculiarly technological, peculiarly North American.

I shall now step back into history. The basic cultural impulse insofar as the United States is concerned derives from the idea of freedom. The word is used here in the sense that Tocqueville understood it. Perhaps, as it has often been said, the basic ethic was Protestant. But one must immediately add that the Catholic immigrant was almost everywhere placed in a situation which made his religious and vocational liberties dominant concerns. In the mill towns of New England, Catholics and Negroes were alike creatures to be exploited; in the Middle West, Germans had again and again to struggle for their civil rights. The culture (not the economic institutions) of the United States bred the great war of

the 1860's, and it has ever since been bent on liberating someone
from something—at home from predatory capitalism, disease, and
even potential exploitation by agents of subversion; abroad from
Communist control and the great evils of poverty, ignorance,
disease, and overpopulation. We have done, and still do, these
things with great uneasiness and of course with some lapses into
exploitation. He whom Latin Americans call the *Yanqui* is a curious blend of braggadocio and humility. The examinations of conscience to which he subjects himself almost continuously, coming
up with such self-characterizations as Ugly American, are, however, seldom taken seriously abroad. What our friends usually see
is a man with a conscience and a pocketful of libidos. At any
rate, I do not believe that we ourselves or anybody else can
understand our present stance unless he grasps what is so deeply
rooted in our culture. We are really at heart inveterate do-
gooders, in spite of our current affluence and obvious ethical
decay.

And Latin Americans? Of course we will agree that in an important sense there are no such people. Anyone who has spent
some time in Rio or São Paulo knows that the breath of the
tropics fills every cranny of men's souls and that here is an
entirely different world from that of Chile stretched out like an
eel from one cluster of mountains to another. Nevertheless one
can from another point of view conclude that there is a Latin
American. He is aware that his culture is of European origin
and still in significant ways pre-Western.

It seems to be that just as the cultural thrust in the United
States has been made in terms of freedom, so also the thrust in
Latin America has been toward independence. Simón Bolívar was
perhaps the most constructive and Platonic genius in modern
history, for all that he dreamed of a kind of Pan-American United
Nations. Perhaps if this country had been prepared at the time to
consider some of Bolívar's proposals in practical terms the course
of history might have been different. At any rate, his dream

faded, while that of our founding fathers did not. Their union was imperfect, has had to be fought for in one manner or other to this very day. But however real and decisive Bolívar's campaign against Spanish rule was, the love for Spanish culture survived. And independence? Of course it is regrettably true that the United States made predatory assaults on Latin American states, sometimes military in character. Yet in the end an impressive amalgam was created—first in the form of an Orgnization of American States and then in that of the Alliance for Progress.

I have thought about the matter a good deal, and though such statements as that which follow must be quite tentative, it seems that while the North American service of freedom is not free of traits of imperialism, consciously realized or not, the Latin American idea of independence has been nationalized to the point of no return. How to get the two in tandem so that real progress can be made is the conundrum. Certainly many people in Latin America today are better off than they have ever previously been, romantic views of Inca culture to the contrary notwithstanding. But we all know that improvement is no palliative when a people starts from a predominatingly low base. The movement can be kept going only through teamwork, and precisely this is lacking. For instance, the attitude of organized labor toward the poverty of the unorganized has sometimes been far from exemplary in Europe and the United States, but in most of Latin America that I have seen it is crass. The average thoughtful person to the south of us realizes all this and is painfully aware that as a result he remains inefficient in comparison with North Americans, Europeans, and the Japanese. It is obvious to him that none of his major problems—in education, industrialization, agricultural production—are anywhere near being solved.

His great continent is also buffeted by culture-forming forces. Pre-Western civilization bubbles up from the subsoil, for example, in the weird macumba and candomblé religions in Brazil, mixtures of pagan rites and superstition-ridden Christianity. But it is the European culture which counts most. We need to take a candid look at its character. It was first felt when the conqueror in the name of profit arrived side by side with the conqueror in the name of the Cross. We can only dream of what the Church in Latin America would have been like if the liberating, civilizing influence of the Jesuits had been felt everywhere instead of being suppressed. What was it actually sometimes like?

Dr. H. Willis Baxley, who as a special commissioner for the United States visited some parts of the west coast of Latin America during the early sixties of the last century, quotes the comments of a European Catholic observer on the prevalent monastic life:

> It is shocking to find them in the processions, while bearing the cross, banners, and candles, having no respect for their robes, nor for the sainted images they carry, nor for religion, nor for decencies demanded by the occasion. . . . On returning to the church two lines of monks are often formed at the portal, through which the crowds pass into the interior, and there too they indulge themselves without restraint, in jest and sarcasm, compliment and repartee; alluring complacent senoritas, white, black, or copper-colored, and addressing to them shameless gallantries; the spectator, I will not say religious, but merely of proper delicacy, turning away with disgust from such unblushing libertinism.

To such depths did the religious establishments of the Conquistadores tumble, largely perhaps by reason of the close union between Church and state, served during many years by the Inquisition.

The Latin American Church of today is a greatly improved, in some respects certainly a heroic Church. It has very much to its credit in terms of religious communities, of education, of popular catechetics, of laborious concern with poverty. It has great and sometimes eloquent bishops. There are Catholic laymen and lay women who can set for all of us an example in terms of service and religious dedication. Of course there are not enough. But sometimes I wonder these days whether the never-ending controversial cantankerousness which now seems to characterize the

Church in the United States would not profit from exposure to
the kind of men and women I have just signaled out.

Of course it has been greatly assisted for a long time. The
same Dr. Baxley from whose book I have quoted wrote on his
own behalf:

> I have not seen anywhere a dispensary at all comparable with that of
> San Andres [in Lima]. . . . It may be said that the *botica* of San Andres
> Hospital is not surpassed by the apothecary shops of the chief cities of the
> United States. Although admitted—by special courtesy to a stranger—to
> the private apartments of the Sisters of Charity, a sense of propriety for-
> bids a reference to the arrangements for their seclusion, other than to say
> that these are remarkable for the perfection of order . . . characteristic of
> these good Samaritans everywhere. The sisterhood having charge of this
> hospital . . . came from France a few years ago on this special mission of
> benevolence. The Superior, bearing the appropriate name Angelica, and
> who illustrates her title by her good deeds, is a lady distinguished alike
> by her accomplishments, exalted character, disinterested charity, and ad-
> ministrative ability.

What this staunch Protestant New Englander did not realize
is that Sister Angelica represented the post-Revolution *aggiorna-
mento* in France, which despite its sterling virtues and readiness
to serve did not dispel the fascination of the ideology of the Revolution for great parts of Latin America. But in France as elsewhere the Revolution was a bourgeois and intellectualist movement and concerned itself with the abjectly poor scarcely at all.
None of the society-changing doctrines of the Anglo-Saxon world
played any role. On the day of President Vargas's funeral I stood
on the veranda of a hotel in Rio looking out over a deployed
machine-gun company to the tiny military airport from which his
body was to be borne, and beside me was Morton Zabell, University of Chicago professor and poet, who had spent several
years in Latin America as a cultural attaché. "How tragic it is for
this country," he said, "that it has never had the tradition of the
British Constitution and the Federalist Papers. All it had to fall
back on are a feudalism and a revolution both ruined by their
excesses."

And so it was eminently natural that when Eduardo Frei fashioned the theory of Christian Democracy in Chile, it was again a French thinker, Jacques Maritain, who supplied the philosophical background. In part this is no doubt due to the dominance of ideological parties. But probably the main reason is that the doctrine of social change, whether in terms of evolution or revolution, continues to bear the stamp of France and Spain. So also does social conservatism. My Notre Dame colleague John Santos, who probably knows Brazil as well as anybody in the United States, feels that the basic social unit is the family, held together by strong ties. This is also a concept that is French, Portuguese, and Spanish in character. Professor Santos believes that it is difficult to proceed from a pattern of intense feeling of family responsibility to a sense of responsibility for the larger society, and he proposes a heavy infusion of the behavioral social sciences. He may be right. I am not qualified to judge. But we might observe that the United States has never been able to export the theory in the light of which the American labor movement has grown so strong, doubtless because its principal component, collective bargaining, recognizes the entrepreneur as an equal partner. In some parts of Latin America he is simply the enemy.

The United States has of course been no stranger to Latin America in either the philanthropic or religious sense. What the great foundations have accomplished in fostering the improvement of medicine, agriculture, and engineering certainly adds up to one of our great national achievements. Recent improvements in agriculture in Mexico are, for example, really spectacular. Nor will anyone who has observed the educational and pastoral mission of the Church question the very moving sublimity of its purpose and the reality of its achievement. But we have not been able to break the grip of the revolutionary ideology, even with the help of the Peace Corps. Perhaps—there is no use raking over old coals—Catholics were poorly prepared for the mission in Latin American countries. Exceptions having duly been noted, we were prone to append the Fourth of July and Armistice Day to the list of religious feast days. We naively assumed that Latin America was a Catholic continent. There was superstition, yes, but that was infinitely better than no religion at all. We made quite a hullabaloo over Protestant missionary activities, not noting that their occasional successes must have been caused by something. And most failed to see thirteen-year-old girls soliciting on dark streets in Lima, saying *Ave Marias* lest they go home without having earned anything.

Of course we have had our successes, and it would be grave self-abasement not to recognize them. Just to mention one of them, anybody who has seen a little of the work of the sons and daughters of Maryknoll will never easily forget it. I believe that we have greatly improved our relationships with many of the Catholic universities, as we certainly have with students who come to study in this country. I can speak only for Notre Dame, but this university does have loyal alumni in many parts of Latin America. Indeed, one of the principal problems is to find the time to communicate with them. Our priests and religious are no strangers to the *barriadas* and the *campo*. Students from our colleges and universities have worked hard and sacrificially in the blighted rural districts.

But, and we might as well be frank about the matter, much of the Latin American present is disappointing from a North American point of view. Of course we ought to provide more economic assistance, perhaps as it is so often suggested by subsidizing higher prices in world markets for staple agricultural and mineral products. It is naturally apparent that the great industrial and commercial centers of the United States generate so much wealth, even as the research establishments produce so much know-how, that it sometimes really seems that they could foot the bill for almost anything. What our vast military establishment costs makes such a suggestion as that just cited seem almost a penny put into the collection box. But by no means everybody in the

United States thinks in those terms. Young couples and the retired elderly, concerned about modest income and persistent inflation, see life differently. The enormous need which exists in our country to solve the problem of rural and urban poverty— a poverty sometimes as distressing as any one comes upon in Latin America—rests on everyone's heart like a stone. Of course, in spite of all this we could do more for Latin America than we are doing. But we need better public relations. We should be encouraged in our expectation of results. We might advertise more effectively the things which are turning out well. What we hear far too much of is hatred for the United States and its institutions, and that sometimes corrodes the dispositions even of the benevolent.

There are real reasons for thinking that our relationships may deteriorate rather than improve. "Student power" in Latin America is not something new. It has led to complete stoppage of instruction for lengthy periods of time in some of the oldest and most distinguished universities. Of late it has begun to spread to Catholic campuses as well. We have, to be sure, witnessed a little of this ourselves, at the universities of California and Columbia, for example, and there exist on many public and and private campuses groups of students who would like to do as well or better. The point here, however, is that in many parts of Latin America "student power" is anti-American and is becoming increasingly so. Perhaps the Camelot affair has helped to fan the flames, but stupid though it was, one should not attach too much importance to it. I have seriously tried to discuss the problem with student leaders in a variety of places. But the only conclusion at which I have been able to arrive is that we did not speak the same language when there was a discussion of social change or even of life goals. Theirs is traditional Spanish and French social philosophy, which may not be Marxist or syndicalist (though it often enough is) but does attach central importance to these currents of thinking, which of course mean very little in this country. At any rate, it is clear that "student power" has become more and more averse to the United States. Currently some of our able scholars fear that professors in some Latin American universities and research institutions will not be able to share in cooperative enterprises because of the risk of being blackballed by their students.

But all is not lost, and there are certainly things we should think hard about. First—and this seems the most important recommendation I have to make—we should seek earnestly to coordinate our efforts with those of our friends in Europe. The French effort is in some ways the least spectacular, but everything one learns about it is inspiring because it derives from a unique consciousness of the missionary difficulty deriving from the estrangement of the contemporary world from Christianity. Let me quote a few words from a recent bulletin of *Dialogue et Coopération:* "Rio is perhaps the most beautiful city in the world. But it is a place where the joy of living, seven magnificent beaches and the Cariocan temperament do not awaken people specially to their apostolic responsibilities." German assistance, through the great efforts of *Miseror* and *Adveniat,* makes possible very impressive achievements, the Catholic University in Rio, for example, to cite only one. In general, for reasons too complex to analyze here, the Germans have entrée to Latin America, true enough though it be that the secularization of its youth has to some extent dried up the sources of religious vocations. Louvain has not only helped raise the sights for our universities but has created and staffed its impressive network of agencies and centers. I may add finally that although for more years than it is pleasant to remember, Spain did not provide what we could comfortably call companions, the situation has greatly changed. It may even be that Spain will become one of the principal centers for the efforts called for by the Second Vatican Council. This is a very cursory survey. For instance, nothing has been said about Holland or Italy. But the conclusion is evident. We have not begun to think seriously about coordination, and in view of the general political and social circumstances it seems imperative that we do so.

Then, again, if we return to Paul Weiss's maxim and ask ourselves just how having a concern with what is "beyond civilization" can affect the Catholic cooperative mission, I believe we shall find the answer in cherishing the hierarchy of values which well up out of a profound and sincere recognition of Divine goodness. This extends all the way from courtesy to generosity, from love of truth to love of goodness, from giving to receiving. Teaching and exemplifying these is now the mission of Catholic education in all its forms. Without having abandoned recognition of the significant importance of the Aristotelian categories or their embodiments in essential Catholic teaching, our outlook must be in essence Platonic or Augustinian. I think this is what is taking place in Catholic universities when they are aware of their true mission. Of course, with very rare exceptions Catholic universities in Latin America do not resemble those of our country. They are private universities which assume that everybody around is a Catholic, and indeed one will meet excellent ones, perhaps more advanced spiritually than one could easily encounter in our establishments. Still, at the Universidad Católica in Lima one would have to look into every cranny of the academic labyrinth to find the torso of a school of theology. The elaborate religious symbolism of North American Catholic universities is completely missing. On the other hand, the Católica in Santiago has a faculty of theology of high quality, though its housing during the Chilean winter is frigid beyond compare. But the liveliest thing I found anywhere was a young North American priest who uses six texts in teaching religion to students, all of them translations of novels by Soviet authors. These, he said, represented six stages in the quest for God. The students in his jam-packed lecture room seemed to agree. Doubtless in religious teaching we need quite simple things which are also profound—as profound as the innermost rhythm of human life itself.

Finally, if Spanish culture plays so great a part in the complexity of the Latin American mind, it is certainly deeply to be regretted that the study of the great Spanish tradition has declined so markedly. We have been so concerned with the Generalissimo (and let me say that I likewise plead guilty to this) that we have on the one hand lost sight of the quality and importance of Spain's contribution to the store of cultural values and on the other to the situation which will exist when the man who led Moorish troops into Spain will have been the major performer in funeral rites. There is nowhere in the United States a genuinely distinguished center for the study of Spanish culture, and there is likewise none which is dedicated to the survey of the future Spanish landscape. I sadly fear that we shall end up in the political and social sense with some counterintelligence escapade unless preparations somewhat nearly adequate can be made. Meanwhile Spain has become, like Italy, far less antiquated in terms of economic and social structure. It has an impressive number of able and well-trained persons, and can indeed become a pillar of European society. But as I have said, its ideology is not ours. Therefore a Catholic Spain, emancipated from the feudalistic corsets of days gone by, could be an ally of very significant strength. I do not much care where a center of Spanish studies is established. All I am suggesting is that one is vitally needed, particularly in terms of our relationships with Latin America. The bishops of the United States do not need to underwrite it. But if their representatives will join with spokesmen for some Catholic university, and with their appropriate hierarchical colleagues in Spain, I am sure that appeals to foundations here and there would be fruitful.

I shall close with a brief biographical note. In the days of yore when I was a student of comparative literature and not an administrator or a servant of the government of the United States, it was taken for granted that the riches of Spanish culture were one of the great heritages of man. The English seventeenth century and our own nineteenth century lived by it. A great vacuum has been created by reason of our current indifference to it. And this vacuum is one of the reasons why we do not seem quite adult to Latin Americans.

We do not all have to turn into revolutionaries. The history of some kinds of revolution is bleak enough. But we do somehow, in spite of very great difficulties, have to become those who put their shoulders successfully to the same wheel.

THE TWO

AMERICAS: COEXISTENCE,

COMPETITION, OR COOPERATION?

JOHN N. PLANK

I had very much hoped to prepare this essay in a constructive, if not an optimistic, spirit, to present a dispassionate, balanced picture of the inter-American situation as it bears upon our theme, to discuss obstacles to effective inter-American dialogue and to suggest ways in which those obstacles might be, if not surmounted, at least recognized and dealt with sensibly. The tenor of what I had hoped to present was to have been reassuring, positive. If the prospects for an easy transition in Latin America from traditionalism to modernity were not bright, at least the transition could be made less painful through enlightened aware-ness on the part of North Americans of the full dimensions of the developmental challenge in the area and the revision of our atti-tudes and policies to take account of those dimensions. I had ex-pected to conclude, of course, on the strongly affirmative note that is appropriate to volumes like this one.

I regret that I have been unable to prepare that kind of essay. My mood is one of deep pessimism, manifested alternately in a spirit of rage and a spirit of despair. Moods change, of course, and I had hoped that before writing this my mood would have changed sufficiently for me to prepare the kind of discussion I have described. But moods do not take orders from our wills—or at least my moods do not.

Let me begin with a quotation: "I am a man: nothing human can be strange to me," said the Latin comic writer. And I would say rather, "no *man* can be strange to me." I am a man; no other man can I regard as strange. The adjective *human* is as suspicious to me as its abstract substantive *humanity*. Neither the human, nor humanity, neither the simple adjective, nor the substantified adjective, but rather the concrete noun: the man. The man of flesh and bone, he who is born, suffers, and dies—above all, dies—he who eats, and drinks, and plays, and sleeps, and thinks, and lives, the man whom we see and to whom we listen, the true man.

Because there is another thing that is also called man, the subject of not a few more or less scientific digressions. And that is the featherless biped of the legend, the political animal of Aristotle, the social contractor of Rousseau, the economic man of the Manchesterians, the *homo sapiens* of Linnaeus, or, if one prefers, the vertical mammal. That is to say, a non-man.

These are the opening words of Unamuno's *On the Tragic Sense of Life*, familiar to many of us. Are they relevant to our theme? Are we not talking about "The Two Americas"? And with a theme so vast, one that obliges us to rise to giddy levels of abstraction, how can we preoccupy ourselves with man, the individual man of flesh and bone? Are we not obliged to deal with cultural syndromes, cultural change, cultural interaction? Do not these conceptions adequately embrace the man of whom Unamuno speaks? How can we handle this topic—or, for that matter, any social or political or economic topic—without abstracting away from the person?

Moreover, our whole tradition of law, of representative democracy, of the economy in its free and planned aspects, depends upon our transcending the person and the intimately personal. And in another dimension so does science, which is precisely the systematic effort to get beyond the discrete, the idiosyncratic, the individual, to general theory, theory applicable, to be sure—if it is good theory—to the concrete case, but as a scientific theory interested in the concrete case only as a manifestation of a more general phenomenon or force. Social science, striving to emulate to the degree its subject matter permits the pure and natural sciences, has accepted the same kinds of criteria: the quest is after probabilistic laws, with the result that data that cannot be statistically manipulated are of dubious scientific value. The social scientist, in an effort to pattern himself after his brothers in the other sciences, tries rigorously to divide himself into man as scientist and man as citizen; he makes a sharp distinction between fact and value, between theory and practice. Somewhere man— Unamuno's man—gets lost in the interstices of the scientist's activity. But who can doubt that the sciences, both the social and the other, have contributed in measurable ways to man's welfare?

Nevertheless, I find myself driven back, willy-nilly, to Unamuno and his man of flesh and bone, the persons of this world, you, me, all of us. And when I look at the men of this hemisphere, I see human tragedy almost everywhere. Therein lies my second reason for calling your attention to Unamuno and the title of his book.

In profound human terms what is unfolding in this hemisphere is tragic in the Greek sense. Forces are at work, influences are at play, over which individuals as individuals have little or no control and that seem to be leading us on irresistibly, inevitably, toward a humanly appalling future. Tragedy, of course, is intrinsic to the human condition, as anyone of Iberian background knows. But the tragedy implicit in the processes of social change now underway in our hemisphere is of an immensity that we can scarcely comprehend. In Latin America one would have to go back to the Conquest and think of the shattering impact of the

Spanish upon established Indian civilizations to find an appropriate parallel for the emerging impact of technology and modernization upon Latin America today. In the United States—where tragedy is not a congenial concept, it being alien to our consciously held national ethos—tragedy has its roots in hubris: our very success is corrupting, dooming us. In the words of Aeschylus: "For when arrogance blooms it bears the fruit of doomed infatuation, whence it reaps a harvest rich in tears. God stands ready to punish overweening pride: he calls men to a heavy reckoning." And the destinies of us North Americans and our Latin American brethren are fatefully interlocked. For as we rush onward toward an uncertain destiny—altogether inadequately denoted by President Johnson in his State of the Union speech as "new and better shores"—we are an agency of impending Latin American human calamity.

I am shocked to find myself writing such words. They are hyperbolic, are they not? And what place does hyperbole have in reasoned discourse? Moreover, what credence is to be placed in voices of doom, which have been heard at every place and in every time? Man survives; more than survives, he improves. Such at least is the prevailing North American view—and, one immediately adds, the prevailing Soviet view also. But I think that at this time hyperbole may be appropriate, a little doom-saying may be useful. Their purpose is the one so powerfully expressed by Oliver Cromwell: "My brethren, by the bowels of Christ I beseech you, bethink you that you may be mistaken."

Let us get into our theme.

Little purpose would be served by simply repeating the standard rundown of elements that perturb inter-American relations. Most of us are already fully familiar with them: that the United States is rich and powerful while the Latin Americans are poor and weak; that the United States is supremely successful as a nation, and so regards itself, while the Latin Americans are conscious of having failed to keep pace either with us or with the

European world with which they feel a cultural affinity and with which they compare themselves; that the United States affects Latin America monumentally, consciously and unconsciously, deliberately and nondeliberately. What is required of us is a somewhat more probing analysis than we have ordinarily undertaken of what we North Americans are, of what the Latin Americans are, and of how we are to a large extent responsible for the traumatic phase through which Latin America is now passing. There is no intention here to assess praise or blame, to allocate pity or scorn. What we are witnessing is the unfolding of a drama in which there are neither heroes nor villains. There are only suffering human beings.

I depart from three fundamental premises. The first is that North American and Latin American cultures are so radically different that any expectation of really effective understanding, communication, and cooperation between the two parts of the hemisphere is probably illusory. The second is that the United States may be playing fully as much a disruptive as a constructive role in Latin America. The third is that technology and modernization are quite as likely to pull Latin American societies still further apart, to rend them still more severely, as they are to bring those societies toward more significant national community. These propositions are patent nonsense to anyone who thinks of welfare in material terms, who thinks development is to be measured by an expanding gross national product, who believes that man is one among three or four factors of production, who calculates in precise statistical ways the comparative costs and benefits of investments in manpower education and training. These propositions are nonsense, in short, to anyone who accepts current philosophies about what the nature and measurement of development are. They are true—or at least I believe they are true—only at Unamuno's level. They are true only at the level where persons breathe, move, and have their being.

For good and ill the United States is at large in the world, a veritable force of nature. Through deployment of military and economic power, through public and private export of skills and goods, through massive diffusion of North American standards, values, patterns, and judgments, the United States is affecting societies everywhere. If the British gained their empire in a fit of absentmindedness, we of this country have been unsettling the world in a fit of explosive national energy unparalleled in world history, one projected to almost every significant dimension: military, political, economic, social, and cultural.

It is not, of course, our primary purpose to be disruptive; very much to the contrary. We ourselves are inclined to think that our influence has by and large been benign and constructive. Our intent, in any event, is to be helpful, our premise being that what is good for the United States is good for the world, and vice versa. If occasionally we feel ourselves obliged to employ brute or concealed force, we justify our behavior as Hamlet justified his harsh words to his mother: we are cruel only to be kind. To the extent that our activity is comprehended within a conscious, coherent design—most of it is not, for what emanates from us is so manifold as almost altogether to escape meaningful coordination and control, but to the extent that a design exists—it is directed toward protecting the weak peoples of the world against overt and insidious dangers (primarily against what we regard as the truly disruptive force, the Communist powers), promoting peaceful change of a meliorative kind, keeping open the world's options, pointing the way toward a brighter future for mankind.

In few other areas of the world have the effects of this extraordinary eruption of diversified power been more unsettling than in Latin America. To assert, as some Latin Americans have been known to do, that the United States is responsible for Latin America's present ills is unwarranted; to assert, however, that the United States, by the manifestations of its presence there and by the power it radiates from North America, is contributing mightily to current Latin American unrest is undoubtedly true. What

is involved here is something far more portentous than the standard, ideologically motivated charges of North American imperialism, North American alliances with reactionary and conservative
Latin American elements. What is involved are such matters as
the influence of the United States upon what enters the minds
of Latin Americans through the popular press, television, radio,
and the cinema. What is involved are the effects in Latin America
of the introduction of North American modes of industrial organization and technique. What is involved are the consequences of
the work of our foundations and universities, our teachers and
researchers, our voluntary associations, our churches. What is
intruding upon Latin America, what is disruptive, is the North
American style, the North American culture. And North American culture clashes with Latin American culture.

Culture clash is of course the very stuff of world history, as the
Latin Americans themselves must be the first to recognize from
their awareness of the lasting effects of the collision between
Christianity and Islam on the Iberian Peninsula and the similarly lasting effects of the collision between Iberians and Indians
in the New World. But culture clash, while its very long-term
consequences may be beneficial—at least they tend to be so interpreted by the dominant party in the encounter, is always psychologically painful, if not to those of the intruding culture, certainly to those of the society upon which the intrusion is exercised.
Moreover, in the specific Latin American case it is precisely because Latin American culture has not yet harmoniously assimilated the consequences of its two earlier cultural traumas that the
region's present situation is so precarious as it experiences the
North American impact. Were Latin American societies today
strong national communities with integrated, coherent national
cultures, the colossal, multifaceted thrust from North America
would pose a challenge, not a threat. Mexico, one of the very few
Latin American countries that has come to terms with its past,
that has developed a "national idea," illustrates this. Mexico has

the degree of national self-confidence, the degree of institutional and structural resilience, to make possible its acceptance of technology and modernization on what it takes to be its own terms and without sacrifice of its national integrity.

Most Latin American societies, however, lack national coherence, a meaningful "national idea," cultural definition. Unable to find significant consensus about what they as societies have been, are, and want to become, they are today in a situation in which they are incapable of either effectively resisting pressures for change excited by North American influences or adequately accommodating those pressures within existing institutions. What we see in the region, therefore, is increasingly widespread restlessness, gradual crumbling of the traditional order, painful and frequently inept efforts to conceive and construct a new order. At the personal level what we see is anxiety, frustration, fear, uncertainty, doubt, insecurity, suspicion—the whole catalogue of symptoms of spiritual and psychological distress. Have we not always seen that in Latin America? We have. But the situation is much graver today than in earlier times.

Can the United States, which so effectively, if often unconsciously, has worked to undermine the old Latin American order, usefully assist in the process of building a new one? Before we rush to answer that question with the resounding Yes that is in the hearts of all of us to give, let us explore a little more carefully the two cultures that are interacting in this hemisphere.

I have said enough to indicate my own discomfort with a concept as broad as "culture" if the use of it leads us to overlook that our real concern is with persons. I confess that I am particularly unhappy with the notion of "two American cultures." If what is meant by the expression is the North American and the Latin American cultures, then I simply cannot accept it, for there is simply no sense in talking about a single Latin American culture. My concern is less with the bizarre inappropriateness of bracketing, say, Haiti and Argentina within one culture (I should have

thought that Haiti and Argentina have about as much in common
as do Afghanistan and Australia). My concern is rather with the
inappropriateness of suggesting that the peasant in the Colombian Chocó shares a common culture with the MIT-trained economist in the president's office in Bogotá. Indeed, I should at a
minimum break almost every Latin American culture into at least
three fairly sharply definable cultures: that of the great number
of persons in almost all countries who are not yet properly incorporated into the national community; that of the traditional-
nationals; and that of the group of men we are coming to call
"modern." While it is an easier matter to speak of a single North
American culture, the recent colloquy between Eartha Kitt and
Mrs. Lyndon Johnson should alert us to the hazards of speaking
so—if alerting is needed in this winter of our discontents.

Who are we North Americans? Presumably we know ourselves
well—at least every other North American is as well qualified as
I to speak to this question—so I shall run through just a handful
of our characteristics that to me appear to be particularly significant in our encounter with Latin America. And the first, the
most important thing to be said about us as a people, as a culture,
is that we are very self-consciously, deliberately, and proudly a
nation. By far the greater part of us in this country feel strongly
that we are participating members of our national community,
and membership in that community is both meaningful and precious to us. Our history has been a history of conscious nation-
building and nation-maintaining around a core of surprisingly
specific and well-articulated ideas. Those ideas, which to this day
undergird our national consensus, inspirited our predecessors as
they worked this superbly endowed North American continent;
they have inspirited generations of us. The result has been—at
least in our own eyes—stunning national success, a success that
has engendered in us a marked sense of privileged destiny,
national mission, and special responsibility. (Parenthetically, it
has to be acknowledged that foreign observers do not always

reach the same judgment. One jaundiced commentator, quoted by Claude Levi-Strauss, is reported to have said: "The United States is the only country of the world to have passed directly from barbarism to decadence without experiencing civilization.")

We tamed our continent, and we forged ourselves as a people. The two processes are intimately related, for our exhilarating experience in dominating, manipulating, exploiting, and bending to our wills our natural environment conditioned our values as a people. But I would stress even more the vast effort we put into Americanizing ourselves, instilling in ourselves "the American idea," "the American way of life." We used every instrument of inculcation, every engine of assimilation: the public schools, the churches, the political parties, the big-city political machines, the labor market. The Americanization of our children began as soon as they could comprehend; the process of assimilation of our huge numbers of immigrants was carried out massively, rapidly, often enough brutally. *E pluribus unum* applied not only to our federal structure; it applied also to the way we handled the challenge of Americanization. De Tocqueville's perceptive eye detected a sameness about us, and he rightly singled out equality as our dominant value with its concomitant danger of the tyranny of the majority. Our South, whose traditions and structure were only awkwardly compatible with those of the increasingly dominant North, was coerced at frightful human cost into formal acceptance of "the American way." Only our Negroes, American Indians, Orientals, and, in the Southwest, Mexican-Americans were excluded from this process. There were historical reasons for this, but, as we all know, there was also a large element of racism in us. A person who was "different" was to be regarded with suspicion, and if the difference extended to skin color, he was probably an inferior specimen of God's work, if indeed the product of God at all.

We, at least those of us who were white, always felt ourselves to be a free people, free to move about within our expansive frontiers, free also to think, to expound. That latter freedom, however, while real enough, was exercised by almost all of us within rather narrow limits. It simply did not occur to us to think "unthinkable thoughts," for the consensus with regard to the evident superiority of "the American way" was overwhelming.

"The American way" evidently needs no full explication here. It was of course egalitarian. It was also individualistic in that the masterless man, the autonomous person, was its basic and only intrinsically valuable component. It was pluralistic in that it took as a premise that the autonomous persons would in the rational pursuit of his own self-interest enter into cooperative and productive relationships with his fellows for the building and support of appropriate institutions and associations. It was buoyantly optimistic, singularly receptive to innovation at the margin, adaptive, flexible, pragmatic, not much given to the long view, very little given to the pondering of ultimate questions. It assumed the near-inevitability of progress; it prized horizontal and vertical mobility. It was materialistic in taking as the measure of success the extent of domination over the consumption of things. It was heavily infused with the notion that work was virtuous, idleness sin. It had an almost limitless appetite for the bathetic and the maudlin; it had little appreciation for the truly tragic.

Success followed upon success—the American way was seemingly invincible. Domestically, without sacrifice of the freedoms we prized, our standard of living soared to levels never before achieved by man. Internationally we assumed a posture of generally benign tolerance of those peoples less favored than we. Twice we intervened in world wars to "save" the values of Western civilization; twice since 1950 we have intervened in Asian conflicts to "save" the future in that region. And throughout our recent history our industrial and other economic power has been growing, our cultural influence has been expanding, our techniques, devices, methods, and patterns have been exported and picked up around the globe. The influence of the Soviet Union has been modest indeed compared with ours; the influence of the Red Chinese infinitesimal. The North American "national style" is the standard with which all people have to contend, either to emulate it or to resist it.

And yet here at home, and quite suddenly, we find the American way showing deficiencies. We might almost say that the American idea is in danger of being killed by its own success. Increasingly the problems posed by cybernation and automation are upon us, the product of industrial and technical advance. Increasingly our young people, accustomed to affluence, are uninspired by the motivational spur of growing material possessions and consumption. Increasingly our evermore intricate and interdependent patterns of production and distribution impose upon us the need for ever-larger firms, ever-greater governmental regulation and control, ever-greater bureaucratization and anonymity of personal function. The American Dream has been realized to an extent its early formulators could not have imagined, but it may become a nightmare unless we engage in some serious reevaluation, some serious rethinking of premises and goals, some reordering of priorities. We shall have to revolutionize our distributive mechanisms, for example, in order to assure those at the margins of our affluence a decent participation in American life. We shall have to rethink our work ethic to adjust to an economic situation in which cybernation and automation will have taken away meaningful employment opportunities for millions of us. In short, we confront a revolutionary challenge of a kind radically new for us and for mankind. Our problem is that of learning to live justly, meaningfully, with abundance.

How remote that problem is from the problems that face Latin Americans! And how radically different our culture is from theirs! What do we have to offer them? What are the bases of effective interaction between them and us? We are in the process of exporting to them production techniques, organizational devices, behavior patterns, and institutional structures that depended for their successful operation in our own society upon values and conditions that soon must be superseded here and that are only precariously established in Latin America.

Earlier I suggested that any Latin American culture today had to be viewed as comprising at least three subcultures: one that can be called prenational, one that is traditional-national, and one that is modern-national. Until recently only the first two of these existed, and neither of them was easily comprehensible by North Americans. The prenational element, the majority in most countries, could a few years ago have been the subject of Edwin Markham's poem "The Man with the Hoe":

> Bowed by the weight of centuries he leans
> Upon his hoe and gazes on the ground,
> The emptiness of ages in his face
> And on his back the burden of the world.

It is the sight of this man, whether we find him in the countryside or in the slums of the city, that wrenches the heart, that causes the upsurge of rage. It is the sight of him that drives men like Father Camilo Torres to the route of violence. This man himself, of course, is not on the route of violence, and if history is at all a safe guide, he is not likely to take it. Men at the margin, at the absolutely critical margin, do not take gratuitous risks: "Better the devil we know than the devil we do not know." But this man is stirring now, raising his head, looking about, questioning, not certain who he is or what he can expect from an environment that is changing in unpredictable ways. What can we say about his culture, the subject of so many anthropological monographs? What it is important to say about it is that that culture is fundamentally different from the culture of other Latin American groups—although there are symbiotic elements between it and that of the others—and that it is profoundly distinct from the culture the Peace Corps volunteer or the agronomist from the Midwestern university brings with him. The world remains broad and alien, in many cases even broader and more alien than the world of his father.

Let me quote from a succeeding stanza of Markham's poem which seems to be directed to the second of our subcultures, the traditional-national:

> O masters, lords and rulers in all lands,
> Is this the handiwork you give to God?
> This monstrous thing distorted and soul-quencht?
> How will you ever straighten up this shape;
> Touch it again with immortality;
> Give back the upward looking and the light;
> Rebuild in it the music and the dream . . .

The traditional-national does not conceive his role as that of agent of redemption. His values are the product in large part of 450 years of use and abuse of men with hoes. This traditional-national still occupies most seats in national congresses, still plays most roles in commerce and the professions, still dominates the land, still confines his activity on behalf of the disfortuned to rhetoric and charity. He does not communicate effectively with the men with hoes because he does not see them as men: his world and their world are often enough physically separate, always psychologically separate. He is disturbed now, though, for change is in the air, and change is always threatening. The institutions and values of which he is the inheritor and which guide his beliefs and actions seem less adequate, less enduring, today than they did yesterday.

In terms relevant to modernization and technology this man is not only an anachronism; he is an obstacle. He has his immensely attractive qualities, but they are not characteristics that make him a constructive nation-builder. He carries within him something unique in this world, a transmuted Iberian cultural strain. Iberian culture, for all that it is not static and not precisely definable, is *sui generis*, not Western European, even less North American. In those aspects of it that interest us here, Iberian culture as per-

petuated in the Latin American environment is incompatible
with the North American culture that supported our own fore-
fathers.

All of us who have read Iberian and Latin American history
know how this distinctive culture evolved syncretically out of
interaction between Christian and Moorish elements on the
Iberian Peninsula during more than six hundred years. The culture has elements of true greatness, true nobility. Its appreciation
for the tragic, the contingent, the fortuitous in man's affairs; its
recognition that man is only precariously placed on this earth; its
enhanced awareness of the worth of the person, particularly one's
own person; its emphasis upon dignity, pride, style; its prizing of
the *hazaña*, the great feat, the enterprise upon which one willingly, recklessly risks all in pursuit of nothing more substantial
than glory—these are values in whose absence mankind would
be the poorer. And yet these are not values that conduce to effective and efficient political systems, coherent economic development, wholesome social dispensations. Particularly in Latin
America, where this cultural syndrome was imposed on a human
base of Negro slavery and Indian servitude and tied to a most
unfortunate landholding and land-use system, the consequences
have been altogether deplorable. Moreover, while we legitimately
stress the positive aspects of the Iberian-Latin American character, it has its negative side too: suspiciousness, envy, the notion
that life is a zero-sum game in which one man's gain necessarily
must entail another man's loss.

Can it be said that we North Americans communicate effectively with Latin America's traditional-nationals? For certain purposes and at certain levels it is evident that we do. We have been
dealing with them for generations in world councils; we have
been dealing with them commercially; we have read their books
and they have read ours. But is there real understanding between
them and us? Scales of priorities between the two cultures are
incompatible: much of what we prize they despise, and vice

versa. Do I put the matter too strongly, too dichotomously? Probably. My purpose, though, is only to highlight the superficiality of most of our associations with these Latin Americans.

It is within this traditional-national cultural group that the greatest conscious resistance to modernization and technology is to be found. And this group will not surrender its perquisites and power willingly—nor, I suspect, is it capable of transforming itself. Why should it? Would we, we North Americans, behave in ways different from the way this group behaves were we to find ourselves in its position? The only remotely comparable situation we have confronted, namely, the full incorporation of our Negro population, is being accomplished only over our strenuous resistance.

There is finally the small, but growing, minority of those whom we are coming to call "modern men." Again note must be taken of the breakdown of communication between groups in Latin American societies. "Modern men"—those who have absorbed North American modes and models or who are working hard to devise more appropriate Latin American variants of those modes and models—are out of effective touch with both the other elements I have been discussing. They sit in government planning offices and plan, but the implementation of the plans, which is the presumed task of the traditional-nationals, does not take place. They devise means for the redemption of the marginal ones, as Father Roger Vekemans refers to the least-favored group, but they have no effective means of establishing living rapport with those marginal ones. They are, many of them, impressive human beings: dedicated, self-sacrificing, capable, well trained, imaginative, bold. But their task is almost an impossible one. Frustrated, some of them are tempted toward the technocratic-authoritarian route of social change, but this route also brings its frustrations as a result of the inadequately articulated structure of most Latin American societies.

We North Americans communicate easily with these "modern

men," and many of us deal directly with no other kinds. We may deceive ourselves into thinking that we are in touch with the real Latin America when we are in touch with them. We should recognize, as they most assuredly do, that they are not representative of their fellow Latin Americans; we should also be aware that the cultural environments within which they work have very little in common with North American environments.

Conflict and suffering are intrinsic parts of the whole process of Latin America's contemporary transformation. The traditional-nationals are not prepared to let most of the society's population enter into the national community; the "modern men" are under constant attack and harassment from left and right; the pace of change is excruciatingly slow; and because of inadequate institutions, lack of consensus, and absence of guidelines, development itself is erratic, uneven, disjointed, and disappointing. There is not, nor can there be, a steady surge toward determinate national goals or even in determinate national directions.

How does the United States fit into this picture? I have already indicated that I believe really close cooperation between them and us to be so difficult as to be impossible. That case can be made without reference to the historical record, which has caused residues of deep anxiety and suspicion toward us among many Latin Americans. It can be made without reference to the shrill cries of the Communists or professional anti-Americans.

Realistically considered, the prospect is for less rather than more cooperation in the future than in the past. We should have no difficulty in understanding why this is so. In the first place, Latin Americans are coming rapidly to realize the limited relevance of our experience, our attitudes, our exportable knowledge to their own situation. Secondly, modernization in Latin America means not only industrialization and urbanization, not only increased and improved production and distribution; it means independence. And independence in Latin America today has only one referent: independence from the United States. Political and economic independence, to be sure, but also cultural independence. As a Latin American friend expressed it to me: "Ni con ni contra sino sin los Estados Unidos (Neither with nor against but without the United States)."

And is that position not thoroughly comprehensible? Do we need to be reminded that what we North Americans have altogether lacked in our dealings with Latin Americans is anything approaching a feeling of equality or humility? We, whether representing our government, or our world of business, our university community, our churches, our voluntary associations—for all that our purpose is solely to "do good"—have moved around Latin America with an air of conscious or unconscious superiority, either benignly paternalistic or arrogantly assertive.

In the academic worlds of Mexico, Chile, Argentina, increasingly in Peru and Colombia, one detects a murmur of protest on the part of scholars against working with North American collaborators. My guess is that the good ladies of the League of Women Voters who for so many years have worked so valiantly trying to teach Latin American women the virtues and skills of democratic organization and government are going to encounter greater and greater difficulty in gaining access to Latin America during the years ahead. My firm belief is that North American trade union organizations will soon be struggling to maintain a Latin American foothold; their claim on Latin American labor will be largely forfeited. I think the role of North American churchmen—whether Catholic or Protestant—is going to diminish rapidly. All of this strikes me as being wholesome.

Let us be altogether honest with ourselves: there has been something psychologically degrading to the Latin Americans in the way we have customarily interacted with them, whether in the cultural sphere or any other. Even if all that we have conveyed to them of our wisdom through our preaching, chastising, and cajoling has been useful and relevant—and we know, of course, that much of it has not been—the relationship has been intrinsically an unhealthy one.

Coexistence rather than cooperation, therefore, is the likely pattern in the future. That does not mean, naturally, that United States influence in Latin America will rapidly and significantly diminish. First, that influence cannot diminish so long as Latin American newspapers are overwhelmingly dependent upon our wire services; so long as *The Reader's Digest, Time,* and *Good Housekeeping* are journals of mass circulation in the region; so long as the United States sets the styles in consumption goods; so long as production and marketing techniques developed in the United States maintain their appeal. But the tone of the relationship will change.

As for us in the United States, can we be wise enough, relaxed enough, to back away from Latin America, increasingly to let them ask their own questions, define their own problems, formulate their own programs, make their own decisions and mistakes? That Latin America can use our technical and financial resources is not in question; of course it can. I am not persuaded, however, that the Latin Americans need—or even particularly want—our patronizing concern, our unwonted interference in areas where our ignorance is exceeded only by our assurance. We are told that when Senator Robert Kennedy visited Mexico City, he saw on a wall the slogan "Dollars si, Yanquis no." There is a great deal to be said for that proposition.

Much more suffering, turmoil, and tragedy lie ahead for Latin America. I do not see how that projection can be avoided. There are few grounds for optimism that massive unrest, painful social frictions, some violent conflict, will not characterize the region during the years ahead as its societies seek their national definitions, their national identities. The real challenge in Latin America was put poignantly a couple of years ago by a Latin American bishop. "The problem of Latin America," he said, "is not to have more but to be more."

What is Latin America to *be?* That is their challenge, not ours. But is not the bishop speaking to us also? Is not our problem also precisely that to which the bishop pointed? Let us look, then, to the beam in our own eye.

THE POLITICAL IDEOLOGY

OF POLITICAL ECONOMY

IRVING L. HOROWITZ

The burgeoning literature on economic development holds to the classical picture of economic evolution as an autonomous system of growth. A prejudice favoring Adam Smith still supersedes the pragmatic acceptance of John Maynard Keynes. This essay will not dwell on those numerous places where theorists on economic development ought to permit some role for government planning in the growth of underdeveloped nations. Rather, it will point up some assumptions that United States policy exhibits in treating the problem of economic growth in underdeveloped countries, assumptions that show a penchant for treating policy formulation in underdeveloped areas as a form of therapy for sick, immature, or retarded colonies, incapable of being trusted to grow freely.

The Metaphysical Bottleneck

The problem for most development theorists is to find out why economic growth has not occurred and to provide these moribund or recalcitrant communities with the tools for "takeoff."[1] In the process they have refined the intellectual sport of searching for missing variables. The search often fatalistically locates a bottleneck. Policy predilections follow which place a strong emphasis on removing a bottleneck to permit what then becomes automatic growth. The current competition among economic theorists thus reduces itself to identifying obstructions which, when removed, will release underdeveloped countries from stagnation and send them into a takeoff state leading to self-sustaining growth.

Guidelines suggested include such diverse notions as increased capital inputs for existent economic infrastructures, capitalization of agriculture and agricultural cooperatives, the extension of marketing facilities, increased agricultural credit, labor intensity technology for the industrial sector, the broadening of the economic middle sector, the development of the ethos of an industrial entrepreneurship, and the injection of achievement motivation among broad strata of the population. To vitalize the developmental process, support of marginal groups with supposed predispositions toward economic development is solicited. But whether such middle sectors can or will support reform in the area of fiscal, administrative, and tax structures is more assumed than demonstrated. For since the rate of inflation is more certain than the rate of profit, risk capital often "flees" into the waiting arms of enterprises in the cosmopolitan centers.

The defining characteristic of latter-day laissez-faire thinking is that once the correct devices are set in motion in any underdeveloped nation, rapid development must follow. The influence of classical economic theory is therefore not quite tucked away under talk of planning or mobilization and is far from being confined to academic environments; on the contrary, it is rapidly becoming the basic principle of United States foreign-aid programs, expressed in Latin America through the International Monetary Fund.

Economists writing in the area of Latin American studies often argue the case that the United States should aid underdeveloped nations, seek maximum yields on capital inputs, and plow back the difference between that capacity and the resources of the country involved. Capital reinvestment could in its proper framework then do the job of economic development. These economists maintain that political and military factors, which are often involved in foreign-aid programs, obscure this pure theory of economic value.

The Depoliticization of Foreign Aid

Increasingly, some of the most powerful admonitions for the depoliticization of foreign-aid programs comes not from the ideological enemies of colonialism but from economic analysts, the custodians of international financial largesse. Economists, in contrast to political scientists, believe that aid for development should be apolitical, because for them economic growth takes place independently of politics.[2]

Underlying the propensity to separate economic from political development are two factors: a predisposition to idealistic interpretation of how change is brought about and institutionalized, and a belief that expertise is best served when separated from politics. Two analysts who have this frame of reference are David McClelland and Seymour Martin Lipset. Achievement motivation, McClelland feels, is endowed with powers of self-perpetuation, and rises by degrees to form an architectonic of values that descend finally upon human agents who are thus rendered participants in development. McClelland's analysis is carried further by Lipset, who sees the notion of achievement as related to marginality, which in turn is linked to a creative form of elite behavior. This nonpolitical discharge of social energy also enhances development by centering on creative elites who can proceed to the manipulation or utilization of the masses.[3] What is actually implied is that deviance issues into entrepreneurial behavior; what is excluded from consideration is that deviance may just as readily stimulate revolutionary behavior.

The conventional assumption here is that if a nation can be induced to alter its values, social development will flow simply from reshaping traditional values into modern ones. Indeed, the very existence of a political apparatus is considered something of an encumbrance for economic development. There is a tendency to cling to a concept of achievement as something which pervades a social fabric outside political machinery. Instead of approaching "achievement" as a stimulant to or an outcome of political mobilization, it is used as a psychological expression of antipolitique.[4]

Latin American economists, for their part, have also sought after an explanation for their continental economic plight which would distinguish economic from political remedies. This is characteristic of Raúl Prebisch, and it defines much of the work of Economic Commission for Latin America (CEPAL) and various United Nations commissions.[5] Thus, while the demands of Latin American economists are often more radical than those of their North American counterparts, the theoretical assumptions with which they operate are quite similar. Indeed, certain notions of how finished industrial goods show a propensity to increase more rapidly than farm goods was actually borrowed from populist economic thinking current at an earlier stage of United States history.

The Transition from Capitalism to Feudalism

Antipoliticization of economic theory has led as a side effect to the justification of neocolonialism. The neocolonial phenomenon has four features: (1) the dominance of United States private capital in the investment sector of the developing Latin American economies; (2) the exploitative character of this domination; (3) the bartering of goods rather than the capitalization of the trade mechanism, that is, the exchange of cheap raw materials for costly manufactured products; and (4) the consistent effort of the United States to prevent domestic economic autonomy within Latin America. The presence of these and other factors (such as the United States voting against the "Conference of the seventy-seven" at Geneva, 1963) indicate that economic rallying and value reorientation can only accompany rather than replace decisions about national development and autonomy.

The magnitude of United States participation in external financing is significant. It is the prime investor. For the period between 1955 and 1961 the Economic Commission for Latin America (ECLA) has calculated that for Argentina, Bolivia, Chile, Paraguay, and Uruguay, taken as a group, net external financing comprised 12.2 percent of gross domestic investment. For Central America, Cuba, and the Dominican Republic, taken as a group in the same period, this percentage reached 17.6 percent. In Brazil it reached 18 percent.[6] The data fluctuate from period to period, but these figures give some indication of how important the external sector has been in the formation of capital in Latin America, and how significant to this sector has been the United States as the prime investor.

The preponderant influence of foreign private capital in Latin America comes about as a result of its selective investment strategy. These investments amounted to 5,765 million dollars for the period between 1951 and 1962. Most of the terminal use of this capital flow was determined by a relatively small number of United States firms. Such businesses performed an inordinately large role in determining the overall investment pattern during this most critical period in Latin American-United States relationships.[7]

Direct United States public capital investment during this period had the important function of reinforcing patterns of oligopolistic participation. Of the total, 33 percent was in the petroleum sector, 31 percent in the manufacturing sector, and 12 percent in the mining sector. The ECLA report pointed out that

the heavy expenditure in the extractive activities reflected the spectacular growth in international demand and prices of primary materials so pronounced in international markets for more than a decade after 1946. In the case of manufacturing the rationale involved a desire to benefit from the growth of domestic demand in countries where population and per capita income levels were rising rapidly after the war, and where preferential tariff treatment was often accorded to the industrial sector.[8]

In other words, between 1951 and 1962 United States investment was heavily concentrated in those sectors strategic to the private investor. Hence it had a more pervasive influence in hemispheric economic affairs than even the overall absolute figures might suggest. Investment in agriculture, social services, or in other parts of the economic infrastructure was negligible. Neither was the investment for heavy goods exports particularly significant, except in those cases where it was part of a complex international cost-accounting strategy.

There are characteristics of United States direct investment in Latin America which make clear the strategic importance of that investment over and above its purely monetary aspect.

First, the size, experience, and financial-technological sophistication of large United States corporations in Latin America often make them the leading investment sector in particular countries, which results in their determining the structure and the direction of investment patterns. Indigenous entrepreneurs were often simply unable to take much initiative, especially in research and technological innovation.

Second, United States foreign assistance was highly concentrated in a few areas. Venezuela, Brazil, to a lesser extent Argentina and Chile, have been the major recipients of foreign aid. Assistance was also distributed unevenly among various sectors within each of these countries. In this way the flow of United States public capital intensified already accelerated patterns of interregional and international income and inequality. Foreign imperialism stimulated patterns of internal imperialism by building up an urban complex and a business class which could reduce the countryside to a one-crop cash product and utter political and economic dependency.

Third, concentration of United States direct investment in the areas of extractive goods for export, such as petroleum, copper, and iron ore, lent itself to a situation where profits could be gained directly from income realized on these exports. No new capital or labor investments are necessary in the extractive fields. This in combination with the concentration of manufacturing investment in those countries where concessions were more easily obtained from pliable local governments meant that United States corporative enterprise was able to minimize restrictions on its ability to garner profits abroad.[9]

Fourth, analysis of United States influence in Latin America entails evaluating the relative participation of this United States investment in its total international investment picture. In order to blunt the argument that neocolonialism exists in Latin America, it is fashionable to point out that the total United States investment in Latin America lags behind the array of investment in Western Europe and Canada. In theory the areas of Western Europe and Canada are far more subject to United States penetration than is Latin America, and therefore, by extension, United States holdings in Latin America, even if they are relatively important to the Latin Americans, are relatively unimportant to the United States. American investment patterns are said not to require a theory of imperialism, since then one would have to argue that the United States colonizes Western Europe as well.[10]

While the factual content of this assertion is correct, the conclusions drawn are misleading. The value of United States holdings in Latin America in 1962 amounted to 8,472 million dollars, or almost one-fourth of the United States total of 37,145 million dollars in direct foreign investment. This is a sizable regional investment proportion by any standard. Moreover, Latin American investment is located in a politically and economically unstable region, where United States power, the freedom of action it enjoys in the region, and the fact that local economic power is restricted by an absence of economic freedom to compete in the

international marketplace, stand in marked contrast to the relationships between the United States and Western Europe, where
investment has not reduced Europeans to dependency. Nor has
economic penetration led Canada into a dependency relation to
the United States.

In other words, the political variable—the relationship between
degrees of national autonomy, independence in political decision-
making, and allocation of resources—is highly significant. There
is a difference between economic investment in a politically self-
directed nation and in one where economic penetration becomes
a means of inducing political dependency, with political decision-making is increasingly oriented toward preserving and
enhancing the influence of the foreign investors. Thus, United
States investment in Great Britain is a relatively nonpolitical act.
United States investment in Chile is not. The chief difference is
that in the former case the conditions of the investment are determined by the receiving nation, whereas in the latter the political
structure is made to protect the investor nation, whose interests
replace indigenous interests as primary. Further economic development for Latin American nations in such a case involves political nationalism and political reorientation, even if an economic
cost need be paid at first.

When one compares the amount of United States investment
in Latin America with that in the rest of the underdeveloped
areas, the strategic importance of Latin America for United States
private enterprise becomes clear, and the relationship between
this importance and factors of international power differentials
also becomes manifest. One of the main architects of United
States Latin American policy has put the matter bluntly and
correctly: in the area of economic relations "The United States,
of course, has a choice, which Latin America does not."[11]

Fifth, we might expand a point already touched on. The ECLA
report omits the fact that the centrality of United States investment in Latin America allows the United States to have a political

role in each of the Latin American nations that it would not possibly acquire in other areas of the world even given an equivalent amount of investment. The absence of local forms of political legitimacy and the shutting off of huge portions of the population from political participation allow the legitimation of an outside source and authority, namely, United States entrepreneurial interests. Therefore, the concept of a primarily economic solution to the Latin American problem tends drastically to underestimate the degree to which investment becomes politically determined.

Sixth, the functional psychology of North American entrepreneurial interests operating in Latin America has to be brought into account since the "investment climate" is fundamental. The following extract from a report presented by Sheldon Schreiberg for the joint Congressional subcommittee on Inter-American Economic Relations is most instructive in this connection. The references are specifically to Central America, since the report was based largely on interviews with United States businessmen in that area. By extension, however, it serves as a barometer of current United States attitudes toward the political structures of the hemisphere.

Political stability, not democracy, I should stress is the import criteria. The U. S. investor is not concerned with abstract political theory. Any government approximating or to the right, of our own politically is acceptable. The impressive record of 35 years of political and economic stability in Nicaragua under Somoza family rule proves a definite asset to its industrial promoters. In the last year, Guatemala has experienced a slowdown in the number of investments it is attracting relative to the other [Central American common] market partners and much of this decline is attributable to widely publicized government instability and Castroite guerilla activity.

The majority of U. S. businessmen in the area believe that the region is now entering a more mature era in this respect. One representative firm believes that—". . . gradual evolution is . . . taking place principally because of the tremendous concentration and increasing importance which the economic sphere . . . has recently taken in terms of the total scheme of things. It has recently been said that businessmen in Central American [sic] will no longer put up with wild political gyrations. . . . There is no question that the economic and business element is beginning to exert more . . . of a stabilizing influence on the political and social life of Central America."[12]

The position of the overseas entrepreneur is usually more important than comments by State Department developmentalists. The financial climate desired by the overseas investor is considerably within his power to create. He is not simply a cog in a vast machine, but in fact provides a lever, usually a considerably larger lever than he can use within his own advanced society. Not only does he command and manipulate wealth and the means to get wealth, but this wealth is far less challenged or subject to economic counterweights in Latin America. The power of oligopolistic combines is thus far less subject to market correction through competition than it would be in the United States proper.

Seventh, it should occasion little surprise that United States corporations seek maximum control over their overseas investment portfolios. This involves freedom from local government control in Latin America. Clearly, these are the same goals that are desired, but less well achieved, within the United States. We should not be surprised that, given normal business impulses, American firms and individual entrepreneurs order their investment priorities, not according to an international long-run welfare ideology, but rather in terms of short-run profitability. The argument for the dominance of United States capital within Latin American economies as a pillar of neocolonialism rests on the recognition that United States business and its overseas executives work out their economic goals according to norms of their own making. They operate in a structural setting in which no significant system of countervailing power exists. Where indigenous development is consciously sought by Latin American nations, the power quotient of opposing agents rises enormously. But the sense of responsibility on the part of overseas investors does not show any corresponding increase.

Moreover, a new approach in overseas investment procedures involves the bypassing of local capital. This can be done through appeal to the "modernizing military." Investment poured into military channels simultaneously holds down the level of United States government financial investment in civilian projects in underdeveloped areas in Latin America, while it avoids the possibility that a local or national bourgeoisie will become countervailing agents, openly challenging United States corporate investment. This latest application of the broadly political approach to overseas economic development is by extension also a noneconomic approach, since it rests on funneling support directly to a military network within the nation, which in turn seeks to stabilize a regime.

A Latin American Trial Balance Sheet

The mere presence of a significant amount of capital investment in Latin America does not in itself prove such investment is more to the interest of the United States than it is to the interest of Latin America. More telling are statistics on net balances of United States capital investment transactions in Latin America during recent years. These are hardly encouraging from the Latin American point of view. According to the ECLA study on external financing in Latin America, net capital flows, including both direct investments and portfolio transactions to Latin America, for the 1951–1963 period amounted to 6.9 billion dollars. The net-income transfers from Latin America to the United States— 95 percent of which derive from interest and dividends paid to private United States firms and individuals—totaled 11.9 billion dollars. This leaves a net balance of nearly 5 billion dollars flowing into the United States.[13] For this extended period the direct effect of United States investment on Latin America's balance of payments, one of the area's most crucial developmental problems, is decidedly negative for Latin America.

The effects of this imbalance between capital export and import were mitigated by a surplus on the public or foreign-aid side of the capital flow ledger in favor of Latin America, but this surplus amounted to only 3.3 billion dollars. This still left a residue and net balance of 1.7 billion dollars in favor of the United States.[13] In other words, capital transfers had the effect of increasing rather than decreasing the debt of the nations of Latin America. Further, United States government funds which were used to mitigate this debit oftentimes were, not in the form of direct cash expenditure or cash flow, but in the form of credit memoranda entitling the Latin American nations to buy further from United States corporate enterprises. Thus, while the government funds mitigated the effects of the negative balance of payments, they also accentuated the powerful position of United States corporate life in the area.

It could be argued that the indirect benefits of United States private and public investment outweigh its negative consequences on the Latin American balance of payments. One way of evaluating these indirect effects is to determine the trend in the relative portion of Latin American export earnings from the United States that has to be utilized for income remittances and service payments on public and private debts in the United States. In other words, is Latin America progressively paying more or less for the use of United States capital in relation to what it earns through its exports to the United States, its principal partner in world exchange and world trade? ECLA studies reveal that by 1963 Latin America was using one dollar in four earned by export sales to the United States for investment income remittances and capital repayment, that is, public and private debt service. Moreover, the trend in this ratio has steadily increased since 1951. The ratio of Latin American obligations to the United States for investment earnings and capital servicing in terms of export earnings in the United States between 1951 and 1963 are as follows:

1951 (17.8%)	1958 (19.6%)
1952 (16.2%)	1959 (20.4%)
1953 (16.1%)	1960 (22.6%)
1954 (17.9%)	1961 (26.3%)
1955 (22.2%)	1962 (27.4%)
1956 (22.2%)	1963 (27.1%)
1957 (24.0%)	

Any discussions of net balances of United States capital transactions in Latin America should also include the fact that the relationship between United States corporate interests and weak Latin American governments favors the overseas corporate establishments and provides many opportunities for paper inflation of the book value of investments and paper deflation of profit remittances abroad.

The existence of statistical manipulation does not lead to an expected overevaluation of United States investment holding in Latin America, since there is also a downward manipulation for tax purposes, that is, the undervaluing of both book value and profits. But then they actually underestimate the difference between United States earnings on its capital inputs in Latin America and the magnitude of these inputs. A final argument respecting the exploitative character of United States capital flow in Latin America has to do with the qualitative composition of this flow and the backwardness it produces within the Latin American economics. Those that seek to defend United States economic interests in the Latin American area usually prefer not to discuss the qualitative aspects of capital flow, but rather tend to draw up superficial lists of benefits that might accrue to Latin American nations from the presence of foreign capital.

From the perspective of the United States Department of State the importance of North American investment in Latin America is reduced to the following terms: first, Latin American governments receive 15 percent of all revenues from United States companies; second, profit remittances by United States companies are only about one-half as large as their tax payments to Latin American governments; third, about 75 percent of the gross revenue of United States companies is paid out to large Latin American factor resources, a type of calculation susceptible to a great variety of statistical manipulation in terms of the data that are put in; fourth, United States companies are held to provide jobs for over 600,000 Latin Americans; and fifth, United States companies have contributed as much as one billion dollars annually to the Latin American economies.[14]

Such figures tend to obscure the fact that United States investment is concentrated, first, in petroleum, which has minimal linkage to domestic economy (except in the form of taxes) since it is highly capital-intensive, employs small cadres of labor, and has its biggest cost outlays in the import of foreign machinery, equipment, and technical personnel; second, in import-substitution manufacturing, which is concentrated in the production of luxury items and consumer durables priced beyond the means of most Latin Americans who are therefore not helped by this form of overseas aid; and third, in mining, such as the copper industry of Chile or the tin industry of Bolivia, which employs only small units of labor and is oriented toward the raw material needs of the highly developed countries. These three investment areas thus afford very little opportunity for an internal expansion of the monetary labor force.

The figures cited by the Department of State thus mean little without interpretation. They obscure the fact that United States investment tends to intensify rather than alleviate income inequalities within the domestic economies of Latin America.

Selective investment procedures also reinforce the tendencies of Latin American economies to maintain a single crop system in order to maximize dollar yields—and these two factors, in tandem, serve to imperialize national relations. The fact that the latter has been of far less strategic importance to the United States than the former has been to Latin America is another instance of why one must take into account concepts of social stratification and power differentials in analyzing the economic relationships between the United States and Latin America. The view is very different once the qualitative aspect of overseas aid is taken into account, not simply because one can alter one's perspective from a North American to a Latin American view, but rather because there are structural consequences of certain kinds of aid over and above the amounts of financing involved.

One does not have to explain the exploitative use of foreign capital in Latin America in terms of a frenzied drive for expansion on the part of a United States commercial community, or in terms of some Machiavellian transformation that commercial interests undergo when they step on foreign soil. Acting as business firms do, endeavoring to maximize both short-run profits and long-run advantages within the economic and political environment in which they operate, powerful United States firms do not require any magical leverage in order to be exploitative in Latin America. Doing what comes naturally in an environment in which they have a monopoly of choice as well as a functional monopoly of capital is itself often sufficient to guarantee positive results for the overseas investor.[15]

The Transition from Old Colonialism to New Imperialism

Let us return to the problem of how the capitalist structures of Latin America are likely to confront, not rising expectations, but falling profits and eventual national fragmentation. Basic to this position is that the Latin American economies are not simply underdeveloped, but capitalist in character. They tend to be fragmented and lose out to the superior organization, research, and resource situation found in fully advanced capitalist nations. Latin American states are not feudal economies tending to become more capitalistic. The role of the foreign neocolonial power, moreover, is, not simply to further the stagnation process, but even to reverse historical tendencies exhibited in the European economies between the sixteenth and nineteenth centuries, a process underwritten by the very nature of American aid programs.

Modernization is in fact a new aspect of colonialism. This aspect cannot be reduced to a traditional imperialist frame of reference. The principal aim of neocolonialism in an age of modernization is not the export of capital as a means of exploiting cheap labor overseas. It is rather that of concentrating investment at home to expand production in the metropolitan country and of seeking to dominate the overseas markets on which it establishes a trade monopoly by a variety of means. Investment itself becomes a key instrument employed in pursuance of this goal. Bluntly put, colonialism and imperialism are no longer complementary to, but rather distinct from, each other. The colonial era required the buildup of a cosmopolitan center in the underdeveloped area because it involved the physical presence of foreign administration. The new imperialism requires only the export of capital to monopolize labor, while it expands production in the metropolitan center by importing raw materials. Colonialism can be resolved by various national liberation movements. But this resolution may not of itself settle the issue of dependency and imperialist control. It may in fact merely allow the dominating nation to develop effective means of control from abroad and thus obliterate the need for physical presence.

Where the United States has had an inherited political leverage, it has not been above exercising frank control of market mechanisms in Latin America to the advantage of its own commercial groups and with the effect of retarding industrial development of the importing country. A clear-cut example of this process was the reciprocal trade agreement with Cuba that existed between 1934 and 1959, that is, until the Cuban Revolution. Under that agreement Cuban import duties were lowered on many United States items. It was stipulated that duties were not to be raised on a longer list of items; strict limitations were put on the application of internal taxes on goods originating in the United States, and exchange control by the Cuban government was prohibited. Cheap United States goods flooded into Cuba under this shield, and almost all possibility of import-substitution industrialization in Cuba was ruled out. While reaping the benefits of a protected sugar market in the United States, Cuba nevertheless became an economic satellite in the very process of trading off its sugar production for imported finished goods. The barter arrangement, then, had a built-in disadvantage. The Cuban sugar economy was protected only insofar as an import-substitution industrialization model was inhibited.

Elsewhere in Latin America the "feudalization" of trade devices was more indirect. Its main elements were as follows:

First, the wedding of the Latin American raw materials export sector to markets in the United States. These exports, coming from countries which are essentially single-crop economies, were characteristically inelastic both in their price system and income distribution. Their production and price control have also been led internationally by cartels such as the petroleum industry.

Second, dependence of the Latin American economy on the United States for manufactured and capital goods served to rigidify these inelasticities because price variabilities of these basic products are significantly greater than they are in the raw material sector.

Third, deterioration in the terms of trade with respect to Latin America is now characteristic. This has meant that when a Latin American nation has entered into a rapid stage of developmental takeoff, it meets the barrier of balance of payments deficits. This was the case in Argentina during the thirties, and is presently very much the case with Mexico. Import-substitution industrialization as an economic device has not been sufficient to overcome this problem, for after a certain stage this kind of substitution process develops its own import gap.[16]

Fourth, where United States capital dominates the industrial sector, this capital is not utilized to stimulate competition within the United States corporate structure. These investments help supply restricted domestic markets and create international imbalances by tariff and import restriction barriers, or they may contribute to an advantageous international division of industry only within the internal structure of corporate life. In any case they do not threaten the industrial hegemony of the United States in the Western Hemisphere.

The Political Sources of the New Imperialism

Socialist critics of the new imperialism in Latin America tend to assume that the chief reasons for United States economic penetration are to ward off the formation of socialist governments and to prevent revolutionary change. The reasoning underlying this view is roughly this:

First, sustained economic development is only possible in Latin America through the procurement of economic and political autonomy. Revolution and the socialist reorganization of Latin American societies are the only means to achieve this autonomy.

Second, revolution and socialism are perceived as threats to United States interests in Latin America not only because nationalization of industry and mining sectors is likely but also because the United States will have to do without a source of cheap and vital raw materials.

Third, since United States policy is ultimately subservient to its own internal commerical interests and the international corporations and cartels, it must maintain the status quo in Latin America, even to the point of using armed intervention.

But this view is oversimplified. It is true that the United States government is subject to pressure from vested interests. Its reaction to nationalization schemes in the petroleum industry of Bolivia, Mexico, Brazil, Argentina, and Cuba gives credence to this view. Its reaction to the confiscation of United States agricultural interests in Guatemala strengthens this interpretation. Similarly, after Guatemala in 1954 it can hardly be argued that the United States does not exhibit hostility to the establishment of an expropriational regime in any of the Latin American republics. The connection, however, between the protection of specific American interests and antirevolutionary politics is often ambiguous. Ideological factors possess a degree of autonomy. Devotion to free enterprise is not always the same as devotion to a particular American industry abroad or to a particular foreign policy pronouncement. The United States was opposed to nationalization of the tin mines in Bolivia in 1952, but not because it represented specific economic interests within the United States. The mines were (at least formally) primarily owned by Bolivian capitalists. It was more likely the case that opposition derived from the fact that for the United States nationalization *per se* is an evil to be prevented if possible. The notion of expropriation as a response to profit-taking never penetrated United States relations with Latin America. The same can be said concerning the oil nationalization program in Mexico in the late 1930's. United States interests in the area were relatively minor. But ferocious American opposition to oil nationalization in Mexico nearly occasioned a severe rupture between the two nations, which only the skilled diplomacy of Josephus Daniels and the crisis of World War II averted.

A serious flaw in conventional Marxian critiques of imperialist policy toward Latin America[17] is that they project the time span of United States penetration so far back, so rooted in American economic development, that the short-run features of Latin American political dependency, the recentness of the phenomenon, are obscured. The intensification of trade imbalances, for example, took place after World War II. The war epoch was notable for the wide degree of latitude in Latin American economic trade policies, not to mention the high degree of profitability involved in extractive and farm products. Only after the conclusion of the war, only as a result of a recently crystallized American political hegemony in the area (and such hegemony did not exist in the pre-World War II period, given the fierce competition engaged in by Germany, England, and other European powers) can features held as characteristic by Marxist critics be seen as genuinely present. Here is an example of how noneconomic factors produced a drastic transformation in the economic relations of the region.

Moreover, the conservative drift of United States feeling in the postwar period, coupled with an increased power and prestige of the military, must be contended with as a factor. This too is not merely a policy outcome from the pressures of a given ecconomic class or interest. Consider, for example, President Eisenhower's report on the prelude to the Guatemalan invasion. It is illustrative of how the internal American conservative ideology created the basis for the action taken. The President apparently acted in Guatemala on the basis of a report by John E. Peurifoy, who submitted the following description of his conversation with President Jacobo Arbenz less than a month after he had arrived in Guatemala as ambassador.

In a six hour conversation he listened while I counted off the leading Communists in his regime, but he gave no ground; many notorious Reds he denied to be Communists; if they were, they were not dangerous; if dangerous, he would control them; if not controllable, he would round them up. He said, in any case, all our difficulties were due to the malpractices of American business. The trips of Communists to Russia were not to get training and instruction, he said, but merely to study Marxism, just in the same way as other Guatemalans may come to the United States to study economics. Meanwhile, they would continue to enjoy the full advantages accorded all Guatemalans, as they were valuable allies to him in the fight for social reform. . . . It seemed to me that the man thought like a Communist and talked like a Communist, and if not actually one, would do until one came along. I so reported to Secretary Dulles, who informed the President; and I expressed to them the view that unless the Communist influence in Guatemala were counteracted, Guatemala would within six months fall completely under Communist control.[18]

In this instance the basic triggering mechanism was, not economic, that is, defense of the United Fruit Company, but rather the ideological commitment that had gained such a foothold in the United States as to restructure its activities in Latin America in terms of control and coercion.

The combination of militarization and conservatism, indeed, is best shown in the counterinsurgency program that became such a feature of the present decade. Defense Secretary McNamara, in discussing counterinsurgency before the Senate Foreign Relations Committee, pointed out that the military program of and for Latin America did not dissolve with the end of Soviet expansionism, but merely shifted gears.

Until about 1960, military assistance programs for Latin America were oriented toward hemispheric defense. After it became clear that there was no threat of significant overt external aggression against Latin America, emphasis shifted to internal security capabilities for use again Communist-inspired subversion or overt aggression and to civic-action projects designed to promote stability and strengthen national economies.[19]

The general easing of internal strains within the United States in the early 1960's did not lead to a relaxation of its hemispheric grip, because the Cuban Revolution was the key intervening variable. This had as a counterpart a civic action and internal militarization approach to the question of hemispheric solidarity, and a continued movement away from strictly economic intervention.

Theories of neoimperialism attempting to identify political outcomes by means of a deterministic economic model suffer from a kind of "softness," despite claims for "hard" analysis, out of their incapacity to face the character and autonomy of hard military factors. The incompleteness of the vested interest explanation of United States power in Latin America is also evidenced by recent developments in United States-Latin American economic relations as well. For almost two decades Raúl Prebisch and the economists of ECLA have tried to construct a strategy for economic development in Latin America built on accepted Keynesian principles of mixed-economy planning by giving frank encouragement to capitalist industrial development as a spearhead of this strategy. This aspect of the Prebisch program is borrowed from nineteenth-century American economic theory which held that the relationship between the industrial and the agricultural sectors of the economy was such that the impoverishment of the agricultural sector, in "financing" the industrial sector, would create a constant drainage effect if things were left in their natural state. Therefore, encouragement for the agricultural sector was, not simply a matter of moral preference, but a downright necessity for protecting the land sector of the economy. This idea received a wide hearing in the United States, and in its latest version underscores the basic ECLA outlook.

ECLA has become an interest group for Latin American development. It has been actively trying to foment policy decisions on the part of Latin American governments and international cooperative agencies in order to implement the Prebisch program. Yet despite the wide acceptance of Keynesian perspectives, and despite the deep roots in the early American economic experience that the Prebisch program shows, ECLA's policy recommendations have met with the strongest United States opposition (and this opposition has been documented on more than one occasion). Its promotion of commodity agreements to strengthen the Latin American balance of payments position and expand its import capacity for purposes of import-substitution industrialization have been and continue to be looked upon with suspicion by the United States. The fear of any truly capitalist solution in the Latin American sphere as one of potential economic competition may even have given so much recent importance to military-sponsored-and-conceived solutions.[20]

It can be argued that there are more radical implications in some of the stipulations of the Punta del Este charter of the Alliance for Progress than anything which has been recommended by the ECLA Commission to the United Nations. Yet the Alliance for Progress was enthusiastically sponsored by the United States, despite the obvious incongruence with its economic policy at the United Nations. A closer examination of the charter of the Alliance, along with an examination of the various Prebisch policies, reveals significant differences. The Alliance had a reform thrust directed at the domestic structures of each of the Latin American nations. The ECLA orientation aims at a rationalization of the international economy. Despite the conservative language of ECLA in contrast to the more radical language of the Alliance, the ECLA argument is one for the overall autonomy of Latin America. The Alliance argument is contrary to autonomy, and aims at benevolent hegemony and domestic reform of a United States-led community of nations.

Survival Proposals

Let me conclude this paper with a set of recommendations and goals attainable without involving a disruption in present international relationships.

1. The most important need of the moment is for the United States to develop a capacity for distinguishing its *national* interests from the commercial interests within the American nation. The United States so often responds to threats of expropriation or reform on an assumption that what is in the interests of overseas United States business firms is necessarily consonant with American national purpose. This has been the characteristic situation throughout the twentieth century. American national policy needs to be further developed so that it does not mistake economic interests of a class for its better political interests.

2. There must be developed a capacity of the United States to distinguish its preferences from what is possible in the Latin American structure, or, further, to distinguish its own preferences from that of other people. Illusions about modernizing militarists in Latin American society, illusions that a middle-class sector will somehow rise above its self-serving propensities to become a democratic bulwark between wealth and poverty in Latin America, illusions that agricultural technology is somehow sufficient to encourage economic development without requiring transformation in the social bases of agricultural relations—these are some of the illusions that need to be distinguished from Latin American reality.

3. There must be a broad insistence that the United States develop an appreciation that its attitudes toward Bolivia and Mexico need to be as carefully differentiated as its attitudes toward Poland and England. Further, that a whole range of social and political systems might be accommodated as acceptable to hemispheric peace and that it cannot raise its own image as a standard for what "ought to be" elsewhere.

4. To minimize military influence and determination abroad, the State Department will need to recover its former strength and prestige with respect to the Defense Department. This would entail a drastic minimization of the role of overseas military missions, overseas paramilitary organizations, and a general decrease of Defense Department control of Latin American policy-making. Until a restoration in this balance is made, hemispheric problems can only be seriously compounded. The politics of economic aid often turns out to be antipolitics, a military definition of the situation. This creates a bizarre condition in which counterinsurgency precedes insurgency in time and acts as a self-propelling, self-destructive prophecy regarding hemispheric affairs.

5. The United States must learn to appreciate the value of the working and peasant classes in modernization. For a long time now there has been an unthinking commitment to the middle classes, without understanding their corruptions and failings as a mobilizing and integrating force. Such a commitment may have hardened with the rise of a Maoist position which places its own emphasis on the peasant and rural classes of Latin America. And given that the Soviet Union claims a longstanding priority to defend the rights of the proletariat and factory-working class, the United States has allowed its prejudices to rigidify. It is possible, and the United States must learn to consider it possible, that the factory-working class remains a viable instrument of mass democracy in the hemisphere, and the examples of Mexico and Chile should certainly provide encouragement along these lines.

6. It is significant to appreciate that any revolution of rising

expectations encouraged by the United States has as its minimal price a corresponding revolution in falling profits. There can be no mass change unless the United States is willing to absorb some part of the costs involved. This may mean higher prices for basic crops like sugar and coffee, and different profit-sharing arrangements with respect to the different nations of Latin America. The costs can be absorbed domestically by increased production and greater technological innovations, but it should be understood that it is unlikely that these will fully compensate for a falling off in the profit margins.

7. The final proposal I should like to make is that nations have the right not only to make revolutions. They also have the right to make re-revolutions. In view of the fact that the United States has had one singularly successful revolution, it has tended to forget the possibility that other revolutions may become atrophied or simply fail entirely. Therefore, the right of remaking revolution, in nations such as Mexico and Bolivia, or even those that had their revolutions much earlier, must be accepted. This right of re-revolution is perhaps hardest to accept. Those Latin American nations like Mexico and Cuba that have come to thrive off the revolution triumphant cannot accept even the possibility that further radical change may be in the offing, while the United States, which has come to reject the idea of unsponsored and unchaperoned revolution, cannot accept even the present initial stage of revolutionary upheavals. It might be that in Latin America a genuine model of stability would require a permanent circulation of elites and a steady responsiveness to mass sentiments by revolutionary rather than by parliamentary forms. If this possibility can be accepted, then stimulating the sorts of political systems which can reach an accommodation with the United States would be greatly enhanced.

Obviously these seven policy suggestions are not likely to be employed in the very near future. On the other hand, they do constitute what I believe to be a minimal set of demands for accepting and surviving social change in Latin America. They also constitute a brief for the vitalization of United States policy, and, surely, most social sectors in Latin America look carefully and sympathetically for exactly this sort of vitality.

NOTES

1. For a sampling of theories see A. N. Agarwala and S. P. Singh, eds., *The Economics of Underdevelopment* (New York: Oxford University Press, 1963); Benjamin Higgins, *Economic Development* (New York: W. W. Norton and Co., Inc., 1959); and Charles P. Kindleberger, *Economic Development* (New York: The McGraw-Hill Book Co., Inc., 1958).

2. This does not imply a view of the exact relationship between economic development and political structures. Recent evidence indicates that this connection may be more remote than formerly supposed. See Irma Adelman and Cynthia Taft Morris, *Society, Politics, and Economic Development: A Quantitative Approach* (Baltimore: The Johns Hopkins Press, 1967). But economists often take their stand on principle, not evidence.

3. Two forceful statements of the view that values and motives determine the rate of economic and social development are David McClelland, *The Achieving Society* (Princeton: Van Nostrand, 1961); in this connection also see McClelland's explicit defense of this "idealist" view in "Motivational Patterns in Southeast Asia with Special Reference to the Chinese Case," *Journal of Social Issues*, XIX, 1 (January, 1963); and Seymour Martin Lipset, "Values, Education, and Entrepreneurship," in Seymour Lipset and Aldo Solari, eds., *Elites in Latin America* (New York: Oxford University Press, 1967), pp. 3–60. For a critique of the psychologistic interpretations of development see Andrew Gunder Frank, "Sociology of Development and Underdevelopment of Sociology," *Catalyst*, 3 (Summer, 1967), pp. 20–73.

4. On the relationship between "achievement" and the role of violence see Merle Kling, "Violence and Politics in Latin America" (mimeographed).

5. For discussions of neoimperialism see Hamza Alavi, "Imperialism, Old and New," in Ralph Miliband and John Saville, eds., *The Socialist Register: 1964* (New York: The Monthly Review Press, 1964), pp.

124–126; Paul Baran, *The Political Economy of Growth* (New York: The Monthly Review Press, 1957); and Bernard Semmel, "On the Economics of Imperialism," in Bert F. Hoselitz, ed., *Economics and the Idea of Mankind* (New York: Columbia University Press, 1964), pp. 192–232. For special application to Latin America see Fredrick Clairmonte, *Liberalismo, economico y sub-desarrollo* (Bogotá: Ediciónes Tercer Mundo, 1963), pp. 247–350; and John Powelson, *Latin America: Today's Economic and Social Revolution* (New York: The McGraw-Hill Book Co., Inc., 1964), pp. 1–10.

6. Figures based on Economic Commission for Latin America (ECLA), *The Economic Development of Latin America in the Postwar Period* (New York: United Nations Publication [E/Cn.12/659/Rev.1], 1964), pp. 35–36.

7. ECLA, *External Financing in Latin America* (New York: United Nations Publications [E/Cn.12/649/Rev.1], 1965), p. 218. In 1950 about 300 firms owned 91 percent of all United States' direct investments in Latin America, exclusive of shipping and export-import firms.

8. *Ibid.*, pp. 214–218.

9. *Ibid.*, p. 218; and U.S. Department of Commerce, Office of Business Economics, Survey of Current Business (August, 1963).

10. For a vigorous argument along these lines see Harry G. Johnson, "The Ideology of Economic Policy in the New States," in H. G. Johnson, ed., *Economic Nationalism in Old and New States* (Chicago: The University of Chicago Press, 1967), pp. 124–141.

11. Adolf A. Berle, *Latin America—Diplomacy and Reality* (New York: Harper & Row, published for the Council on Foreign Relations, 1962), p. 7.

12. Sheldon L. Schreiberg, "The United States Private Investor and the Central American Common Market," in United States Congress, Joint Economic Committee, *Hearings, Latin American Development and Western Hemisphere Trade* (Washington, D. C.: Government Printing Office, 1963), p. 267. Quotation is from Robert Shepherd and Richard M. Kline, *Central American Common Market: Opportunities Plus* (Atlanta: Conway Research, Inc., July, 1964), p. 92.

13. ECLA, *External Financing in Latin America*, pp. 216–217.

14. U. S. Department of State, *Our Southern Partners*, Publication 7404 (Washington, D. C.: Government Printing Office, 1962), p. 47, cited in J. Lloyd Mecham, *A Survey of United States-Latin American Relations* (Boston: Houghton Mifflin, 1965), pp. 191–192.

15. See Otto Feinstein, "A Changing Latin America and U.S. For-

312 *Political Ideology of Political Economy*

eign Policy," in Otto Feinstein, ed., *Two Worlds of Change* (New York: Anchor-Doubleday, 1964), pp. 375–420.

16. For a discussion of United States-Latin American trade relations and balance of payments problems see ECLA, *Economic Development, op. cit.,* pp. 33–47, 121–144; and Raúl Prebisch, *Towards a New Trade Policy for Development* (New York: United Nations Publications [E/Conf/46/3], 1964). For a discussion of the limitations on import-substitution industrialization see David Felix, "Beyond Import Substitution: A Latin American Dilemma," Washington University, St. Louis, March 7, 1966 (mimeographed).

17. See, for example, Andre Gunder Frank, *Capitalism and Underdevelopment in Latin America* (New York: Monthly Review Press, 1967).

18. Dwight D. Eisenhower, *Mandate for Change, 1953–1956* (New York: Doubleday & Co., Inc., 1963), p. 442.

19. U. S. Congress, Senate Committee on Foreign Relations, *Hearings, Foreign Assistance Act of 1963* (Washington, D.C.: Government Printing Office, 1963), p. 175.

20. For an exposition of Prebisch's views see Raúl Prebisch, *Towards a Dynamic Deveolpment Policy for Latin America* (New York: United Nations Publication [E/Conf/12/680/1], 1963), and Prebisch, *Towards a New Trade Policy for Development;* and for an analysis of the practical outcomes of the Prebisch framework see Irving Horowitz, *Three Worlds of Development: The Theory and Practice of International Stratification* (New York: Oxford University Press, 1966), pp. 179–186.

MARKET PROBLEMS IN
INTER-AMERICAN RELATIONS

GUSTAVO ROMERO-KOLBECK

Over the past two decades our world has been divided, in terms of economics and trade, into two great sectors. On the one hand, the so-called industrialized nations, such as the United States, have since World War II enjoyed unprecedented development. But at the same time the developing and underdeveloped nations seventy-seven countries in Asia, Africa, and Latin America— have found it difficult to achieve a rate of growth sufficient to keep pace with the population explosion.

The basic reason for this development gap is the characteristics of world trade, which really amounts to the trade transactions and capital movements between the developed nations. Within this system are the developing countries, desperately attempting to find the means by which they can acquire the capital goods essential for their development.

These developing nations, unfortunately, are for the most part exporters of raw materials and normally depend on one or two basic crops for their foreign exchange and hence for their capital imports. In recent years the gap between the developed and the developing nations has grown wider because of the trend in prices. Goods which are being imported by the developing nations constantly cost more. At the same time commodity prices in the world market over the past decade have generally tended to decline. This deterioration in the terms of trade has resulted in lowered purchasing power for the developing countries.

The developed countries maintain, however, and with some justification, that while the cost of machinery and equipment they export has increased, the productivity of this equipment also has increased. They also deny that they are responsible for the decline in commodity prices. Yet year after year they offer more of their own commodities on the world market, while their technological advances make it possible for them to find synthetic products with which to replace the commodities offered by the developing nations. Regardless of which side we may take in this argument, the fact remains that over the past few years there has been a notable decline in the export income of the developing nations. As a result, these nations have found their already small role in global trade steadily reduced in terms of percentage participation. In the last ten years, the exports of the industrialized nations have risen by close to 80 percent. In the same period the total exports of the developing countries have actually declined. In 1930, at the depth of the Depression, Latin America's total exports amounted to sixty dollars per capita. In 1966, the last year for which complete figures are available, the per-capita value of exports from Latin America had been reduced to just half of its 1930 level.

It is, therefore, easy to understand the difficult situation which the developing nations have with their balance of payments, particularly since their capital goods needs are greater every year. In Latin America, for example, petroleum accounts for 93 percent of Venezuela's annual exports, while coffee comprises 55 percent of Brazilian exports. Similar proportions are found in Chile for copper, in Bolivia for tin, in Argentina for beef and wheat, in Colombia for coffee, and in Guatemala for coffee and bananas. If in any particular year the world-market price for one of these products declines even moderately, it can result in an economic crisis in any of these nations, where balance of trade and balance of payments positions depend heavily on export sales. As exports decline and a reduction in imports of capital goods is required, a lower rate of economic growth for the country involved results.

The idea naturally comes to mind that the best way to escape this trade and development dilemma is to diversify the economy in order to export other products, and so moderate the impact of price fluctuations. Unfortunately, there are two basic obstacles which make such a diversification over the short term practically impossible. In the first place, any diversification requires economic development and a much greater importing of the necessary capital goods. Second, any developing country which begins producing manufactured goods for export finds itself in competition with the industrialized nations. It is almost always impossible for the developing nations to compete on the world market with manufactured goods of the industrialized countries owing to the production, marketing, and price conditions which these latter nations enjoy. It is thus extremely difficult for the nations of the so-called Third World to diversify their economies and thus improve their terms of trade and internal growth possibilities.

Mexico is one of those developing countries which have sought to diversify. Thirty years ago petroleum and minerals accounted for 45 percent of all Mexican exports. Today a group of eight products represents this 45 percent—but all eight nevertheless still are commodities. Cotton, for example, accounts for 20 percent of total exports at present, followed by sugar, coffee, corn and wheat, minerals, cattle, and the like. Despite Mexico's great strides toward industrialization in recent years, exports of manufactured or semimanufactured goods still make up only 20 percent of exports.

As the result of the negative situation described above, the developing nations several years ago began a campaign aimed at convincing the industrialized countries to take action to improve their terms of trade and their prospects for an improved rate of economic growth. This led to the 1964 meeting in Geneva of the first world-trade conference under the auspices of the United Nations. This was the first meeting of its kind since 1945, when agreement had been reached on establishment of the General Agreement Tariffs and Trade (GATT).

As soon as the United Nations announced plans for the Geneva meeting, the developing nations began laying the groundwork for their position at that conference. The Latin America nations, for example, held three preconference meetings in order to unify programs. The first, held at Rio de Janeiro, included Cuba among the participants. The position of that nation within the Latin American community made it impossible to reach conclusions which could even be considered by the industrialized nations. A second meeting, without Cuba, was therefore held in New York City, at which the Latin American countries reached agreement in principal. This in turn led to the third and final meeting, held at Altagracia, Argentina, where these countries, once again without Cuba, reached final accord on the so-called Charter of Altagracia.

This document had two fundamental characteristics. First of all, it called for a basic change in the criteria governing trade relations between the developed and the developing nations. Since the Roosevelt period, virtually all world trade has been carried out on the basis of two principles: that of reciprocity in international trade dealings and that of the most-favored-nation clause, which is the keystone of United States trade policy. The principle of reciprocity is based on bilateral trade agreements. It required that any benefits granted by one nation to another in its trade relations must be returned. The most-favored-nation clause refers to the granting by one nation to another of more favorable trade benefits, benefits which are then often extended to other nations with which the country has bilateral trade agreements, but not necessarily on a completely reciprocal basis.

These two principles, institutionalized by GATT at the world level, have been dominant principles in world trade during recent decades. They establish the policy of equal trade treatment between nations, regardless of the state of development or the ability to trade of the countries involved. This policy is one to which the Charter of Altagracia most strongly objects.

The second basic characteristic of the charter was that for the first time the nations of Latin America joined in presenting four petitions which they considered could span the ever-widening development gap.

These four petitions were

1. That existing international commodity agreements, fixing minimum world prices on specific primary products, be extended to cover a wide range of additional products;

2. That the developed nations provide preferential trade treatment to the developing nations in the export of semimanufactures;

3. That when a developed nation grants preferential trade treatment to a developing nation, it does not demand reciprocity nor does it automatically apply terms of the most favored nation clause to the detriment of the terms of trade of the developing nation; and

4. That the developed countries agree to search for a formula which will improve financing conditions for the developing nations, to alleviate these latter countries from the burden of meeting heavy short-term debt payments.

It is well known that there already do exist several international price agreements regarding commodities such as tin, cotton, wheat, and coffee. What the Latin nations were urging was that these agreements be expanded in order to incorporate other basic commodities for which price floors and therefore a degree of price stability would be fixed. In general, these agreements are reached between the producing and the consuming countries, and usually include escape clauses which allow the industrialized nations to ignore them under certain conditions.

The second point aims at protecting those fledgling industries which are beginning to crop up throughout Latin America, and assures them of a possible, although small, export entry into markets of the industrial countries. The third point would establish a new look in world-trade relations and policies, since it calls for an elimination of those principles which long have been established for trade between the developed and the developing nations. The final point merely seeks a better deal for the developing nations when they solicit and receive financial help from abroad.

Let us move on now to the Geneva conference, which as far as the developing nations were concerned proved a failure. The developing nations won all the votes, but their proposals meant little since the industrial countries meeting either voted against these or simply abstained. Since the 1964 conference only one of the proposals put forth at that meeting by the developing countries has been accepted even in part by the industrialized nations.

What has happened to world trade since the Geneva conference four years ago? With the exception of more meetings of a similar nature, very little. On the first proposal, the only accomplishment has been an agreement in principal to study the possibilities of an international pricing accord for cocoa. As far as point two is concerned, no industrial nation has as yet approved any preferential treatment of any kind for imports of semimanufactured goods from developing countries. Only on point three—that of trade reciprocity and the most-favored-nation clause—has any action been taken, and only to a small degree as the result of approval of Article Four of GATT and the Kennedy Round tariff negotiations concluded last year. Concerning point four, that of easing financing conditions, the World Bank studied the problem at length and decided to send the proposals back to a special committee for further study.

In that area in which progress has been made, that of the

terms of trade, improvement has been small. The Kennedy Round for the most part improved trade conditions only between the United States and the European Economic Community. It is estimated that the developing nations are only affected favorably in 1 percent of the total annual trade value of the articles involved.

The GATT charter does include a statement to the effect that when a developed nation approves preferential trade treatment for a developing country, it should not necessarily expect reciprocity. This clause is not an absolute one, nor is it being universally applied. But it does signify the creation of a new concept on nondirect trade reciprocity, and is thus an important first step.

In 1965 the Organization for Economic Cooperation and Development (OECD), an organization of twenty developed countries with its head office in Paris, created a group of experts to work on a possible system of preferences that could be offered to the developing countries. In November, 1967, that work was practically finished, and the OECD had a session to approve a program of preferences that was offered in the second United Nations Conference on Trade and Development (UNCTAD) held in February, 1968, in New Delhi. The proposition involves a system of preferences for manufactured and semimanufactured exports from the developing countries, with limitations to protect the industries of the developed nations. Representatives of the seventy-seven developing nations met in 1967 at Algiers to begin work on a coordinated policy for the New Delhi meetings.

In view of the relatively minor concessions granted the developing nations since the Geneva conference, the nations of Latin America—Mexico included—feel that their only real opportunity for economic development and improved trade lies in the creation of an economic union similar to the European Common Market. Obviously, such a common market for Latin America cannot be achieved overnight if for no other reason than the wide differences in the level of development of the nations involved. A number of steps toward the eventual creation of such a common market have, however, been taken already, the first of them was the signing of the Treaty of Montevideo in 1960 which resulted in establishment of the Latin American Free Trade Association (LAFTA), with Argentina, Brazil, Chile, Mexico, Uruguay, and Peru as members. Since then most of the Latin American nations have become LAFTA members, with the exception of the Central American countries, which in turn formed their own common market organization.

The Treaty of Montevideo contained three fundamental agreements. The first called for an elimination, no later than 1973, of all tariffs on regional products. The second dealt with the establishment of industrial complementation agreements for zonal industries. And the third called for preferential development and trade treatment for the region's less developed nations, such as Paraguay, Bolivia, and Ecuador.

During its first seven years of existence two major problems have cropped up which have severely limited the progress of LAFTA. First of all, there has been little progress in the negotiations which would eliminate zonal import duties on select products which already are being produced in one or more of the Latin nations. This problem has crippled LAFTA tariff negotiations from the beginning down to the negotiation session at montevideo in December, 1967. The basic reason for this stagnation is understandable. Any process of economic integration implies an accelerated development in the region involved and a resulting reduction in zonal protectionism. Since industrial development in Latin America is to date very modest indeed, it is difficult to achieve agreement on widespread tariff cuts if these endanger the very life of those industries already in existence. This is one of the crucial differences in the development of a Latin American common market as opposed to a European Common Market.

The second problem is the tremendous difference in the degree of development of the Latin American nations, which makes complementation agreements extremely difficult, particularly since there is relatively no capital available for the development of new industries on a zonal or regional scale. Despite these problems and others the presidents of the Latin American nations met in April, 1967, with President Johnson to try and reach agreement on the economic integration of Latin America, with a Latin American common market as basis. It was illogical, perhaps, for the Latin nations to take on the tremendous challenge of economic integration, considering how little they have accomplished so far with LAFTA. The most reasonable explanation is that the Latin nations felt that the greater challenge would speed up progress. However, because of this the LAFTA program has been relegated to a position of lesser importance. The goal now is economic integration and a common market, going far beyond LAFTA's proposals. The LAFTA idea of free zonal trade by 1973 has now become just one part of a larger process.

At present important aspects of Latin American economic integration are being widely, at times heatedly, examined. LAFTA clearly needs a hefty push to establish itself as the base for the forthcoming Latin American common market, a push which includes the creation of a common external tariff program. Another problem is the integration of the Central American Common Market (CACOM). Here, agreement has been reached on the integration process, and CACOM is establishing its formula for a common outer tariff, a formula which would require the Latin American nations to freeze their tariff barriers at present levels as far as regional trade is concerned.

It should be emphasized here that at present LAFTA, economic integration, and a common market are virtually the only hope left for real development in the Latin American economies. One should keep in mind the long history of vicious circles in the economies of these nations in order to understand why Latin America really has no other alternatives than those we have just been discussing, in a world in which no outside powers offer any substantial aid. All the Latin American nations, to one degree or another, are faced with a situation in which the majority of their population is inefficiently employed in agriculture and is left outside the region's economically active sector. In virtually every Latin American country this has created a weak and thinly based market structure, so that the area is not able to build up and sustain large-scale and low-cost industrial development. Industrialization in Latin America, therefore, is at best a modest reality, unable to use modern technology because of the huge volumes of production and consumption required in order to amortize the necessary investments.

Because of this vicious circle the industry which does exist produces very little and is not able to absorb the region's excess manpower. As a result, Latin America's rural population continues to live from the field, on a subsistence basis, with limited incomes depressed still further when the export market for the product involved is weakened by world market conditions. Under such conditions it is not possible for Latin American industry to compete in the world market.

It is possible that economic integration in Latin America could, over the long run, offer a solution to this vicious circle of subdevelopment. By reducing zonal tariffs these countries would expand their existing national markets. Then Latin American industries could produce in volume and reach levels of productivity involving the use of modern technology. It is then probable that some of these industries could reduce costs to a level where their products are competitive on world markets.

The Latin American nations could thus develop their economies at a much greater rate once the integration process is begun. Integration implies more aggressive fiscal policies and a wider distribution of income, which in turn would give the Latin American governments access to greater revenues and allow for increased investment in economic and social infrastructure. But economic integration will also mean that the governments will need greater amounts of foreign exchange in order to acquire the

machinery, equipment, and materials indispensable for industrialization. As this industrialization process gathers momentum,
however, it will result in a considerable amount of imports substitution, which will reduce foreign exchange needs and broaden
still further the base for Latin America's own production activities.

With regard to this development process the forecasts are
promising. The United Nations Economic Commission for Latin
America (CEPAL) has estimated that, using the program of
import substitution, the minimally acceptable growth rate of 3
percent capita per year could be achieved with 30 percent less
need for foreign exchange.

These factors establish quite clearly that the Latin American
economies will have to achieve their own development, since
there is nothing on the horizon which would indicate additional
assistance in meeting this goal from the industrialized nations of
the world. Unfortunately at present there does not really exist
any such thing as meaningful international economic cooperation. In recent years the concept has become so elastic in its
application that it covers such matters as technical assistance and
manufacturing licenses to the developing nations, as well as
international credits and the flow of direct foreign investment. As
a result, there is at present no real definition of the term nor
is there a workable theory of it.

Such programs as direct foreign investment, foreign loans, technical assistance, and manufacturing licenses are really nothing
more than bilateral business agreements between a developed
and a developing nation which have nothing whatever to do with
a true spirit of international economic cooperation. What may be
passed off as cooperation is really nothing more than international paternalism which the industrialized nations apply toward
underdeveloped areas in general and underdeveloped countries
in particular. Why this paternalistic attitude? It seems that the
industrial countries have unilaterally decided that the only way
out for the developing nations, in other words the only road open

to them, is the repetition of the same process which the industrialized nations used to get to the economic positions they now enjoy. But the industrial nations have never stopped to analyze whether present conditions will allow for such a repetition.

For the most part the industrialized nations of today underwent development by opening their doors to foreign capital and foreign human resources, persons who supplied these nations with both resources and know-how. For the most part this possibility no longer exists. Instead we have the establishment of gigantic international business and industrial consortiums, which move both capital and people, but with no idea of putting down permanent roots. The head office of these consortiums is located in one of the developed countries, and decisions on whether or not to set up operations in any of the developing nations depend almost exclusively on the need for satisfactory returns.

For these reasons international paternalism makes it virtually impossible for the developing nations to take alternate roads to economic development. Thus the developing country is limited to that growth which international paternalism is willing to allow it. Any nation which deviates from the traditional development norms laid down by this international paternalism program runs the risk of being labeled as extremist, at which point all aid from the industrialized nation automatically ceases.

This whole system is the result of an outdated philosophy of economic liberalism, one of the most hated economic doctrines which the world has produced. Under this system international economic cooperation can never become a reality, since liberalism does not take into account the glaring lack of equality between the industrialized nations and the developing countries. The idea of equal economic treatment between these two blocs is meaningless as long as economic relations are based on actual inequality.

As an example, let us look at the system of international credits as it presently operates. When an international agency for economic cooperation such as the World Bank approves a credit for

Paraguay, it sets up a wide range of preconditions and interest rates using the same system of criteria that it would use for granting a loan to France. This certainly is not economic cooperation. After all, it seems hard to believe that the World Bank is not aware of the vast differences between the economies of France and of Paraguay. Paraguay obviously needs longer repayment terms, easier interest rates, allowance for partial local financing, and so on, all of which are absolutely necessary concessions for the developing nations of the world. But these characteristics are not part of the World Bank's statutes. Why? Because the bank must sell its bonds in the industrialized nations in order to finance its operations, and the industrial countries will never agree to the easier financing terms which the developing nations really need.

The attitude of the private sector is the same. If a United States company approves a manufacturing license or technical assistance agreement with a company in Honduras, it will demand the same terms it would seek from a company in West Germany. In other words, the international operations policy of this company is universally applied. Apparently the large international firms have not yet realized—or perhaps they do not want to—that the economy of Honduras and that of West Germany have nothing whatsoever in common.

The dismal truth of the matter is that it has not been possible to produce a new philosophy in international economic relations which establishes firmly that it is impossible to demand equal economic treatment in dealings between nations which economically are not equals. International jurisprudence deals harshly with the stronger nations when they abuse and deal unjustly with the weaker countries. But as far as international economics and trade are concerned, the practice of equal treatment remains very much in vogue, even when it is obvious that the development and trade conditions of the developed and the developing nations have nothing in common. Actually, of course, what has happened in international economics is that while humanity continues to give lip service to the idea of cooperation and solidarity, it still is governed by the principle of business is business.

The essential theory of international economic cooperation I think should be similar to the principles of fiscal policy. There should, in other words, be a progressive system in which the tax burden depends on the amount of income received, which of course is the only just system. What must be achieved is a new spirit of international economic cooperation in which the cost of capital and services to the developing nations is made under more favorable conditions than those for the industrial countries. Until this is done, today's "spirit" of international economic cooperation will continue in force, with no benefit to the development efforts of the lesser developed nations.

Since my audience is largely Christian and Roman Catholic, I would like to mention here Christian social doctrine and how its principles could be applied to the responsibility of the businessman in the industrial nations. This could be a major element in the evolution of a new philosophy in the field of international relations. Many of the executives who direct the major companies, as well as the international financing and development agencies of the world, are for the most part practicing Christians, although it often seems that they forget this the moment they sit down to discuss international economics. The decisions which can mean a more favorable treatment for the developing nations must come precisely from these directors. These executives are, therefore, in an excellent position to formulate a new, more human philosophy relative to the disequality which exists between the countries of the world. Such a philosophy would, of course, have a tremendous impact on the world economy.

The Christian faith consists not only of religious practices, and its followers should not feel that they have fulfilled their obligations merely by observing faithfully these religious practices. To the contrary, the greatest significance at this period in world history is the putting into practice of the theory of social responsibility, the social responsibility of Christian business leaders who are willing to understand and work to correct the tremendous imbalance of development which exists among the nations of the world today.

If this feeling of social responsibility became widespread and effectively practiced, it would open a new era in the attitude of business and financing executives of the industrial nations toward their brethren in the developing countries. This change in mentality could mean the flourishing of a new, humanistic philosophy in international relations, which could lead to the development and economic well-being of these developing countries.

UNIVERSITY COLLABORATION
AND CULTURAL DEVELOPMENT

ROBERT J. HENLE, S.J.

I conceive technical assistance at the level of higher education to consist in helping to establish or develop educational, cultural, research, or service programs appropriate to a university, and to institutionalize these programs both in themselves and as parts of a strong university. The strategy of this sort of technical assistance is thus to achieve multiple and self-augmenting results. It does not aim, for example, to do actual nursing except by way of demonstration. Rather, it would aim to establish a model hospital, a nursing school, in-service training programs to prepare and provide competent teachers, and to help build institutions which could recruit and hold the teachers needed to maintain a high-level nursing program and conduct the health research needed in a given country. As another example, it would not aim at undertaking to assist in the teaching of high-school science courses, but would instead seek to establish in-service programs to improve the existing teachers of science in the high schools and set up training centers which would attract future teachers of science

328

who would be better qualified than their predecessors.

The aim of technical assistance, from the very beginning, must be to make itself unnecessary. It may develop into a continuing cultural collaboration, and this is a most desirable outcome. Technical assistance wherein a university or a group of universities gives "aid" to institutions unable, alone, to develop themselves rapidly enough to meet the needs of the modern world, is helpful. But the program must from the beginning look to a termination in which it can be adequately maintained and advanced by a staff of trained and experienced nationals.

It is easy to fall into the trap of building oneself into the institutions being aided. Care must be taken not to allow the aid recipients to become chronically dependent on outside help. Their independence and their personal responsibility must be encouraged. Every contribution that they can make should be recognized and accepted.

If the assistance program is to have permanent and useful results, it should be planned with a total view both of the host institution and of the host country in mind. Developing countries need institutions which embody what we have often called the concept of the "land-grant" college. These institutions must provide for their society the leadership and services appropriate to a university and needed by that society. Hence, there should be an assessment of the true needs of the host country and a determination of priorities. There should be an assessment and evaluation of existing institutions. It is generally better to strengthen existing universities rather than to establish new ones. All the strengths, actual or potential, of the country should be identified and used.

In a very special way, the assistance program must relate to the economic development of the country. We face here a vicious or a beneficent circle—whichever way you want to consider it. The most important element in economic development is certainly trained manpower and human leadership. But programs to produce the necessary manpower are expensive, and underdeveloped economies cannot afford them. This is, of course, one reason why technical assistance financed from outside the country is presently necessary. But the development thus brought about must face fiscal realities. While institutions are being developed, plans for long-range, in-country financial support should simultaneously be developed. The program of development should not be over-ambitious in relation to the possibilities of support. If the strategy of the program does not take into account these fiscal realities, technical assistance can leave behind institutions which, for lack of funds, will slowly decay or disintegrate. On the other hand, once a rhythm of development is established, the universities will contribute to an increasing gross national product and, in turn, will be supported at higher levels by the growing economy. Once possibilities and goals are determined and matched, a program should be laid out in a series of steps or stages leading to a fore-seeable phase-out of each part of the program. The program, moreover, must be flexible, capable of being continuously revised.

In dealing with institutional development, the changing of atti-tudes and ideas and the selection and preparation of people involve so many human factors that the plan must be open to stra-tegic waiting and strategic acceleration in accordance with actual developments within the institution. This sort of development cannot be planned and staged as can the building of a material object; nor, as it moves along, can it be evaluated in the same fashion. The building of a road can fairly well be evaluated in terms of the relationship of miles completed, the time required for completion, and direct costs. In the kind of thing we are deal-ing with here there are often periods in which slow preparation is made for change. Often there are sudden breakthroughs, when changes begin to roll rapidly forward and a great deal appears to be achieved in a short time. The upshot of this is that while some kind of intuitive and qualitative evaluation can be made during the progress of a technical assistance program, its actual success can only be determined on termination, when it becomes apparent that developments have or have not taken place.

After the plan has been laid out and funding provided, an adequate staff is to be inserted into the institutional situation abroad. As far as possible, the American university staff should not find themselves put in positions of authority or top direction. This cannot always be avoided. Sometimes a program has to be initiated, and there is no one locally who is prepared to be in a directive position. But the responsibility for institutional direction should, as far as possible, be in the hands of nationals, not of the American team. This is necessary to maintain the temporary character of the technical assistance program, but it is also vitally necessary in order to develop the kind of institutional responsibility that will be necessary to make the changes authentic and real and to keep them alive after the program has ceased to function. Psychologically, too, it is an effort to recognize, as far as possible, that the responsibility for development is really a local responsibility and that the program development is a collaborative activity, not simply an imposition of foreign ideas and foreign structures.

On the other hand, however, the American staff should not act simply as external consultants. I know that there are people in the United States Agency for International Development (AID) and elsewhere who maintain that university staff people should be simply consultants and should not involve themselves directly in the activities of the university. It is my conviction that this is a mistaken view. The American staff will achieve acceptance and will be able to produce much more effective results if they actively participate in the normal university activities in the institution to which they have come. In other words, a person who comes to help develop a science program should not simply talk with faculty members and lay out plans and curricula. He should actually teach science; preferably he should begin with redevelopment of the basic courses. If possible, he should collaborate in this teaching with local counterparts. Often, however, local counterparts do not exist and must be developed. The teaching of the course not only is the development of a new course and a new program but is a demonstration to students and faculty what a modern scientific course ought to be and can be. We all know that in education, demonstration without supervised practice and experience of what a laboratory course is like is fairly futile. The technical assistance staff assigned to a university should therefore enter into the university and identify with the departments and faculties and schools where they are to work. They should undertake the role of a university person, adapting to local conditions but attempting to introduce those modifications which will move toward the goals of the program.

The staff members should not consider themselves superior individuals who are there to tell others how to improve, but rather should act as co-workers within the institution by collaborating with national counterparts on equal terms. Such an interrelationship brings about changes on both sides and produces a situation of mutual learning and mutual understanding. If it is done with tact and intelligence, the activity of the staff can thus become a source of cooperative strength by building into mutual respect and establishing a basis for continued collaboration after the phasing out of the technical assistance. If this sort of relationship is not established, I doubt that any true internal development can really take place.

An essential part of this activity, of course, is the selection of nationals from the host country to be given experience, in-service training, and formal training abroad, and who eventually will replace the American staff and undertake to maintain and promote development. In the whole matter of technical assistance the critical factor, from the standpoint of long-range success, is the selection and preparation of in-country personnel. Too often equipment and material aid are given to institutions abroad without provision for an adequately trained staff to handle the equipment or to deal with the materials. We have all seen American equipment in Latin America standing idle because staffing was not planned along with provision of the equipment.

As I have indicated above, a technical assistance program in a university should aim to make itself unnecessary. It should aim at establishing a strong institution with well-developed programs and with such a group of faculty and administrators that they themselves will be qualified to undertake the future development of their own institution and country. I do not mean that this can be done entirely without further outside help, because all institutions, even the most developed, need stimulation and assistance from outside. But this is quite different from the phase in which an institution is dependent upon outside help for fundamental development or even the beginning of development.

Here I would like to offer, from our own Saint Louis University experience in Quito, what, to my mind, is almost a classic example of a successful piece of technical assistance. When I first visited the Universidad Católica in Ecuador with a view to working out a plan of collaboration and assistance between that institution and Saint Louis University, I found that one of the great needs both of the university and of the country was preparation in English and particularly in the teaching of English. English has long been a second language of Ecuador, and is required in the second ary schools and most university faculties. Teaching, however, has been so bad, the teachers so poorly prepared, that the students for the most part spent many years in English language study without really mastering the language. For this reason the development of an Institute of Languages and Linguistics was proposed as part of our technical assistance goal. At that time there were three teachers of English in the Universidad Católica. None of them had any training in the teaching of English, either as a first or as a second language. Two of them had studied in North American high schools, but had no advanced degree. The third had an advanced degree, but it was in economics. There were,

of course, no tape recorders, no electronic laboratories, no teaching aids, and practically no books. In this case it was impossible
to find anyone who could serve as the initial director of the institute. We therefore were forced to supply one. But, fortunately, we
were able to do this by appointing a Mexican who had completed his doctoral training at Georgetown University's Institute
of Linguistics.

We opened this institute in October, 1963, with a twenty-four
place electronic laboratory and various teaching aids. We were
so swamped with students that the other members of our staff
who had not been specifically sent to teach English had to take
sections so as not to turn too many students away. We have since
established a second electronic laboratory. (The equipment has
been paid for by the United States government, but the buildings
were constructed with Ecuadorian funds, so that even the physical development was a collaborative one.) We have selected,
interned, and educated a full-time director and an assistant director. We have provided a large number of local teachers, and
we have also provided Ecuadorians a background in American
studies, so that the program is not merely pure linguistics, but
also involves the cultural background of American society. Thus,
we are making a contribution to a better understanding of our
culture through North American literature, politics, and cultural
history. Finally, in June, 1967, the institute had become so fully
developed, and the Ecuadorian staff so competent, that it was
possible to terminate the technical assistance for this part of our
program and to turn the institute over to Ecuadorian management and staff. As I have pointed out, when I originally visited
the Universidad Católica there were three teachers of English, all
of them untrained. At present the Institute of Languages and Linguistics has thirty-five teachers, twenty-one of them teaching
English. The institute offers eighty-one different courses; fifty-
four of them are in English. In addition to English, the institute
now provides Spanish for non-Spanish speakers. It provides

courses in French, German, and, more recently, Italian. The total enrollment as of the first semester of 1967 was 1,350. A good number of these are from outside the university, from embassies and business, but still this is a very large number in a university which has a total of only 1800 students. This institute is a proud showpiece of the university, and one of its most effective programs.

I said above that technical assistance looks to making itself unnecessary, that is to say, aims at developing an institution which can stand on its own feet and undertake to do its own planning and development. Obviously, as long as technical assistance is still needed, the goals of the program have not been reached. Now, of course, it is true that for many, many years universities in underdeveloped countries around the world are going to be in need of some kind of technical assistance. But, as we move forward, this technical assistance should more and more metamorphose into what should be a permanent international relationship between universities, namely, collaboration on a basis of diversity, mutual assistance, and equality.

Modern education, and particularly higher education, must more and more be thoroughly international. One of the ways in which this can be achieved is to provide, for as many students as possible, some kind of a foreign experience in which the program is carefully planned and the students carefully prepared so as to get maximum benefit out of the experience. This should not be just a hasty trip abroad or a people-to-people living visit. It has got to be a planned educational experience. In order to provide the experience appropriate to various student interests and abilities, universities are going to have to have collaborative relationships with many centers in different countries and different cultures. Hopefully, wherever technical assistance has been rendered, a relationship of this sort can thereafter be continued on a basis of mutual understanding and exchange. Personally I am not in favor of sending young people of college age, that is to say, from seventeen to twenty-one, to a foreign country, and particularly to a quite different culture, to receive the whole of their university-level education. I think that every person should spend this central period of education in his own culture. But there should be provided within it a summer, a semester, or even a year abroad to counterbalance the exclusiveness and the parochialism of one's own culture.

To enlarge on this, I think that young people, especially those coming from an underdeveloped country to the United States and spending four and sometimes five, six, or seven years in continuous education in America are, as a rule, to a large extent deculturated. They are not thoroughly Americanized, and they are not prepared, really, to fit into their own culture on their return. I know there are a lot of exceptions to this, and I should not want to make any absolute rules. But, by and large, I would be much happier if the money that is spent on full collegiate education away from home for young people from underdeveloped countries were instead diverted to local institutions where a high-level, first-rate education could be provided without removing these young people totally from their culture. However, as I said above, it seems to me that more and more a foreign experience and a genuine educational experience will be part of the education of young people around the world. Collaborative relationships between universities can facilitate this and make it more effective.

When we come to the graduate and advanced professional levels, I think the situation is different, particularly if the people that come from underdeveloped to developed countries are already well established in their own countries and actually have a job or solid prospects of one. Here, of course, we face the problem of the "braindrain." There are certain countries and certain fields in which it is undesirable to bring potential professionals from one culture to another where the stages of development are too widely separated and where the particular profession in question is well rewarded in the United States and Europe and only meagerly rewarded and partially used in the home country. Many a country around the world right now, for example, has a very low remuneration and respect for nurses, and very difficult, almost impossible, working conditions for them. A nurse who has an opportunity to learn English and be trained in the United States very often does not return to her home country. In this case the collaborative arrangement between universities can be more complicated. A third-country institution could be involved in a training program cosponsored by an American institution and other Latin American institutions, for example. A good example of this kind of arrangement is the library science program in Medellín, Colombia. Here future librarians can obtain preparation which is not as long as that in the United States, which is better adapted to Latin American conditions, which does not require a knowledge of English, and which is much less expensive than a similar American program. On the other hand, continuing relationships between an institution like the library school in Medellín and other institutions in more developed countries will constantly improve that school and also help it maintain itself at the level of current developments in library science.

Another form of collaboration which is of great importance is that of centers for special types of research. No university has or can have its own campus research resources in a variety of fields. A country like Ecuador offers a magnificent living laboratory to biologists, a laboratory with resources beyond what most United States universities could provide at home. A center sponsored by a local university and cosponsored by universities abroad could open up magnificent opportunities for research for students and professors from many countries, at the same time developing Ecuador itself.

Then there is also the exchange of professors. This, of course, has multiple effects. For one thing it offers an opportunity for a professor to get firsthand acquaintance with an area which he has studied, to see a different way of running universities, to be stimulated by different kinds of interests. As the international experience of our students grows, and as international interest expands, it is going to be more and more important that our professors also have an opportunity for a foreign experience which will give a realistic base to much of their international thinking. A professor of comparative political science who does not leave the United States for many, many years at a time can become only artificially acquainted with the political systems that he is comparing. A professor of urban affairs needs firsthand acquaintance with the problems of Mexico City, of Bogotá, of Tokyo, in order really to put the American problems in perspective.

An exchange professor is also a great advantage to the foreign institution and students. He can bring to the students of a different culture a different approach and a different background, even though he is teaching a basic discipline. His own cultural orientation will give his teaching a different character than that of a native professor teaching the same program. All this will help to introduce an international character into institutions and to open the minds of young students to the multicultural world in which they live. The exchange of professors is also related to the development of cooperative research programs and the use of the research centers mentioned above.

All the activities so far mentioned are dependent upon the parallel development of counterpart institutions in Latin America. I should like to emphasize for a moment the importance in this matter of the university-to-university contract. It seems to me that technical assistance through university-to-university contracts and agreements is, perhaps, the single most effective way to create institutions within developing countries and to provide technical services from bases within those countries. The amount of money it would take to bring all the private universities of Latin America to a level of self-sustaining and self-initiating service to their countries would be almost infinitesimal compared to the cost of a war, the cost of destruction. As of September 30,

1967, there were fifty-four AID-financed university contracts for assistance in Latin America. The total dollar amount for these contracts was only 37.5 million dollars, the cost of a few bombers. Many of these university contracts were not precisely directed to the development of university-level institutions abroad. Many of them are assisting in different kinds of technical development. Hence, the university-to-university programs which are designed to develop university centers for the provision of the human resources needed in the development of most countries is a very small part of our foreign-aid program. It is my opinion also that the great foundations, while they have done many fine things in Latin America, have not made use of university-to-university assistance contracts to any great extent. I believe their programs would be vastly improved were they to do so.

At the present time the cut in the United States foreign-aid budget is having a disastrous effect on many of our Latin American programs, and particularly on the budget for university assistance. It appears to me, too, that there is an ambiguous policy stance in the United States with regard to this type of in-country assistance and the instrumentality of the North American university contract. I would strongly urge that additional appropriations be allocated to this program and that it be given a much higher priority in the Alliance for Progress. If properly planned, university development assistance can have an impact on the development of Latin America out of all proportion to the amount of money invested.

The success or failure of these interuniversity undertakings depends, in large measure, on the kind of persons who address themselves to these tasks. I would like to point out a few qualities which I think are of extreme importance. First, the person should have some reflective knowledge of his own culture, particularly of the social structures and the value systems within his culture. Unreflective persons who simply grow up within a culture unconsciously identify with everything which is commonly accepted in that culture, and accept and live with it as an absolute norm. If they find themselves up against a quite different culture, they may react in one of two ways. They may simply condemn all differences without any distinction whatever, and consider these differences to be a mark of their own superiority. Or, being more intelligent, they might come through the experience realizing that many of these differences are in favor of the other culture and that others depend on rather arbitrary and parochial factors. In order to avoid cultural shock and dislocation, persons preparing to work in another culture should have a critical self-evaluating understanding and appraisal of their own culture.

We should, furthermore, not depend upon experiential contact with another culture to create an understanding of it. There should be a definite preparation for any experience in another cultural setting. As far as this can be done in advance, an understanding of the foreign culture should be communicated. Social science, the humanities, anthropology—all should be used to engender an understanding which, after experience, can come to be deep and realistic. Moreover, it would be well if, while actually engaged in activities within a new setting, the persons have opportunities to discuss with more experienced and better-trained people the meaning of their cultural experience.

Persons studying or teaching need, therefore, to have a non-culture-bound respect for human beings. They must be prepared to honor man in whatever style of life he is found. I am not arguing here for cultural relativism. I am not saying that there are not different levels of civilization. I am saying that every group of human beings has developed a culture, a social structure, a set of values, an art, an *ambiente,* and that in every culture there are deficiencies and evils which reflect the imperfection of man and his history of sin; but that in every culture, even in degraded cultures, if there be such, and certainly even in very simple cultures, if there be such, there are many things which reflect the almost divine potentialities of the human race. Every culture is a way of being human; every culture is a style of living humanly. It is only through a knowledge of many cultures of man that we can really come to some understanding of the rich potentiality of human nature. Robert Redfield expressed the point this way:

In effect, I am saying that man is one kind of being, while also this one kind is modified, developed, or emphasized in particular groups, into many different kinds of being. I am also saying that the one kind of being he is, while being also many kinds, is a being composed of sentiments, desires, and mental dispositions that animals do not have and that provide a basis, in some part of the nebulous whole, for any people to feel akin to any other people.[1]

These persons, therefore, must be prepared to rise above their own culture and to view man's cultures from a somewhat detached point of view. Yet this stance will be ineffective if it remains a purely intellectual attitude. Persons who are going to be effective must be prepared not only to understand differences, and even to appreciate them, but to love the people who are different. A charity that can break through cultural limitations is necessary. The man who deals with peoples of other races, nations, and cultures with contempt in his heart will display contempt in gesture, voice, and eye. He will create and nurture hostilities. The successful person will be the one who brings sympathetic understanding, enthusiastic eagerness to cooperate, and warm affection to those he works with and for.

Given these understandings and this basic disposition, persons going to Latin America ought to attempt to adjust their style of living to those with whom, for whom, and among whom they will be working. This has been the great strength of our Peace Corps volunteers and of some of our missionaries. To work with and among persons from whom one nonetheless lives apart in isolated luxury is self-defeating.

Persons to be engaged in this work should also possess the necessary tools and technical skills: first of all, language, the skills of communication; and, second, the specific technical skills for the job to be done. These skills should be possessed in the fashion of a master, that is to say, with reflective understanding of them. Otherwise they will be applied to new situations mechanically, and will generally result in the artificial imposition of forms incompatible with the new culture. All of these have to be adapted, and the more so, the more humane and social the techniques are.

One final word. We are all working to lift the level of all the peoples of the Western Hemisphere. Ideally, it seems to me, we should aim at a common socioeconomic base so that we can share the wealth of the hemisphere in a fair and democratic way. Inevitably and rightly a certain cosmopolitan common culture will develop, particularly at the level of the academic community. This culture will be in some sense a second level of culture. We hope that the rich diversity of cultures and cultural traditions, whether they be Inca or French, Portuguese or American Indian, German or African, will be maintained, refined, and will contribute to the rich diversity of styles of being human in our own hemisphere. Thus we look forward to effecting a unity in diversity which will make of this hemisphere, in the words of Jose Martí, *nuestra American,* our common America.

NOTES

1. Robert Redfield, "The Universally Human and the Culturally Variable," *Journal of General Education,* X, 150–160.

OUR LATIN AMERICAN POLICY

EUGENE J. McCARTHY

The United States was conceived by radicals and born in revolution. Our assertion that all men are created equal is certainly
more radical than any announcement ever made by Karl Marx or
by any Communist since. Yet we now seem to believe that revolutions are always alien and always dangerous.

The Alliance for Progress was a truly revolutionary concept. Its
1961 threshold was correctly defined as the beginning of a Decade
of Urgency. It sought to change feudalistic landholding patterns,
to reduce poverty and social injustice, and to improve education.
The Alliance was the high-water mark in our recent Latin Amer-
can relations. Under its terms the American republics, with aid
from the United States, agreed to work together for the social and
economic development of the region and promised to carry out
a series of reforms, particularly in the field of agriculture, and
tax and fiscal administration. This was not another foreign-
aid bill; not a simple plan to bundle men, money, and machinery into known dimensions. It was and is a compact by which

343

the United States commits itself to underwrite a social revolution in our hemisphere.

Now the Decade of Urgency is more than half gone. It is proper that we analyze the Alliance for Progress. But it is even more important that we should analyze the progress toward alliance. It was bold to announce an alliance, not to secure but to achieve. The Alliance was, above all else, a recognition that people everywhere who live in poverty and in ignorance belong to the twentieth century as much as we do, and that it belongs to them also. The Alliance was a statement of our intent to see that they share in the good of that century. It was a blueprint for bringing about through justice what the world has often accomplished only through war and bloodshed.

The Alliance proposed that the revolution should be carried out by the Latins themselves, not through Washington. It is the Latins who must, as Adlai Stevenson said, "take the bold, brave, and difficult steps" that have to be taken. The Alliance is not a total failure. It is not a dramatic success. It has fallen far short of its potential. Why failure in our hemisphere, called by John Kennedy "the most critical area of the world"? Why so little success if we believe "no work is more important for our generation of Americans than our work in this hemisphere," as stated by President Johnson?

The war in Vietnam is draining off our military, our economic, and our moral energy. Despite this, we can and must look at Latin America. The Alliance gave us focus, and President Kennedy's courageous confrontation in 1962 grouped Latin America with us in an atmosphere of excitement and hope. The clash of cymbals in the overture caught the attention of the world, but the performance has been disappointing. The spirit and thrust of the Alliance must be recovered.

We must ask ourselves whether we are nothing more than pretenders. Whether we deserve the mantle of greatness that we sometimes claim. Whether we are worthy of the power we hold.

What should we do? What can we do? What can we say to ourselves here today are practical goals, even in the shadows of a war that shakes our spirit?

The modest goal set for the Alliance, as you know, projected an overall increase in per-capita gross product of 2.5 percent annually. This week the Inter-American Committee of the Alliance for Progress revealed that the hemisphere once again failed to meet that target. Growth averaged only 1.6 percent.

Economically, we must give our increased support to the developing Latin American regional and subregional common market efforts. The Central American Common Market is proof that it can be done. The Latin American Free Trade Association, which also became operative in 1961, the same year as the Central American Market, still has a long way to go. And a third grouping, the Andean Common Market, has shown exciting indications of success.

The Alliance has itself admitted that only through regional economic agreements will the Latin American economy move ahead at the pace it must. Here then is the crux of our work in these years of urgency. Yet how much time has our government given to the attainment of these goals? And what minute percentage of its talent and brain power has gone toward the perfection of planning in this area? All of us know that other targets get today's attention.

Still in the economic field, and intricately woven into the future of all people, is the development of the heart of the Latin American continent. For most of us Latin America, like the western stages they build for Hollywood, is a row of false fronts built atop rickety and empty one-story buildings. It is a chain of cities, all of which lie near the coast. The great interior of the continent is an unknown to us as Tibet. I can see nothing that is being done to reduce that ignorance.

Here are the millions of acres that can feed a growing population. Access roads, better communications, rural electrification, and rural responsibility need money and planning. Why is our focus so often only negative, attempting to reduce the problem by reducing the potential? Our enthusiasm must be caught up in the creative functions of the Alliance: the imagination to bring into production those millions of acres of top-soil-rich land that are the heartland of the continent south of us, and the willingness to do so even if it costs us money, effort, and time.

But more is needed. I would suggest the following as a basis for United States policy:

One, increased access to our markets, with the possibility of import concessions to companies that will give substantial investment guarantees to the Latin American countries.

Two, reduction or elimination of tariff barriers. In 1965 we concluded with the Canadian government a tariff-reduction agreement involving automotive products which is expected to benefit the industry on both sides of the border. This special arrangement was justified by the Administration on the basis of our special relationship with Canada. Our relationships with the Latin American countries generally are no less extraordinary.

Three, a better market at stable prices for Latin American tropical products such as sugar, cotton, bananas, and coffee. The primary products of the Latin countries, which are the chief source of foreign exchange earnings, are, to a considerable extent, frozen out of the European market by the preferences granted by European countries to developing nations which were formerly their colonies.

The problems of Latin America are not only economic; they are also political.

In the early sixties the United States applied limited political pressures in favor of democratic forces. In the Dominican Republic in 1961, in Peru in 1962, and in Haiti, Honduras, and the Dominican Republic again in 1963, nonrecognition, along with the suspension of economic and military assistance, were used against governments that had assumed power by nonconstitutional means. Further, in the Dominican Republic in 1961 the United States used diplomatic, economic, and even military pressure, including the stationing of warships off the coast, to discourage the return of a rightist dictatorship.

Since 1964 the great power of the United States has frequently been thrown behind unrepresentative elements, and, on at least one occasion, military intervention has been employed. When military coups against constitutionally elected governments occurred in Brazil, Bolivia, and Argentina, no real effort was made to deny recognition or aid. Our Latin American policy has shifted to one in which the emphasis is on stability. Intervention in the Dominican republic in 1965 was justified on the basis of a supposedly imminent Communist take-over.

The United States intervention in the Dominican Republic raised many issues. It called into question some of the basic precepts of United States foreign policy. Because our intervention was contrary to the United States position as it was generally understood and accepted in Latin America, our willingness to stand by our treaty obligations was questioned.

We must again prove, when opportunity presents, our adherence to the principle of nonintervention. We must move to deemphasize the power of military forces in Latin American political life. Our diplomatic missions should be at least as powerful and influential as our military missions.

The United States must continue the attempt to curb the escalation of the senseless arms race in Latin America. Given the pressing developmental needs of Latin America, it is appalling that in some countries over 18 percent of the budget is consumed by the military. The United States, along with other arms-producing nations, cannot escape responsibility. In addition to an ever-expanding program of military assistance, which is currently almost 100 million dollars, our government has extended United States credit assistance for the purchase of arms by the Latin American military. Until recently Latin American countries were

buying between 100 million and 150 million dollars worth of
arms. The United States should stand firm in its stated commitment to stop a hemispheric arms race. We should not give in
to cries that if Latin America is to have arms, they must be
American. The Administration should not hesitate to suspend
military aid to intransigent military or unrepresentative governments which are unwilling to hold elections and start necessary
political reforms.

The Organization of American States (OAS) should be revital-
ized and reorganized. Latin Americans have lost confidence in
the OAS. The greatest blow to the OAS, and to its basic principle
of nonintervention except by collective action, was delivered by
the United States in its unilateral intervention in the Dominican
Republic. The OAS headquarters should be moved from Washington. Such a move would have more than symbolic value. At
present many Latin American nations send one man to Washington who serves both as ambassador to the United States and
ambassador to the OAS. Too frequently the man who represents his nation before the United States is unable to perform
adequately his functions before the OAS. In one role he is
called upon to maintain good relations with Washington; in
the other he must often voice his government's difference with
the United States.

The United States should drop its quest for an inter-American
peacekeeping force which would only appear to serve United
States interests. Few Central or South American nations see it
as being in their interest to cooperate in the creating of a permanent military force staffed largely by Latin American troops, but
armed and financed and, they therefore suspect, ultimately controlled by the United States.

The United States is reluctant to commit itself by treaty or to
allow too much authority over inter-American economic affairs
and control of Alliance funds to be vested in a body in which the
United States is outnumbered by nineteen votes to one. We did

not commit ourselves by treaty to the Marshall Plan and were not members of the Organization for European Economic Cooperation which planned the recovery of Europe. We should consider similar procedures and relationships with Latin American countries. There is little real hope for reform of the OAS and for making it an effective instrument of hemispheric cooperation unless the United States is willing to give up some of the political leverage we gain by keeping tight control over determining "who gets what" in the Alliance.

The Alliance can never be a truly cooperative effort so long as it continues to operate as one supplier and nineteen receivers. It is up to the United States to initiate measures to check its natural domination of the OAS, acquired by virtue of its overwhelming power and large financial contribution to the OAS. To those who fear change it may seem foolhardy for our government to loosen its control, to permit the OAS to become a hemispheric forum for disagreement as well as cooperation. But to those who would restore confidence in the OAS this will seem a small sacrifice in the long run.

Finally we must reexamine our policy with reference to the place of Cuba in the pattern of the American States. Our policy of containment of Cuba is as negative as the past, as sterile as yesterday. From it flow the guerillas that operate at Castro's direction, killing the innocent, taking their only pride in death and destruction. And from it flow, just as strongly, the increased expenditures for arms for Latin countries, based on the theory that they have to defend themselves against Cuba. But can Brazil use sophisticated jets against peasant guerillas?

Cuba should be offered the chance to return to the family of nations to which she belongs. This does not mean that the United States should retreat an inch in its dedication to democratic principles, nor in its condemnation of the evils that have attended Cuba's march toward communistic failure. It does mean that we should move forward, looking toward the end of still another situation in which we are now bogged down, without a clear way out, without any signal for tomorrow.

Let Cuba select a group of its own Latin neighbors at her own choosing to act as an international commission. Let Cuba, in open talks with this commission, move toward a fuller life for its people, unshackled from the chains in which she now is caught. I believe that such a commission, working through the Organization of American States, could find proper guarantees so that Cuba would accept its international obligations, free its political prisoners, and begin to move toward freedom.

We have a positive role to play in Latin America: in part because of our location, because of our cultural and economic ties, and in part also because we have exploited Latin American countries and have failed in our responsibility to give assistance. There is nothing wrong with being "big brother" if we understand what a "big brother" should be, and what we should do and not do. Certain functions are honorable and properly ours. We should not shun them. Others will never be ours, and we should not claim them.

Our policy must not betray our heritage, nor forsake our belief in ourselves as the true radicals and the true revolutionaries, believers in that greatest radical belief—freedom. This is what should set us apart and mark our role in history. I will end by calling to your attention a warning sounded by President Eduardo Frei of Chile in an article in *Foreign Affairs* of April, 1967:

> The Latin American revolution, as a force for rapid and substantial change, has been germinating for the last decade; it is now a permanent and dynamic torrent which is weakening the political and social institutions of the continent. The form taken by this drastic change will depend on the time which elapses before the forces of revolution are finally released. The greater the delay, the greater will be the accumulated pressure and the greater the violence of the eventual explosion.

APPENDIX

LATIN AMERICA—SOME BASIC STATISTICS

COUNTRY	INDEPENDENCE	AREA, SQ. MI.	POPULATION	DENSITY/SQ. MI.	CAPITAL
Argentina	1816 Spain	1.1 million 2nd in LA	22.4 million 3rd in LA	21 20th in LA	Buenos Aires* 7.2 million
Bolivia	1825 Spain	420,000 6th	3.7 12th	9 22nd	La Paz* 460,000
Brazil	1822 Portugal	3.3 million 1st	81.3 1st	25 18th	Brasília 190,550
Chile	1818 Spain	290,000 8th	8.6 7th	30 15th	Santiago* 2,338,860
Colombia	1819 Spain	440,000 5th	17.8 4th	40 13th	Bogotá* 1,532,568
Costa Rica	1821 Spain	19,500 18th	1.4 20th	73 8th	San José* 331,874
Cuba	1899 Spain	44,000 14th	7.6 8th	173 6th	Havana* 1,506,760
Dominican Republic	1865 Spain	18,900 19th	3.6 13th	192 5th	Santo Domingo* 476,058
Ecuador	1822 Spain	105,000 10th	5 9th	49 11th	Quito 389,000
El Salvador	1821 Spain	8,300 21st	2.9 14th	354 4th	San Salvador* 370,800
Guatemala	1821 Spain	42,000 16th	4.3 11th	103 7th	Guatemala City* 520,500

Guyana	1966	Gr. Brit.	83,000	11th	650,000	23rd	8	23rd	Georgetown*	161,000
Haiti	1804	France	10,800	20th	.7	10th	435	2nd	Port-au-Prince*	300,000
Honduras	1821	Spain	43,000	15th	.2	16th	50	10th	Tegucigalpa*	138,097
Jamaica	1962	Gr. Brit.	4,400	22nd	1.8	18th	402	3rd	Kingston*	392,180
Mexico	1821	Spain	762,000	3rd	40.9	2nd	54	9th	Mexico City*	5,371,450
Nicaragua	1821	Spain	57,000	13th	1.7	19th	29	16th	Managua*	371,641
Panama	1903	Colombia	29,000	17th	1.2	21st	43	12th	Panama City*	339,900
Paraguay	1811	Spain	157,000	9th	2	17th	13	21st	Asunción*	376,500
Peru	1824	Spain	496,000	4th	11.7	5th	23	19th	Lima*	1,864,815
Trinidad-Tobago	1962	Gr. Brit.	2,000	23rd	980,000	22nd	490	1st	Port of Spain*	175,100
Uruguay	1828	Brazil	72,000	12th	2.7	15th	38	14th	Montevideo*	1,364,750
Venezuela	1821	Spain	352,000	7th	8.7	6th	25	17th	Caracas*	1,637,093

*Also largest city.

LATIN AMERICA—SOCIAL AND ECONOMIC CONDITIONS

COUNTRY	PER-CAPITA INCOME	DOCTOR	TEACHER	CAR	PHONE	RADIO	T.V.	LIFE SPAN	LITERACY (PERCENT)
Argentina	$614	670	113	32	15	3	16	59	86
Bolivia	$154	3,700	197	314	187	6	no tv	50	32
Brazil	$196	2,700	225	91	65	9	37	53	49
Chile	$483	1,800	198	100	36	4	254	52	85
Colombia	$292	2,000	237	135	41	4	44	45	62
Costa Rica	$385	2,600	119	67	68	6	46	56	88
Cuba	$323	1,200	173	81	33	6	15	53	78
Dominican Republic	$269	1,681	305	163	125	12	69	50 (est.)	64
Ecuador	$199	2,800	209	334	111	8	122	52	60
El Salvador	$275	4,700	261	123	137	7	105	59	48
Guatemala	$284	3,600	283	143	214	17	95	44	29
Guyana	$291	2,600	195	61	66	16	no tv	50	80
Haiti	$ 80	10,600	682	711	1,034	46	910	33	10
Honduras	$216	not avail.	220	280	226	9	262	45	45
Jamaica	$429	2,200	299	33	40	6	87	64	85
Mexico	$402	1,800	258	64	60	9	37	57	65
Nicaragua	$282	2,800	269	149	115	11	258	50	40
Panama	$448	3,100	156	48	31	3	12	62	78
Paraguay	$193	1,700	145	162	151	12	no tv	45	68
Peru	$262	2,200	189	102	90	9	54	50	61
Trinidad-Tobago	$630	2,600	151	19	26	8	47	62	82
Uruguay	$478	1,100	321	18	15	4	15	67	95
Venezuela	$728	1,300	186	29	35	3	21	66	80

Appendix 355

MEDICINE IN LATIN AMERICA

(Data from *Statistical Abstract of Latin America, 1963* [UCLA]
and CIF, *Latin America in Maps, Charts, Tables* [1964])

HEALTH FACILITIES (1957 TO 1960)	PERSONS PER MD	PERSONS PER DDS	PERSONS PER HOSPITAL BED	DAILY CALORIES	PERCENT ANIMAL SOURCE
United States	784	1,998	101	3,100	41
Mexico	1,730	20,166	875	2,725	13
Costa Rica	2,557	8,871	135	2,555	21
El Salvador	5,406	17,413	480	1,975	12
Guatemala	6,367	26,546	660	2,175	10
Honduras	13,978	—	750	2,190	8
Nicaragua	2,819	12,843	510	1,985	15
Panama	3,216	11,989	245	2,370	19
Cuba	1,028	3,399	300	2,870	27
Dominican Republic	8,037	—	390	1,950	11
Haiti	2,820	—	1,500	1,875	8
Argentina	1,660	1,805	160	3,360	33
Bolivia	5,269	5,868	480	1,880	16
Brazil	2,054	4,038	310	2,815	17
Chile	1,588	2,924	185	2,610	19
Colombia	2,367	8,221	380	2,225	16
Ecuador	2,607	9,205	—	1,935	11
Paraguay	1,799	—	615	2,355	25
Peru	2,145	7,274	500	2,040	14
Uruguay	2,423	—	175	2,945	39
Venezuela	1,330	7,261	395	2,255	15

INFANT MORTALITY

	DEATHS/1000, 1960	PERCENT OF POPULATION 0–15 YEARS	65 PLUS	LIFE EXPECTANCY, MALE, AT BIRTH
United States	25	31	9	67
Mexico	70	42	3	38
Guatemala	85	42	2.5	41
Cuba	38	36	4	–
Brazil	170	41	2.4	39
Peru	97	44	4	46
Ecuador	90	43	3.5	50
Bolivia	91	40	4	49

MALARIA

	NUMBER OF KNOWN CASES (1958)	RATE PER 100,000
United States	0	0
Brazil	23,000	37
Panama	5,200	524
Colombia	79,000	651
Haiti	26,000	758
Honduras	–	922

INFLATION—A MAJOR LATIN AMERICAN PROBLEM

Among the reasons for Latin American instability and lack of satisfactory growth in the postwar years has been the galloping inflation that has been suffered by a number of these nations. With their predominantly one-crop economies vulnerable to price declines and competition, with their people demanding more government expenditures for development and social welfare, with many of them run by corrupt and inefficient military regimes, a number of Latin nations have been stretched on the rack of runaway inflation. In the chart below (taken from the *Congressional Record,* July, 12, 1967, p. 8596) the nations of the world are listed in the order of decreasing monetary stability. Note that three Latin nations (and the United States) are at the very top of the list: Guatemala and Honduras, with their regimes determined to keep their currencies at par with the dollar no matter what the social cost, and oil-rich Venezuela. But note also that seven of the last eight nations in the chart, most of them major countries, are from Latin America. Inflation rates of 10 to 30 percent, continued over a decade or more, are a grave problem for these countries and their people.

	INDEX OF VALUE OF MONEY (1956 = 100)		ANNUAL RATE OF DEPRECIATION %	
	1961	1966	1956–1966	1965–1966
Guatemala	102	100	0	0.7
Venezuela	93	90	1.1	0.1
Honduras	98	86	1.5	1.6
United States	91	84	1.8	2.8
Luxembourg	94	83	1.9	2.5
Canada	91	82	2.0	3.6
Australia	90	82	2.0	2.7
Greece	91	81	2.1	4.8
Thailand	88	80	2.2	3.7
Belgium	93	80	2.2	3.9
South Africa	91	80	2.2	3.6
Germany (Federal Rep.)	92	79	2.3	3.4

	INDEX OF VALUE OF MONEY (1956 = 100)		ANNUAL RATE OF DEPRECIATION %	
	1961	1966	1956–1966	1965–1966
Portugal	92	78	2.4	4.9
Switzerland	94	78	2.4	4.6
New Zealand	88	77	2.6	2.4
Ecuador	94	76	2.6	5.2
Austria	90	75	2.8	2.1
United Arab Rep.	95	75	2.9	8.2
United Kingdom	89	74	2.9	3.8
Italy	92	72	3.2	2.3
Ireland	89	72	3.2	2.9
Norway	88	72	3.3	3.3
Netherlands	88	71	3.4	5.6
Pakistan	84	70	3.5	6.7
Iran	75	70	3.5	–.4
Philippines	92	70	3.6	6.0
Denmark	93	69	3.6	6.9
Mexico	78	69	3.7	4.0
Sweden	85	68	3.8	6.3
Japan	88	66	4.0	4.0
France	74	62	4.7	2.6
Finland	79	60	4.9	3.8
China (Taiwan)	62	58	5.2	2.2
Israel	82	58	5.4	7.2
India	83	57	5.5	9.7
Spain	73	49	6.9	6.0
Vietnam	99	46	7.4	38.6
Turkey	58	45	7.7	7.8
Peru	66	41	8.5	8.4
Korea	70	33	10.5	10.6
Colombia	63	32	10.8	16.4
Bolivia	31	25	13.0	5.7
Chile	38	10	20.6	18.6
Argentina	20	6	24.5	24.2
Brazil	29	2	31.0	31.8

THE ALLIANCE FOR PROGRESS

(Data from Simon G. Hanson, *Five Years of the Alliance for Progress* [Washington, D.C., 1967])

I. *The U. S. kept its pledge to provide 1 billion dollars in public funds per year.*

GRANTS
AND LOANS AUTHORIZED

Fiscal 1962 –	$1.2 billion
1963 –	.96
1964 –	1.2
1965 –	1.1
1966 –	1.2

Actual disbursements, because of Latin America's failure to meet conditions that would assure effective expenditures, were somewhat smaller, but still averaged 800 million dollars a year. The International Coffee Agreement provides another 400 million dollars a year in a concealed subsidy.

In 1966, excluding Mexico, 93 percent of aid funds were grants, and only 7 percent loans.

II. *The target figure of 3000 million dollars in private United States investment was not met.*

U.S. DIRECT INVESTMENT
IN LATIN AMERICA:

Fiscal 1960 –	$258 million
1961 –	214
1962 –	*minus* $24
1963 –	11
1964 –	83
1965 –	180
1966 –	190

Why American businessmen did not invest in Latin America: Expropriation in Cuba frightened many. Investment in Europe was more attractive. There was anti-U.S. investment feeling and action in Argentina, Brazil, Venezuela, and other countries. Inflation and political instability made for an unattractive climate.

III. *The target of 2.5 percent per-year per-capita growth in GNP was not met.*

GROWTH IN GNP	TOTAL	PER CAPITA
1950–1955	5.1%	2.4%
1955–1960	4.8	1.9
1960–1965	4.4	1.5

Because of declining commodity prices, inflation, and political troubles, Latin America grew more rapidly *before* the Alliance for Progress than after.

IV. *The only relatively prospering countries were Mexico, Peru, Panama, and the Central American Common Market. The rest of Latin America was stagnating.*

	PERCENTAGE CHANGE IN TOTAL GNP			PERCENTAGE CHANGE IN GNP PER CAPITA		
	1950–55	1955–60	1960–65	1950–55	1955–60	1960–65
Costa Rica	7.4	4.8	3.9	3.5	1.1	0.2
El Salvador	4.5	3.9	7.7	1.8	1.2	4.2
Guatemala	2.3	5.3	6.2	−0.9	2.2	3.1
Honduras	4.1	4.4	4.8	1.0	1.3	1.7
Nicaragua	8.3	2.3	8.3	5.5	−0.8	5.2
Central American Economic Community	4.5	4.4	6.3	1.4	1.3	3.0

Argentina	3.1	2.6	3.0	1.4	0.9	1.3
Bolivia	0.8	—0.1	4.3	—1.5	—2.4	2.0
Brazil	5.7	5.8	3.3	2.6	2.7	0.2
Chile	3.0	4.2	3.9	0.7	1.9	1.6
Colombia	5.5	4.0	4.4	2.6	1.1	1.5
Ecuador	5.3	4.4	4.3	2.3	1.4	1.3
Mexico	6.2	6.1	5.9	3.1	3.0	2.8
Panama	–	–	8.1	–	–	5.1
Paraguay	2.9	2.4	3.8	0.7	0.2	1.6
Peru	6.0	4.3	6.6	3.7	2.0	3.7
Uruguay	–	—0.1	0.4	–	—1.4	—0.9
Venezuela	9.0	7.1	5.2	5.1	3.2	1.6
Latin America (17 listed countries)	5.1	4.8	4.4	2.4	1.9	1.5

V. *Hanson's Conclusions*: "Five years of the Alliance for Progress found Latin America losing ground politically, economically, and socially in its response to the challenge of the times. And five years found Latin America increasingly willing to avoid the basic decisions as long as the alternative of drawing on the United States treasury remained open."

INDEX

A
Acción Popular, 93
Adams, John, 61
Adams, John Quincy, 62
Agency for International Development (AID), 73, 331, 339
Agrarian Reform Corporation (CORA), 139
Agustín I, 44
Albornoz, Rodrigo de, 55
Alexander, Robert, 137–138
Alexander VI, Pope, 213
Alianza Popular Revolucionaria Americana (APRA), 89, 90
Alliance for Progress, vii, viii, ix, 39 f., 48, 65, 66, 76, 115, 116, 135–136, 138–139, 256, 306–307, 339, 343–344, 359–361
Althusser, Louis, 30
Andean Common Market, 345

Aquinas, Thomas, 244
Arbenz, Jacobo, 304
Arendt, Hannah, 16
Arévalo, Juan José, 65
Asimov, Isaac, 79

B
Bandung Conference, 178
Basic Education Movement (MEB), x, 134, 163–165
Baxley, H. Willis, 257, 258
Belaunde, Fernando, 88, 93
Bergson, Henri, 242
Berle, Adolf A., 292
Board of Trade, 44
Bolívar, Simón, 60, 61, 254, 255, 256
Bolton, Herbert E., 39, 49, 50, 65, 66
Bonaparte, Napoleon, 61
Bonilla, Frank, 87
Bosch, Juan, 90